D0855329

Girls *with* Slingshots

created and illustrated by

Danielle Corsetto

PART TWO

IRON
CIRCUS
COMICS

Cover Design
Danielle Corsetto

Colorist
Danielle Corsetto & Laeluu

Collection Design
Allyson Haller

***THE COMPLETE GIRLS WITH SLINGSHOTS*, VOLUME 2**
This volume collects comic strips from the Girls With Slingshots website, originally published from 2004-2015.

www.girlswithslingshots.com
www.gwscomic.com if you're lazy

Published by Iron Circus Comics
www.ironcircus.com

First edition: December 2017
ISBN: 978-1-945820-08-3

Graphic Novels / Humor

Printed in China by Global PSD

americanforests.org
GLOBAL
RELEAF

AMERICAN
FORESTS

REPLANTED
PAPER

For Laeluu, my first intern, who
colored everything I didn't want to color, and humbly
taught me what commitment looks like.

DOOOOOOM

TABLE OF CONTENTS

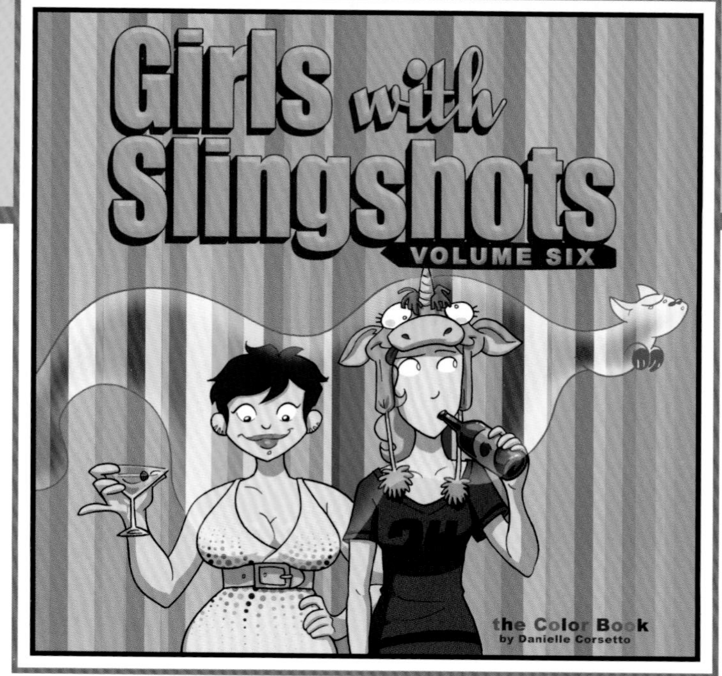
Girls with Slingshots
VOLUME SIX
the Color Book
by Danielle Corsetto

VOLUME SIX STORY ARCS

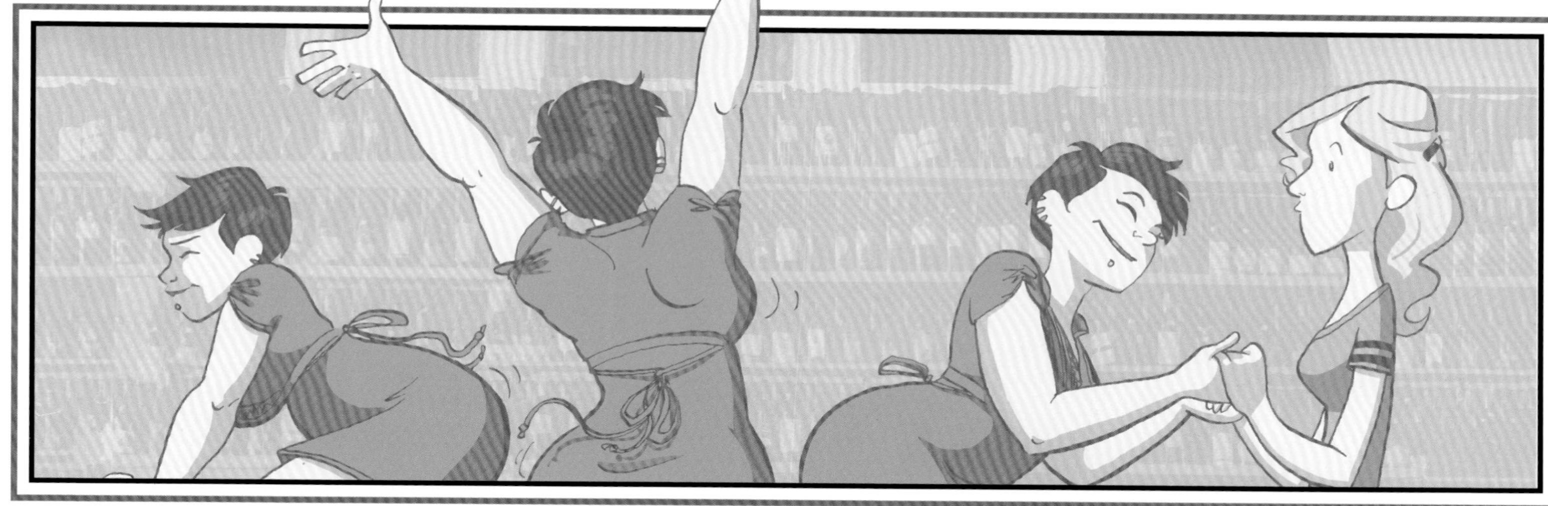

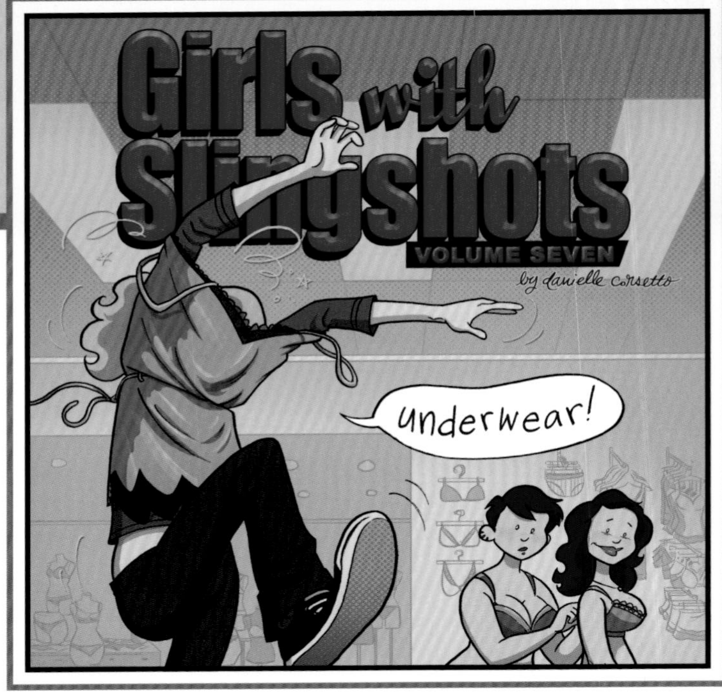
Girls with Slingshots
VOLUME SEVEN
by danielle corsetto
underwear!

VOLUME SEVEN STORY ARCS

mrow?

Girls with Slingshots
VOLUME EIGHT
by danielle corsetto

VOLUME EIGHT STORY ARCS

FEELINGS!

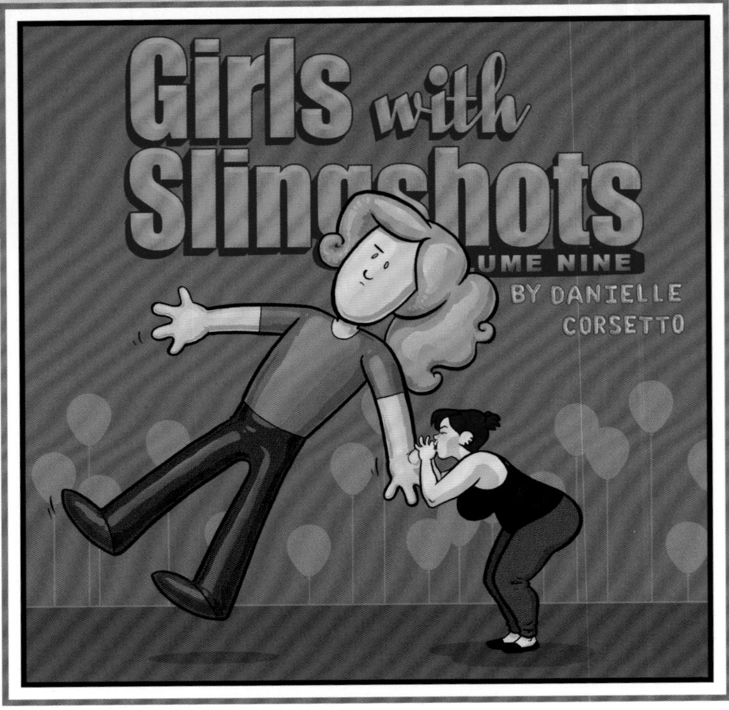
Girls with Slingshots
UME NINE
BY DANIELLE CORSETTO

VOLUME NINE STORY ARCS

GLoooop
pat

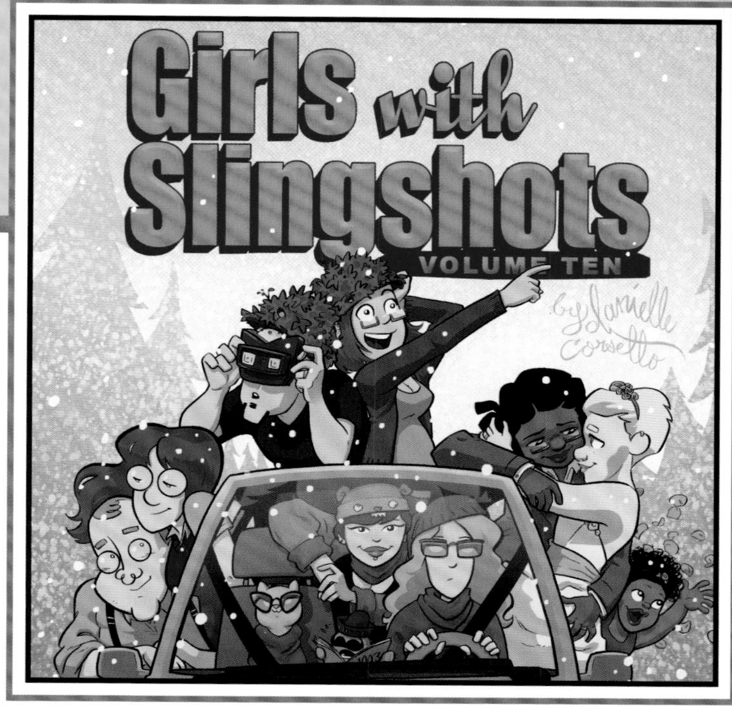
Girls with Slingshots
VOLUME TEN

And the cats in the cradle
and the silver spoon

VOLUME TEN STORY ARCS

INTRODUCTION

Oh good, you're still here! I'm glad the puke didn't deter you. There's still a little more puke to go.

It may seem a little backwards that this is the book I decided to dedicate to Laeluu, even though the whole first book was colored by her. But this one has strip #1551 (page 171), which is the first GWS strip she ever colored. I received an email from her, this college student living in the midwest, asking if she could be my intern for a semester in 2013. I couldn't imagine what an intern a thousand miles away could do for me, but a friend suggested I send her the inks to one of my comics and see how well she could color it. I sent her the inks to #1551 with sparse instructions, and she sent it back looking nearly identical to the one I'd already finished. I gave her the internship, and she colored two strips a week for me shortly after that. When her semester-long internship ran out, I asked if I could hire her to keep going, and she accepted.

Unfortunately I didn't think to have her sign her name in the panel gutters until 2014, but you can see Laeluu's signature next to mine in a number of the later strips that she colored, separated by a little dot of color. (That dot, by the way, is the color we use to apply shadows to the strips—usually a **warm putty color**, depending on the lighting. And now you know.)

So the book you just read was colored by Laeluu after she'd already become a seasoned colorist by working on the latter 500 strips in the series. This second book starts off a little clumsily, because it chronicles the beginning of my journey with digital coloring. Let me give you a little backstory.

REALLY OLD
DVD's

In March of 2005, less than a year out of college and about six months after I started GWS, I quit my job at the newspaper so that I could devote myself to freelance illustration and caricatures, which gave me some extra time to work on GWS. In 2007, I self-published a print-on-demand collection of the first 200 strips (if you still have a copy, I apologize for whatever's left of the cheap binding). They sold so well that I started replacing the living room furniture with boxes of books in order to make room for them. After all the Christmas sales were shipped out, I decided this was a sign that things were going to go well for GWS, so I moved into a house and upgraded from beans and hot dogs to asparagus and chicken.

That was the year I decided to pursue GWS full-time, three years after it began. (Interestingly, I later discovered that it wasn't uncommon for a newspaper cartoonist to take three years to make enough income with their comic to pursue it full-time, even after signing with a syndicate.) "Webcomic" was still a new word back then, but I was inspired by forerunners like Scott Kurtz (*Player vs Player*) to give it a go.

You may be wondering why I'm practically outlining my resume in this backstory about coloring, but my work status directly affected the look of the comic. I was doing everything by myself for the first thousand strips—with invaluable help from assistants and friends—and I spent most of my time trying to turn a "comic" on the "Internet" into a "job" that made "money." This required creativity, which I loved! But it also required a lot of time, and the more time I spent trying to turn comics into income, the less time I spent on the comics. I simplified my style, and sometimes even moved the scenes to a less-complicated setting, or dropped out the backgrounds entirely, in order to save time.

AAAA

Strip #1001—the first one in this book—marks a turning point in GWS. I was in Montreal when I posted it, meeting with Ryan Sohmer of Blind Ferret (*Least I Could Do*, *Looking For Group*) to talk about what his company could do to alleviate the burden of my everyday work so I could focus on what mattered to me most—the comic.

By then I'd already started updating GWS five times a week, which had been a game-changer; updating twice more a week meant that I could share the quiet little moments and superfluous jokes that happened in between the plot-driving strips. But I was jealous of my cartoonist pals like Jeph Jacques (*Questionable Content*) and Randy Milholland (*Something Positive*) for posting their comics in full color. I had colored a few GWS strips before, but it always took me forever, in part because I was still learning, and I didn't have the spare time to learn.

After my trip to Montreal, I decided to trust Sohmer's claim that I'd soon have more time to focus on the comic, and immediately started posting GWS in color. He delivered; I never had to pack or ship massive amounts of merchandise from my house again, and the comic was published in color until the end.

It was at this point that I started taking the strip more seriously. I tried to stick to my five-times-a-week update schedule, and began considering the reader's experience; story arcs now began on Mondays, and ended on Fridays. Longer arcs still had some sort of soft conclusion by Friday's update, so that when readers picked back up the following Monday, they didn't feel like they'd been dropped into the middle of a conversation. Now that I was collecting every 200 strips into a book, I aimed to accomplish that same feeling of a soft conclusion every time I hit a multiple of 200. None of this was really necessary, but it gave the strip a more thoughtful rhythm for its readers to settle into.

As you'll notice when you hit the cast page, this book introduced a lot of important new characters. I like to introduce characters the same way people are introduced to us in real life: without knowing anything about them aside from whatever they decide to share... which is usually a polished lie. My friend and mentor Michael—to whom the first book is dedicated—calls this "sending your representative." Thea was an especially good example of this; when she's first introduced as Hazel's boss, she is accomplished, confident, imposing. Once we got to know her better—and her career crumbled suddenly beneath her—we became intimately aware of her insecurities. (Thea's one of my favorite characters for this reason.)

This approach sometimes results in characters' stories going in the opposite direction than I expected them to. Without resorting to spoilers, let's just say that Keith and Joshua both surprised me very, very much.

I decided to end GWS in 2014 for a number of reasons. I was in my thirties still writing about characters in their drunk twenties. My daily update schedule kept me from creating more thought-out plots. Keeping up with changing technology remained exciting, but a little tiresome to prioritize. Most of my income was coming from advertisements, to which I had some moral aversion. Aside from all of those, it just seemed like the right time to wrap things up, and two thousand strips was a tidy goal for the ending.

The fun thing about ending a series you've been working on for a decade is that you finally get to write all the stuff you'd been waiting to write. Weddings, ridiculous honeymoons, long-anticipated romance, mystery characters who've been hiding in the background, road trips with the discovery of ancient history at the end... (Am I being vague enough? I don't know who's reading this introduction, so I don't want to spoil anything if this is your first time!)

I ended Girls With Slingshots with the door open, just in case I wanted to return to their world someday. But if that day never comes, I hope you'll feel welcome to return on your own.

♡ Danielle

Danielle Corsetto
www.gwscomic.com

CAST

HAZEL TELLINGTON

JAMIE McJACK

McPEDRO

JAMESON

blog
blog
MAUREEN

ZACH

THEA

CHRIS

MELODY

CLARICE

ERIN

DARREN

TYLER

CANDY

ANGEL

FLUFFY

SPRINKLES

SPECIAL KITTY

GHOST KITTY

PURR
GOOPY KITTY

MIMI

Mimi Massacre . . . . ABV 9%

She slammed into Thea's life during a roller derby bout and it was love at first collision. Don't let her grown-up job and house fool you; she loves cartoons, rainbows, and sparkly things.

Drinks: *The blood of her opponents. Or, anything a college kid would like.*

JIM

(I think that's his name) . . . . . ABV 7%

Hazel's ex-blind date, and Jamie's ex-secret-admirestalker. Utterly forgettable to any woman who piques his interest, which is most of them. Jim has some opinions about the term "nice guy."

Drinks: *Whatever will impress the girl next to him.*

MAYA

Thea's Big Sis . . . . ABV 3%

Maya's most recent adventures include becoming a single mom and surviving breast cancer twice, but she prefers to be identified by her sweet-ass dance moves and excellent taste in double mastectomy-friendly clothing.

Drinks: *Whatever Gabby doesn't finish.*

CAROL

YOUR Mom . . . . ABV 0.005%

Hazel's doting mother and lifetime librarian. Carol makes the best mac and cheese on the block, but don't be fooled by her domesticity; she's more street smart than you think she is. Or, wait. Is she?

Drinks: *Wine coolers, on special occasions.*

TUCKER

The Librarian Whisperer . . . . . ABV 1%

Pseudointellectualism is the name of my Tucker cover band. He spends his free time in places that have books, hoping they will serve as bait for the poet of his dreams.

Drinks: *Absinthe, heavy on the water, extra sugar cubes.*

FIONA

Jamie's Little Big Sis (Underage)

Fiona is like... nine, right? Jk, jk, she's nineteen-going-on-pinup. Jamie's little sister is all grown up and ready to find someone who will appreciate her love of sci-fi stories and lacy underthings.

Drinks: *Any pink virgin drink, pile on the garnish.*

GABBY

Aspiring Flower Girl . . . 100% Fruit Juice

Maya's daughter and Thea's niece. Little Gabby has her mother's sly fire, her Aunt Thea's smarts, and a classic little-girl interest in wearing pretty pink dresses. Don't touch her hands, they're sticky.

Drinks: *From a big-girl cup.*

BEATRICE

Grumpy Librarian . . . . ABV 2%

Carol's young book-shelver and Clarice's closest frienemy at the library. Vitriolic about the things she doesn't like, which is most things. You didn't do anything wrong, her face just looks like that.

Drinks: *Red wine if a book strikes her fancy.*

JOSHUA

AKA Franklin Quimby . . . . ABV 1.2%

Joshua reads... a lot. He spends most of his days in the library, drumming up wonder (and sometimes infuriation) from the librarians over how he pays his bills. But that's a secret he rarely shares.

Drinks: *A mild port, if tea is unavailable.*

KEITH

AKA Mall Santa . . . . ABV 4%

Keith is a Santa-in-Training who spends most of his time surrounded by children, either as the man in the red suit, or the man who runs the local afterschool program.

Drinks: *Immediately after the last parent picks up.*

VINCENT

Or Maybe Victor? . . . . ABV Rare

Your friendly neighborhood ice cream slinger. His involvement in Hazel's high school life is... well, fuzzy... was he even in her high school? He's not even in the yearbook...

Drinks: *Apology cocktails made by Angel.*

GREGORY

Hazel's Dad . . . . ABV TBD

He's still alive... I think?

He may be a murderer... I think??

Drinks: *Probably. Probably* ***a lot.***

Girls with Slingshots
VOLUME SIX
24
the Color Book
by Danielle Corsetto

VOLUME SIX

strips 1001-1200

HATS
PHARMACY

1001

murr

Hm? Oh--
okay, I guess you can--

--come up--

--hey-

AAAA

1002

The kittens must go.
Did you know that sometimes you sound like a Disney villain?

They are driving me crazy. There are kittens EVERYWHERE!
Well, I think it's been eight weeks. Now you just need to find them all homes.

I've found a home for them.
Oh! Someone is buying ALL of them? Who?

Mr. Burlap Sack and Mrs. Bottom of the Lake.
Hazel, how are we friends?

1003

Oh hey, speaking of the kitties, I did a little more research and it turns out Davan only gets ONE of the kittens. You get to sell three.

ka-CHiNG
Now, don't go spending money you don't have yet. I ALSO found out that with hypo-allergenic cats, you--

--you have to--

Where are you going?
To quit my job!

1004

Clarice! I quit!
I know.

You know? How?
I just got a text from Jamie. It says, "Don't let Hazel quit."

Oh. Huh.
Well, in that case...
Yeah.

I quit anyway.
That's the spirit.

Did you just buy something expensive?
Why yes, that was my new expensive mattress that was delivered two minutes ago.

Hazel. You're NOT going to be rich. I called Davan and he can't prove that the father is hypoallergenic. Unless both parents are official, it's just a litter of normal, everyday kitties.
Whuh -- buh -- but, expensive mattress --

You'll have to take it back.
Buh, but I, uh --

You ripped the tag off.
I wanted to do this all my life!

1005

Clarice! I need my job back.
Nope.

Ha ha. So, should I start back up tomorrow?
NO, you should start looking for a new job.

Wh -- you mean I'm FIRED?
No Hazel, you QUIT, remember?

But, but I didn't think it through!
Hey, look at that! You solved the Mystery of Where Hazel fucked Up.

Does that mean I get my job back?
No, it means you learned something!

1006

Come ON Clarice, it's not like you filled my position in one DAY.
You should tell that to the new girl.

New g -- SERIOUSLY? Where did you find another GIRL to work in this slum?
I have a friend who needed a job.

Well, you could save yourself the training period if you'd fire her and take me back.
Over my dead body.

OH -- CANDY -- Hi -- um, would you look at that, I suddenly don't need a job anymore!
You gals have the NICEST DAY.

1007

C-CANDY
C-candy? Do you mean c-coffee?

N-No, C-CANDY --
C-camping?
C-coughing?

C-Cock ring?
C-Cock-licking?

CANDY'S BACK, YOU DICKS
Haha dick jokes
WAIT, CANDY?

1008

1009

... so I guess Clarice gave her Hazel's job at the porn shop.
Huh. Okay.
Wow, you're taking this really well.
I'm not afraid of Candy anymore, Jameson. She only ever mattered to me when she mattered to you.
Oh.
And now that she's out of our personal lives, she no longer poses a threat to us.
C'mon, let's go to bed.

1010

GLOOUP
YAAA!!

Oh, it's you.
Bleah

Can't you do anything like a normal cat?
murrfle
Oh excuse me, like a normal boneless pink gelatinous blob with cat-like features?

1011

Blah blah blah, "came to pick up two kittens," signed Davan.
Aww, this must be tough for you. No parent should have to choose between their children.
murr

Here, how about I choose for you, so you're not plagued with this burden.
murr?

Why don't you take Expensive Appetite and Expensive Continued Dental Surgery.
murrfle
You're welcome. Feel free to rename them.

1012

Bye, kitties! Bye, Chugga-Chugga Teddy Something!
Shloop

Shloop
Impressive.

Shloop
BANG

BANG
BANG
BANG

murrfle?
I don't have a bigger drain!

They're GONE?
Right down the drain.

Which ones did he take?
The two gooey pink ones. Special K wouldn't fit, what with his ginormous headgear.

Oooh I wish I could've said good-bye to them.
Good news, you'll get to say good-bye to the last two.

Really?
JAMIE LOOK A BRA SALE

FREE KITTIES

1013

Angel, pour me something cheap and delicious. I'm broke.
Hey, cuz.

YAH! Robyn! Whatre you doing here?
Visiting you.

If you'd wanted to visit me, you could've come to my apartment.

But you basically live here.

That's not true.
Where are you now?

Didn't I like you for a short time?
Yeah, but you were reeeeally drunk.

1014

So I give up. Why are you here?
Aunt Carol told me you have kittens.

Who the hell is Aunt Carol?
Uh, your mom?

YOUR mom!
Hazel, your mom's name is CAROL. She's my AUNT.

Psht, YOUR mom's my aunt.
you win.

1015

When the hell did you talk to Aunt My Mom?
We just chat on facebook from time to time.

PSSSHT FACEBOOK my mom's on FACEBOOK?
Yeah, I'm pretty sure I've suggested her as a friend to you like, five times.

Oh, I thought that just meant "in general."
Hazel, your mom really wants to be your friend.

Then she should get off facebook.
You can be in our farmville co-op!

1016

1017

Wait, you said "kitties." Are you adopting one of them?
Maybe, I'm not sure yet.

Well I just dropped them off with Jamie – she'll have them at the florist's.
Oh yay, I like Jamie! I'll visit her tomorrow.

You're gonna drive all the way home and come back tomorrow?
Of course not, silly, I'm gonna stay on your couch.

Robyn, you can't just invite yourself
I'll tell your mom.
Take my bed, I'll sleep on the couch.

1018

Robyn!
Hey Jamie! I hear you have adorable homeless kitties.
FREE KITTIES

Oooh are you gonna adopt one? You should adopt Special Kitty, he's hilarious.
Hm..
ROBYN!

Robyn! It's Jim! Jim from the Christmas party! Christmas Party Jim haha WOOPS who put that pot there?

Y'know, I have an awful lot of "special" in my life. I'll take the other one.
Haha. I'm not normally this clumsy WHUP
CRACK CRASH

1019

So uh, how've you been?
I'm sorry, do I know you?

It's-- it's Jim! We talked all night at Hazel's Christmas party.

HoHoHo It'sh SHANTA LUSH Hic
is that duct tape?

Hazel had a Christmas party?

1020

Hey Angel, is there a drink for losers who are completely forgettable to women?

Angel! Do you have a drink for celebrating first kisses? 'Cause I'll need three, haha!

Oh! That used to be my drink!
?

Congratulations on your fruity pink "first kiss."
Hey, don't I know you? You were at Hazel's Christmas party, right?

Oh good, I'm only memorable to dudes.
Hey, you should hang out with us tonight. We have a "guys' night" every Tuesday.

Oh, uh... I would, but I don't really keep up with cars or sports.
Cars or--?

OH, nonono, we just talk about GIRLS.
I'm in!

1021

Hey guys, I want you to meet Jim.
Hi, Jim.
Oh! Jim! I remember you.

Whoa-ho-HOA, is that a "first kiss" you're drinking?
Maaaaaybe!

Oh, DISH, dude.
Well, I took her out to a nice hibachi place...

You know anything about cars, Jim?
AUGH

1022

Okay! I've got every pet-thing I'll ever need. I am prepared for the pet-pocalypse.

Oooh, I'll miss you, little guy!
Aw, we'll see you again. Hey, by the way, did I really talk to that guy all night at Hazel's Christmas party?

Ooo... yeah, yeah you did, but don't worry about it. It's Jim, he -- well, it happens to him a lot.

Jim? Who's Jim?
Or perhaps it runs in your family.
Jim? I thought his name was Josh?

1023

Bye Robyn, bye Jamie, bye Expensive Laptop that never was.

HAAZ'L!
GAA!

Oh, right, drinking at home, talking cactus, blah blah blah.
Thahr's a GHOST!

There's a ghost.
Thahr's a ghost, Ah've seen eht, and eht goes "DOOOOOM"

McPedro, is this ghost white?
Wit' a black nose, an'--
--WHISKERS. It's the CAT, McPedro.
Bu-but, but--

DOOOOOOM

1024

1025

So, you made it to first base with Melody, huh?
There may have been a second base involved.

Oh reeeally!
She may have accidentally flashed me her left nipple when she bent down to pick up her purse.

Chris, that's not Second base.

I'm, uh, on a 15-base system.

1026

Hey guys, Chris and I have a question about baseball.
YOU have a question about baseball. I am perfectly secure in the values of my 15 bases.

Oh not THIS again.
I don't know anything about the sport OR the-- y'know, sport.

Hold it -- Angel, you're a girl; enlighten us?
Jameson, I'm a lesbian. Our first Base is "She's not straight."
Oh, yeah, that's my foul Ball. I hit a lot of those.

1027

So, not much luck with the ladies, eh?
HA! That's an understatement.

Half the time, they ignore me. Like I'm a piece of furniture, only less useful.

If they do talk to me, it's only until some douchebag catches their eye, and then they vanish.

Apparently the only people who want to hang out with me are lesbians and--

--guys?

1028

When I open my eyes, I will see... an empty box!

---with a kitty inside.
mow?

How are you still here? People think you're cute!

Lots of people think he's cute, but none of them have the money to cover his health issues.

FREE

Guess who just got a JOB!

You got a job?
Yeah, I joined a group of interpreters. I'm gonna be their ASL girl!

Oh Maureen, that's great! Congratulations!
thanks!
Does it pay well?

Uh-yeah, as a matter of fact!
Good. Can you interpret Kitty?

OH HAI MAUREEN MY HED IZ EXPENSIV I CAN HAZ UR HOME AND MONIEZ?

1029

Hey, Sugarcube!
Hey, Half-and-Half! How was your day?

Um-- well, I have one thing I know you'll like, and one thing I'm not sure you'll like.
Oh. Okay, what's the thing I'll like?

I got a JOB!
HONEY! That's GREAT!

mow?

1030

So- we're-- pet-sitting?
N-no...

He needed a home! And I thought--
You thought you'd adopt him without talking to me?

um...
Sweetie, we're a COUPLE now. We're sharing the same life. Which means--

AWWWWWWW

1031

So, we can keep him?
Well, I mean, you DID just get a job, so..

I will totally pay for everything!
Heh, you may want to start with litter boxes! Where is he gonna--

SQUIIISH

Oh wait, I think I know.

1032

1033

Hello hello, your pet-sitter has arrived.
Thea!

Ooo, check out your haircut!
You like it? I wanted to look my best for uh, y'know, my show.

Where is this show, again?
Uh, Westchester, near London.

Westchester... Why does that sound famil
Directions are on the table gotta go bye!

1034

Hello, roomie!
Where've you been all day, Miss Sunshine?

Playing with Jamie's kitty while she's away.
Man, you lesbians sure love playing with-- wait, what do you mean, "she's away?"

Uh, she's out of the country for like, a week-
Out of the country--

I was wondering why she hadn't asked you to watch the ca
ERIN

1035

mmm

ill be landing in about twent
SHK
wow

I've never been to England...

...I've never been out of the country!
→CUSTOMS

Please have your passport ready.
Oh

'Morning, Miss. What's the purpose of your trip?
Oh, um... I'm having a photo show in Westchester, but.. if you need to know the real purpose..

My ex-girlfriend is going to school here, and I'm -- well, I still have feelings for her, so I kind of stalked her on facebook so that

That's, that'll do, Miss
I brought my diary if you need the whole story.

14 Top Street, Miss.
Are you sure?

um.. hello?

Oh my god-- are you a customer?
We're open! We're open!

I'm -- your exhibiting artist?

1036

I--I see you got my photographs.
YES and they're even more lovely than we'd expected! Though I can't see shit through these old things.

Th- thank you.
We're bloody thrilled to have a new show here; it's been ages!

Oh- has it?
Since the 80's, dear.

I say we put the kettle on an' get to know our artist over tea and biscuits!
Oh splendid!
Geez guys I sure wish I could, but ahem I uh, have work to do See ya!

1037

CAFFÉ NEMO
Friday
8-10 Microbial Ecology
11-3ish lab
3ish-5ish research at Caffé Nemo's

Newsfeed
Faceb
Erin Eli

Please come please come please come

1038

J-- JAMIE??
ERIN!

Wha--

um

What are you doing here?
Having.. coffee?

1039

1040

But--why are you having coffee in ENGLAND?
I-- ah--
fumble fumble
I'm having a show! It's at the Greystone Gallery, the-- the opening's tonight, if you wanna--

um
Okay, maybe I'll see you there, maybe, I hope!

1041

OOH it's so CHEERFUL in here now that you changed all the light bulbs, Jamie!
Who knew they were all burnt out!

Did--did you guys PROMOTE my show at all?
Well of course we did, love! You saw the postcards.

Yes, but... did you DISTRIBUTE them?
Oh. Huh.
I did give one to my Mother, God rest her soul.

1042

RIIING
Yell-ow.
WUHUHUHUH!
JAMIE? Hang up, it's like a billion dollars to call from
I can't, you're the only one who knows what I'm doing out here!

I take it things aren't good.
Things are miserable! My show's a flop, and Erin, she--she's not coming SOB!
She's not coming? Are you sure?
The opening started two hours ago, and NOBODY'S come in!

Well yeah, most people don't start going out until, like, 9:00.
But, it IS 9:00--
CREEEAK

1043

What's going on?
It's—it's Erin!

See? I told you she'd com..
Hey, Jamie.
Erin! You came!

Yo.

—with someone.

Jamie, your photography – you're so GOOD.
thhhanks

You -- you always said you'd have a solo show, and that I'd be there with you...

Why didn't you tell me about this until now??
Why did you have to bring your new girlfriend??

1044

Girlfriend? She's not my girlfriend.
she's -- not?

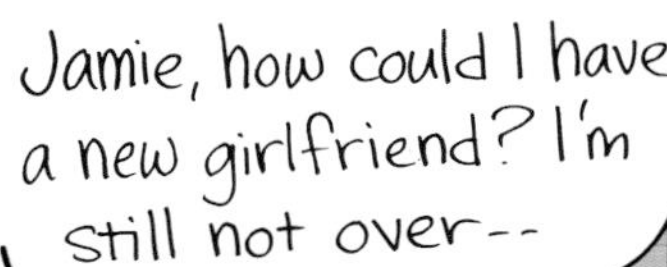
Jamie, how could I have a new girlfriend? I'm still not over --

um..

Oh f'cryin' out loud, y'both stupid f'r each other!

1045

Seriously, I'm not even gonna charge ye', this was so easy. Y'both in love; case closed.
Case... closed?

Jamie, I brought her here because I was confused. You haven't talked to me since I left, and suddenly -- you've got a show! In my town! And you never told me?

But -- you said you were uncomfortable with -- y'know, what we did in the airport, so... I thought you --

I never wanted to end things, I just --
Waitaminute... Romance Detective Jane??

1046

mph Er, yeh?
°gasp° It IS you! I've read so much about you!

How'd you --?
I'm a certified Romance Detective, too! But she's legend-ary – one time, she --
ahem Yes, well, lovely t'meet y' gals, I've really gotta scram --

Oh – y'both think th'other's gay, but y've been secretly in love wit' each othe' f' twenty years. Have fun wit' it.

HAROLD
mph mph Mmmm
Wow, she's good.
Real good!

1047

1048

So, you thought I wanted to end things between us because I didn't want... y'know... sex?
Well..

And you call yourself a Romance Detective.
Heh. Well yeah, I got my magnifying glass and everything!

Looks like you need to turn that magnifying glass...
the other way.

Oh, I guess that doesn't really do anything.
And you call yourself a bio major.

1049

Wow, I'm so glad this was one giant miscommunication.
Me too. So--what now?

Well, what do you want?
Exactly what we had before. What do you want?

Exactly the same thing.
Erin, can we be Cffs?

What's a Cff?
Cuddle friends forever.

1050

You look really sleepy. Are you jet-lagged?

Ooo, jet lag, I've heard of that.

Aww, Jamie, you should really get to bed. Where are you staying?
Uhh, staying? I, uhh.. kind of.. didn't really..

1051

Hey Jameson!
Hey, Sunshine! How was your trip?

Oh man, it was so--

Make that to-go.

Upstairs.

Are-- are you mad?
Mad? No, I got all my "mad" out the first three days. Now I'm just-- I'm just--

sigh
Jamie, why do you hide all this Erin stuff from me? I mean, Thea knew, Jameson knew, Angel knew EVERYTHING--

I'm your best friend! Do you know how that makes me feel? It makes me feel, um... what's that word, it means-- vulnerable, not happy--
Hurt?
AUGH is there a less-pussyish word than "hurt?"

1052

If I'd told you about my trip, you would've just discouraged me from going.
What? No I wouldn't have.

Yes, you would have! Hazel, admit it, you're squicked out about me being with a woman.

You've always been a little homophobic.
What? No I'm not, I love the gays!
Erin and I made out.
EH
SEE?
I was just -- stretching my face

1053

Look, just because I don't wanna think about two girls "doin' it" whatever THAT entails doesn't mean I don't support you.
Who made you a Happy Clam card?
you did

Who told you to have a long-distance relationship with Erin?
Oh-- I guess you did.

Right. So, next time you leave the country, could you please TELL ME so I can worry myself sick about you like a normal best friend?
Okay.

1054

DOOOOOOM

Dammit, Sprinkles, knock it off! You're starting to freak me--

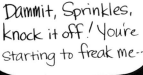

You're not Sprinkles.

SHff

1055

1056

THEA THEA
THEA THEA
MOOOAN
WHAT
the the
WALL
G-G-GHOST

What the hell
are you talking
about, dude?
YAWW
WWW!!
COFFEE

AAAAAAAA
AAAAAAAA

1057

Okay. Okay.
We both saw it.
So, either we're
both crazy, or
this place is
haunted.
Geez, first
the cactus,
now this.
COFFEE NOW

What do you
mean, the cactus?
UM UH,
cactus?
I didn't--

AAA THAHR'S
A GHOST!
WE
KNOW!
COFFEE NOW

We're both
nuts.
Yup.

1058

One coffee--
uhh, BLACK!
COFFEE-N

Umm... walk, home--
you want to walk
back home? Okay!

You--want me to--
hehe, umm, really?
Okay--

Oh wait that means
you're HUNGRY.
YES
YES
YES

1059

Hey Chris!
How's things
with the
lady friend?
Really great!
Melody says I
have a toddler's
grasp of ASL now.

Oh--
that's--
I figure deaf toddlers
have, like, 2-3 years
on me, so I'm doing
pretty well.
Heh, yeah man.
So, is it safe
to call her
your girlfriend
now?
I am happy to
announce that
you're speaking
to the proud
boyfriend of
Melody, yes.

The proud,
terrified boyfriend
of Melody.

What's terrifying about Melody? I thought you WANTED to be her boyfriend.
I did, I do! I just-- I'm really rusty.

At being a boyfriend?
At... doing... BOYFRIEND things.

Oh. OH.
Yeah.
Does someone need advice from a pro?

I don't plan on sucking her dick, Darren.
Bummer for her, I bet you're really good at it.

1060

So you guys haven't, uh...
Not yet.
How long has it been since the last time you
Three years.

Oooooooo.
Wh-- it's not THAT bad!
Yes it is, honey.

We're gonna have to start him on Book 1.
Guys
You see Chris, when a man loves a woman...
AUGH

1061

Nah, seriously man, it's like riding a bicycle. You'll remember.
I was never very good at bicycles.

Wellll, sex isn't actually bicycles, so... you'll be fine.
But, the first time I'm gonna be all clumsy and awkward!

The first time's SUPPOSED to be awkward!
It's never been awkward for me.

Yeah, me neither. Don't take advice from us, Chris.
OH, except don't go for the bunghole without asking her first. I hear girls HATE that.

1062

Oh brilliant, it's snowing.
I thought you liked the snow!

Not when it gets my hair all wet.
Aww, you need a hat like mine!

A dumb bear hat?
Of course not, silly! Something that'll suit you. Look, they have hats in this shop.

1063

1064

I can't believe you bought me this.
It's an early Christmas gift!

for you.
Yup! Hey, am I gonna see the Ghost Kitty or does that only happen at night?

Wha-- how did you--
Thea told me, doofus! I don't know why you bother trying to hide shit from me.

To keep you from doing things like
HEEEEEEERE GHOST KITTY GHOST KITTY GHOST KITTY

1065

I kind of doubt it answers to "here kitty."
I wonder where it came from?

Dunno. Maybe someone's vengeful cat died here a long time ago.
Maybe one of Sprinkles' kitties died here.

Uh, we gave away all of Sprinkles' kittens. Alive.
No no, I mean... maybe there was a stillborn.

I'm pretty sure I would've noticed the smell of a rotting corpse, Jamie.
Don't lie to me, I've seen your fridge.

1066

I think momma cats do something strange with stillborns—like, hide them or something?
Let's look it up.

type type type
Stillborn... cat... Hmm, "the mother cat (or 'queen') will often dispose of a stillborn kitten by... eating...

Lick

YAAAAAA!

1067

Great. Awesome. My cat is a cannibal.
And your house is haunted!

Well this couldn't possibly get wors--
ka-CLICK
Hazel?

I can't afford rent this month.
GAH, why did I say that?
There's more.

♫ JINGLE BELLS JINGLE BELLS ♪
GAH!
snap snap

Alright ladies, if Thea and I are hosting the Christmas party again this year, we're gonna need some help.
We're broke.

Well, Jameson and I can supply coffee and dessert.
I'll make hors d'oeuvres!
I'll think of something.

And the booze will be supplied by..
A true philanthropist.
A team player!
Someone who's guilted into it.
ME.

1068

Merry Almost-Christmas!
Thanks for helping out, guys. Sorry we couldn't really afford to decorate.

Oh that's okay! I grabbed some decorations from the café.
I brought popcorn of questionable expiration dates to string!
I've got scraps from the florist's to make paper ring chains.
Aw, it'll be an Economically and Environmentally Sound Christmas.
Also known as a "Po' People Christmas."

1069

There's only one thing this party needs and that thing is BOOZ
Clarice. Anybody seen her?
Not in this weather.

CREEAK
It'f fnowing.
Clarice!

Waaait wait wait wait.

Not funny.
Hilarious.
I want a pony.
And a cocktail!

1070

KNOCK KNOCK KNOCK
Who's that? I thought everyone was here.

Hi.
Oh! Hi, I'm Jamie. And you are--
My landlady?

Hazel, I have good news and bad news. The bad news is, you're being evicted.
WHAT?

The good news is, I made you snickerdoodles.
Yaaay!

1071

1072

You can't evict me right now!
I'm not evicting you RIGHT NOW. I'm giving you a month, because I'm nice.

But--I've lived here practically forever!
Hazel, you haven't paid me in TWO MONTHS. There's this thing about renting, you have to pay your rent or you don't get to rent anymore.

But, it's CHRISTMAS!
Merry Christmas, I'm not kicking you out 'til February.
Thap'f acfually a weally expenfive gift if you fink about it!

1073

Okay, our New Year's resolution is to PAY OUR RENT. We're gonna list the best and worst ways to do this. Are you ready?
As ever.

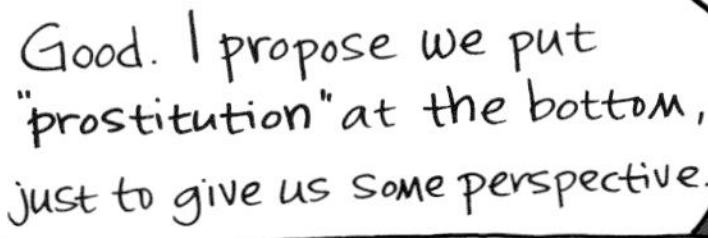

Good. I propose we put "prostitution" at the bottom, just to give us some perspective.

Ha! Why don't we kick it up a notch and make it "prostitution w/ animals."

Eww, yeah! Wait, but... animals don't have money to buy sex.
No, but their owners do. Particularly dog & horse owners.

How do YOU know all this?
Hazel, have you ever seen the Internet with SafeSearch turned off?

1074

Hey gals! Whatchya up to?
We're making a list of things we can do to make rent.

Ooo, what're your ideas?
At the bottom of the list we have: prostitution, drug dealers, bank robbers, Scientologists, middle school teachers-

Those are your ideas?
Well no, those are just things we DON'T want to resort to.

Oh! What're the things you ARE willing to do?
Ahh let's see.. "win the lotto."
Theoretically, that one has the highest profit margin.

1075

AUGH this is RIDICULOUS! We're both either over- or underqualified for EVERYTHING.
We could go back to school and get degrees in something that isn't ENGLISH.

That's it, time for Plan B: GREGSLIST.
GREGSLIST? I thought you said no prostitution?

Thea, they're not ALL sex jobs. Look: "Office Manager, 30 hrs/wk."
"Job description: Hold my penis."

You just need to filter those out.
If you filter out "penises," the results go from "520 in your area" to "none."

I've gotta run. I have an interview for another shit job I'm not gonna get.
Go get 'em, Tiger.
Bye, Thea!

Hey! Jameson! I don't suppose the coffee shop is hiring?
Nah, I don't think we need any more help.

No offense, but I don't want to HELP. I want to get PAID.
Uhh yeah, that's not really how it works.

GAAAHD this country is EFFED UP!
Yeah, I can't wait 'til the recession is over and everyone goes back to being paid to do NOTHING, like old times.

1076

sigh
I don't wanna lose this place. I've been here forever. I'll never find another place like it.

DOOOOOOOM

Sometimes change is GOOD.

1077

Well, I got the job.
Wha--you did? What kind of job is it?

The kind we're not gonna discuss.
What, do you work for the CIA or something?

Or something.
WOOOW, the CIA! I bet they gave you a weapon. Can you tell me what kind of weapon they gave you?

Hot dogs.
HOT

1078

THEA! You're doing great work, great work, could you do me a favor?
Yes, boss?

Oh no no, just call me Dick.
Uh, yes Dick?

Thea you've gotta really get in there, be excited about those wieners, get EVERYONE excited about the wieners!
Uhh yes, Dick.
You gotta be pro-wiener, wieners make people happy! Imagine EVERYONE here with a wiener in their mouth!
Please stop calling them wieners.
HOT

1079

1080

HEY! I need one BIG FAT WIENER over here! hee hee
I'll shove a big fat wiener straight up your BUNS, you--

Jamie?
Nice outfit!
AUGH NOOOO
HOT

What, you're not happy to see me? 'Cause your hat sure is.
Jamie, you can't tell ANYONE I sell hot dogs for a living.

What, you want me to tell 'em you sell tacos instead?
Tacos? Why would that--
LESBIAN JOKE! Haha, GOD I am ON today!

1081

What are you doing here, anyway? I didn't know you were into basketball.
Basketball? I'm here for the Roller Derby, silly!
HOT DOGS

Roller Derby?
Yeah! You didn't notice all the girls on roller skates?
HOT

GIRLS
ON
ROLLER
SKATES?

I can't believe you've never heard of
LESBIANS ON WHEELS
HOT

1082

Oh my god, I'm wearing a wiener on my head.
Did you just now realize this?
HOT DOGS

There are HOT, potentially GAY women EVERYWHERE, and I have a wiener on my head.
Ooh Thea it's not THAT bad!

HEADS UP, WIENER LADY!

BOOM

1083

WHOA hey, are you alright?

Sorry 'bout that, I blew right past the suicide seats.

WOOOOW, wiener wipeout.
It's-- it's okay.

Oh good! See ya, cutie!

1084

You met someone at your CIA job?
I was body-checked by someone, and she happened to be hot, yes.

Body-checked? Was she trying to escape or something?
Uhh, technically, I guess you could say that.

Thea-- are you falling in love with the enemy?
Hazel, I can't discuss this with you, you already know too much.

LESBIANS IN HEAT
CIA

1085

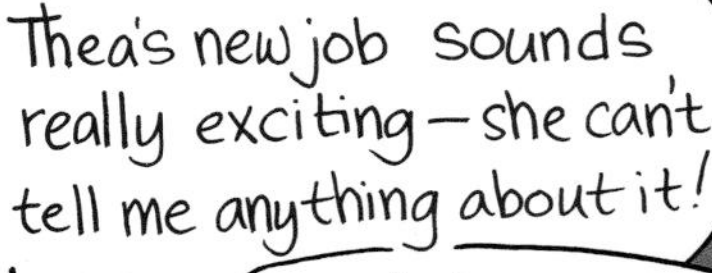

Thea's new job sounds really exciting—she can't tell me anything about it!

Oh! That's -- mysteriously vague.

Hey, how's your job search going? Any bites?
Oh. Um--

You know you only have a week until your rent is due.
Yeah, I'm -- I've got some jobs lined up, I was just gonna follow up with them today.

PLEASE GIVE ME MY JOB BACK

1086

Hazel, I can't give you back your job. It's Candy's job now.
PLEEEASE?

Look, we can't hire any more people here, but I just turned down a high-paying job that nobody wants--

I'll take it.
You don't even know what the
is yet.
I'll take it.

GOD DAMMIT

1087

We meet again.
Welcome back, Tits.
Aren't you like, twelve now? Why do you still need a babysitter?
Well, thanks to you and Miss "Bookstore," my mom thinks that if I leave the house I'm gonna get someone pregnant.

I seriously doubt that.
I know, right? Why would I bother tryin' to get laid when I have the Internet?
"Hey Tiger, wanna see me take my top off?"

Are you paying for porn with your mother's credit card.
Not telling.
Where is your modem.
Same answer.

1088

Well I'm back from my JOB.
You got a job?

Yeah, it's--
uhmmmm, it's also with the CIA.
OH, like-- My job.

Yeah, actually, I think it's in your-- division... or, sector--
Oh REALLY. That's funny, I didn't hear about any job openings in my... divisor.

That's because my job is more top-secret than yours is.
MY JOB IS ACTUALLY VERY IMPORTANT

1089

Sooo I wonder what teams are skating tonight
Skating? OH, like roller derby! Naw, tonight we have a wrestlin' match!

Wrestling..
Yeah, wrestlin' people love their wieners! Let's get out there an' put some wieners in their faces!

HOT WIENERS!

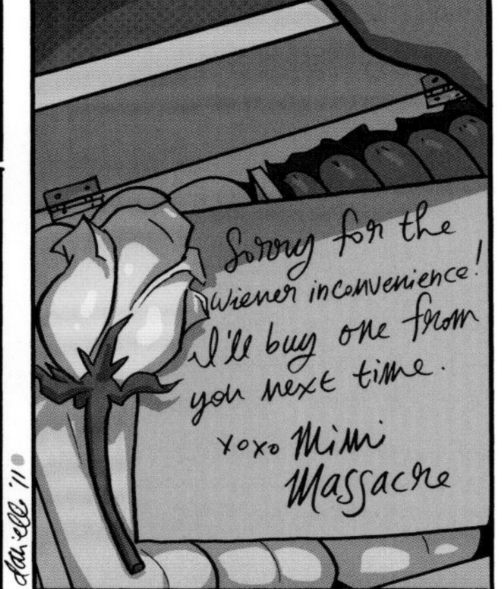

Sorry for the wiener inconvenience! I'll buy one from you next time.
xoxo Mimi Massacre

1090

Your groceries and giant penis have arrived.
Oh good, I was hungry in that double-entendre sort of way.

So are we cooking for two, or--
Yeah, Thea's out at her job until ten.

Speaking of jobs--
UGH, speaking of jobs let's not talk about mine, because it'll make me cry.

I brought your favorite wine and a towel for my shoulder.
You are better than the best boyfriend.

1091

...but then I found the modem and hid it, and forced him to play Scrabble with me, which he of course filled with dirty words.
But I totally kicked his ass.

feel better?
Yeah, thanks for listening, Sweetie.

I guess it could be worse. He could not be potty-trained.
It could be worse, you could not have a job.

Heh, it could be worse, I could have less than three days to make rent.
It could be worse, you could be broke and sober.

You know what I'm gonna say, but I know what you're gonna say back.
I don't want to borrow money from you, Zach.

Just to tide you over..
::Sigh:: What's the point? I can't afford this place now, and it's not gonna magically change by next month.

So, what are your options?
Move in with my mom, or maybe someone else.

I bet your mom would really like that.
...yeah.

1092

Did we have to come to an auditorium filled with strangers to discuss my shitty life?
This'll TOTALLY cheer you up!

What is "roller derby" again?
Okay, the girls with the stars on their heads skate around the rink as many times as they can.

Sounds boring.
EXCEPT, the other girls try to either block 'em or help 'em!

Oh, well that makes it WAY more exciting.
They sell beer here, you'll be fine.

1093

Did you say Thea's coming, too?
No no, she works here.

What? No she doesn't, she works for the--
HOT DOGS! Get yer HOT DOGS here!

See?
EEP! Hazel!
HOT DOGS

OOOH right, Thea has a dangerous job selling hot dogs.
Haha, yeeeah, it's a good thing I haven't had to use these hot dogs on anyone yet, haha

1094

Well, I've gotta jet! Y'never know what kind of scum will need a wiener.
Be careful out there!

What the flip was that all about? I've never seen you wink so much in my life.
Oh, umm my contact--

You don't wear contacts.
Look, let's just say that Thea's job is more than meets the eye.

::gasp:: Does she turn into a TRUCK?
That's classified.

1095

1096

Sooo, have we got a new roller derby fan?
-and then BAM, like bowling pins! And then, that one girl, with the mohawk--

I knew it would cheer you up.
Cheer me up? Why? Was I in a bad -- mood-- wait--

Jamie--
And that's why I got you drunk--

I'm sad and I forgot why!
I'm sure you'll remember as soon as I drink all the wine in your house.

1097

So I said that I could either move in with my mom or, y'know, him, and he basically said my mom.
Hm.

Well... Hazel, moving in with Zach doesn't exactly solve the money problem. In fact, it makes it worse.
Pshht BALLS.

Oh. Oh, balls, I see. Well, it all makes sense now.
YES. Balls, cock and balls. In my house, all the time.

You're cute when you drink so much that you let your vagina be your logic calculator.
EWW I'm not drunk enough to hear the word vagi-- vageee, vageena pass me that bottle.

1098

So um, does your CIA job pay enough to--
Hazel-

:sigh: I don't have a CIA job, either.
I know. We're both terrible liars.

So I guess this is the end.
The money's due tomorrow, right?
Yep.

Well, let's just enjoy our last day in the

GODDAMMIT!

1099

So what're you gonna do?
For now? Move in with my sister. You?

Move in with my mom, I guess. I asked Zach, but--
Whoa wait, I thought Zach lived with his parents?

He does. I was thinking we could, y'know, get our own place.
But, you're broke.

AUGH, if you people could just live in my pants for one day!
We'd tell you to do laundry, at your mom's.

Who wants brownies?
Oo!
Hi, Miss Tellington!

Oh Hazel, you've hardly packed!
I know. I'fe been depweffed.

Ooh honey, I know it's hard. I'll pack up the kitchen.

Whapf?
This explains a lot about you.

1100

WOW.

You really haven't moved anything in here, have you?
Well, sometimes, when I dust--

Thank you for letting me stay here, Mom.
Oh honey, it's your home, too!

1101

We'll pick up your furniture tomorrow.
If you need anything, just yell!
I'll leave the nightlig in the bathro
click

kid sister kid sister wherever I go, you're gonna go

hey hot dog girl!
sigh stupid wrestling match
hey! I need a hot dog!

Alright, HANG ON! I'm outta dogs, I'll be right back
WHUMP
oof

Oh shi-SHOOT, I'm really sorry!
Haha that's okay!

gasp
It's you!
Payback's a bitch!

1102

1103

I-- I'm surprised to see you!
I told ya I'd buy a hot dog!

Oh-- right!
Um, actually, I'm fresh outta dogs. Can you give me like, ten minutes?
Sure! I'll come with you.

Oh-- uh
Am I not allowed to see where the hot dogs come from?

No no, you **can**, I'm just not sure you **want** to.
I've seen a bone pop outta my elbow and I'm still in derby— I think I can handle it.

1104

So, is there a derby bout tonight, or...?
Nah, I was just on my way to a Palentine's Day party and I was hungry.
BEEP
BEEP

Palentine's Day?
Yeah, all my single pals go bar-hopping on Valentine's Day. It's a tradition!

Man, that sounds... perfect.
You should come! It's open to anyone. When do you get off?

In half an hour! Uh, I guess it's a good thing I brought a change of clothes.
Ooo, does that mean I get to wear the wiener hat tonight?

1105

I've never even SEEN this bar before.
Really? It's our favorite! Hey guys! This is Thea!
Hey
Hi, Thea!

Wait, is this the Hot Dog Girl?
Umm yeah!
George, gimme a Guinness!

Aaand what would you like?
Oh-- um-- the cheapest beer on the planet?

It's on my tab, silly, get whatever you want!
Wow, I guess you really are wearing the wiener hat tonight!
Gin and tonic, please!

1106

LAST CALL!
Oh man, I haven't been this drunk since I could afford liquor!
Haha! Can I call you a cab?

Nooono, I live right down the street!
Then let me walk you home!

D'wanna come up for some coffee?
Sure!

jingle
jingle

I-- I forgot I don't live here.
Lucky for you, I know where I live AND I've got coffee. C'mon!

mMng

Good morning.
Good morning!

Did we--
Let's just say if you're pregnant, I'm not the father.

1107

I'm sorry I got so drunk last night.
Don't be! You were really cute.

So... last night, we--
We snuggled.

We only snuggled?
It was a lot of snuggling.

I-- I would like very much for this to not be a one-night snuggle.
Then I will snuggle the shit out of you tomorrow night.

1108

Where are the boys? I thought they were coming to help you move the couch?
I told you, they won't be here until nine.

But... it's 8:45
Yes, Mom, not EVERYONE thinks that "on-time" is the same thing as "late," just you.
I'M HERE!

huff puff
I'm here
Ooh there you are, Zach! Hazel thought you were going to be late.
MOM

It's too early to lie to you, Miss Tellington. I'm only early to impress you.
And honest, too!
MOM

1109

Hey guys, I'm sorry I'm so late.
Good timing! Your bed is going next.

Hi.
Hi, Sir Drinks-A-Lot. Since when can you afford enough booze to make you look like that?

Wait, you're hungover, but you're glowing.
mm-hm.

Are we officially over Angel?
Oh we are so over Angel.

1110

1111

knock knock!
Come in!
Oooh, I love it, it's so cute!
Very spacious!
Hi Hazel! Just showing the place to this nice family.
Oh.

Ooo, the red couch would look so nice in that corner.
It would!
Uhh, Actually, that's like, the dining area.
Oh, but it can be whatever it wants to be!
I can't believe you're LEAVING this place!

1112

Thanks for dropping me off, Mom.
Hi, Miss Tellington!
Hello, dear!

Did you pack a pair of clean undies?
MOM
Well, I'm just remembering that time in fifth grade..
MOM

Oh I guess you're not having your period right now, anyway. Have fun, girls!
We will!
VROOOM

So, what're we doing while we wait for Zach to pick you up?
My mom packed us matching Happy Pony cross stitch kits.
SCORE.

1113

Man, cross stitching is AWESOME.
I think adults created alcohol to make stupid kids' stuff fun again.
knock knock knock

Come in!
Is Hazel ready to be picked up from daycare?

Here. I made you something.
It's -- a pony?

It can be a death pony.
How much red do you have? It needs laser beam eyes.

1114

Have a good time at your "sleepover."
Oh, we will.

Waitaminute— did you seriously tell your mom you were staying at Jamie's tonight?
No, I told her I was gonna put your wing-wang in my hoo-hah.
So, yes.

Hazel, I don't feel comfortable lying to—
Did I tell you that Jamie and I went bra-shopping together?

I-- AH--
follow the boobies, Zach.

Hazel, we can't do this all the time.
Well yeah, that position would eventually make my vagina fall out.

No, I mean we can't lie to your mom every time you wanna sleep over.
Oh. Well, I hope you like sleeping alone, then.

Hazel--
Hey, you could've moved in with me, but NO. Now I live with a full-time chaperone.

What th- how am I getting yelled at for trying to be nice to my girlfriend's mom?
Your girlfriend's mom thinks your girlfriend is still ten years old.

1115

So, what's all this 'I could've moved in with you' talk? You never asked me-
I brought it up with you, and you thought it'd be nice if I lived with my mom.

I thought your mom would like it if you moved in, but I never said I wouldn't move in with you.
You may as well have.

sigh Hazel, did it ever occur to you that living together goes beyond sharing a bed? But we never talk about our future, because every time I bring it up, you--

ZZZZZ

1116

Hey, Mom.
Oh! Good morning!

I thought I was picking you up from Jamie's this afternoon?
Nah, Zach dropped by, so... how's Sprinkles adjusting to her new home?
Murr

Oh just fine! The other one is a little skittish, though.
Other one?

You never told me you had two cats!
DOOOOOOM

1117

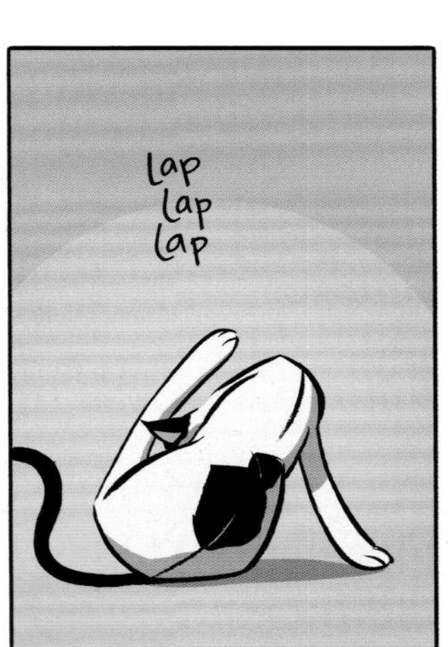
lap
lap
lap

Heeey, kitteh. What's 'at import'nt thing yeh're doin'?

Eht looks REAL IMPORT'NT! An' TASTEH, even!

Yeh're LICKIN' yehr BUTT!
Yeh're a BUTT—LICKEHR!

Says the cactus who plays with his own soil.

1118

1119

AND I'm off work!
Woohoo! Let's get drinks!
HOT DOGS

I'm gonna go change, but I'm keeping the wiener hat on, 'cause tonight I'm taking you out!
Ooh!

um

Literally?
figuratively.
Oh thank you!

1120

Oh my goodnesh theshe are delishish
I knew you'd like 'em! Crispy Crunch shots are my fave.
Wan' me t' buy some more?
Hmm... nah, let's go back to my place.
Okay... HAAAY, guy what tends bar! I'd like to close th' tab that's been feeding this lovely ladie

Haha, you're so drunk!
Drunk 'bout YOU
Card's been declined, Ma'am.

1121

Tha-- that can't be right. Run it again!
I ran it three times.

It's okay, Thea, I can get it. You can take me out next--
NO, but--but I'm wearin' th' wiener hat tonight!

It's OKAY, I promise! Stay right here, I'll be back with my wallet.

1122

And then you left?
Oh, Thea.
It was humiliating! I should be able to pay for her drinks!

Wait, is there a Lesbian Code for who "should" be paying?
Yeah, what makes you the "dude?"
I'm older than her. I finished college--

But wasn't SHE the one who made all the first moves?
She is totally the dude.
BUT I'M ALWAYS the DUDE!

What'd we miss?
Oh, Thea abandoned Miss Meals on Wheels because her credit card bounced.

You left her with the tab?
I panicked! What would you do if you offered to buy someone drinks and your card was declined?

Let 'em pay for it.

Can I join your club?

1123

...and then my card got declined.
Ooh, shit.
AUGH, my worst nightmare!

See? I knew you guys would get it. All the girls were like, "WAH WAH WAH, if she invited you in the first place, and she expected to pay--"

Oh wait, she invited you?
You walked out on a girl who wanted to pay?
Call her right now and apologize!

1124

Maya, I wish you were a lesbian.
Aaaa, words I never wanted to hear from my sister.

Not like THAT. I just wish I had other lesbians to talk to about ...girls.
Mm, I don't envy you there. So far every man I've dumped has claimed that we're "complicated."

Mama, what's a lesbian?
Aunt Thea's trying to figure that out, too, baby.
Hey!

1125

So I thought I'd make your favorite mac & cheese dish for your birthday dinner Thursday.
Mm, your mac & cheese is the best mac & cheese.

Do Zach's parents have any food allergies?
That's-- an unrelated question, I hope?
Oh, was it supposed to be a surprise? Zach made it sound like it wasn't a surprise.

What did you
SURPRISE!

1126

1127

Look, if my mom can convince your mom that it's okay for you to sleep over here, then you won't have to lie to her about it anymore.

Dinner with your parents is NOT my idea of a birthday gift, Zach.
That's why we're doing it on Thursday. before your birthday.

Thursday IS my birthday, Zach.

-- that's ... why ... I'm gonna ...
Spike our moms' drinks and laugh with me when one of them passes out face-first into the cake.
... yes, sweetie.

1128

Tom and Estelle, it is SO nice to finally meet you both!
Well thank you for having us, Carol!

So, where's the birthday girl?
'M right here

Oh my.
What. S'My birfday.

1129

You look, um--
It's m' birfday.

Sigh. Right.
So, you gonna turn some water into some wine, or what?

Won't have to. My mom brought booze.
Yeah, but my mom NEVER drinks
HAHAHA HAHAHA

Let's hope they'd have your DAUGHTER'S nose!
HA! Well, hopefully they WOULDN'T have her bladder control! Once, when she was five, she
MOM!

1130

Well, that was delicious, Carol.
Oh I'm so glad you could join us!

Ready to go, Hazel?
OH-- uh-- I mean--
Oh, are you staying with the Mazzeos tonight?

Uh--if that's -- you know--
Here, let me give you something special for tonight.

Tell me those are condoms.
Sad Puppy cross stitch kits.
We can add death ray eyes.

I SOWWY

:gasp:
for Me?

It was supposed to be a surprise!
Well, now I'm the surprise!

1131

Ooh I LOVE puppies!
I--I hope this makes up for--

Shhh.
...sorry I couldn't afford our drinks... sorry you had to pay the bill...

Ooh, Thea

You apologized for all the wrong things!

1132

I--I, what did I forget to apologize for?

I bet you can figure it out if you think about it.
:GASP: for leaving you at the bar!

And what else?
for... for being a failure.

for THINKING you're a failure.

1133

Thea, you don't have to buy me things to impress me.
But... it's embarrassing that I can't.

Oh that's just silly. I'm not dating you to get free stuff, I'm dating you 'cause I like you.
You like a hot dog vendor.

Don't judge...
I have a crush on the hot dog vendor.

Wow, I didn't know you could blush!
It's a secret blush.

1134

1135

So, did you grow a pair?
I am still without testicles, but I did apologize to Mimi, yes.
And what did she say?
.. sigh.. Exactly what you told me she'd say..

That she doesn't care about your money, she just likes me, I know I know.

TOOOOLD YOOUUUU
YOU-- are going to make a fine teenager one day, you know that?

1136

ZZZXXZZ

DOOOOOOM

DOOOOOOM

THAT'S EHT! Ah'm sick o' this cryptic "DOOOM" shite! Ef Ah hear eht one more time..

DOOM
EEE!

1137

Seriousleh! What th' fehck are they DOOOOMin' about?
McPedro! Watch yer fuckin' language.
I didn't even notice they were saying "DOOM." I thought they just meowed funny.
Ah'm gonna get to th' bottom of this.

My sentient Scottish-Irish cactus is off to solve the mystery of why my cat and her stillborn ghost-baby like to say "DOOM."

1138

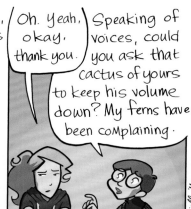

I picked up some of that wine you liked that Estelle brought over.
Oh! Thank you, dear. I'll save it for a special occasion.
Mom, do you ever hear, um... voices where you know you shouldn't?
Mm... well, sometimes I hear Grandma's voice in my head, when I'm missing her.
Oh. Yeah, okay, thank you.
Speaking of voices, could you ask that cactus of yours to keep his volume down? My ferns have been complaining.

...
Yes.
Yes, I can, Mom.
Thank you.

So apparently my mom can hear McPedro, AND her own plants.
WOW, I thought your mom didn't drink?

She doesn't! Maybe she was BORN drunk.
Maybe you don't have to be drunk to hear plants after all. Maybe we're just drunk all the time.

Nah.
The born-drunk thing makes more sense anyway.

1139

Hazel.

C'mere, I need you.
Hi, Clari-- oh..

I need your mom to help me get a job at the library. Candy's driving me nuts at the porn store and I can't take it anymore.

Can't you just fire her?
sigh Yeah, but then I don't have a good excuse to chase my dream.

1140

Wait, you want me to hook you up with a job at the library so you can quit the porn store.
Yes.

Instead of firing Candy and giving me back my job.
GAH, I thought you were too drunk to make that connection.

I'm a high-functioning drunk, Clarice. You know that.
Yeah, but I've been counting bottles, and you've crossed your faux-Sober Threshold.

Eight? Holy shit. I leveled up!
Congratulations. Great timing.

1141

I must be the greatest friend in the world to be doing this for you.
You are, you are.

Hi, Mom.
Oh! Sweetie, what a pleasant surprise!

Mom, I'd like to introduce you to my friend Clarice. She-
OH, the DANCER!

Ah, n--
YES. Yes, the dancer.
Oh I hear people practically beg and scream for you!

1142

1143

You told your mom I'm a dancer?
No, I told her you're a dominatrix.

WHAT?
Kidding. Just putting it into perspective for you.

Anyway, now you've met my mom. Since you're being a dick and not giving me back my job, the rest is up to you.
I'm gonna go home and sleep off this hangover.
Leaving me to wonder why I don't replace Candy with someone as responsible as you.
uRp
Exactly.

1144

Tobin's Spirit Guide?
Shh, Ah'm doin' research on th' GHOST KITTEH.

McPedro, Tobin's Spirit Guide is a fictional book made up by the creators of Ghostbusters.

Believe me, I know. I asked for one for my 8th birthday.
They got me a rain stick instead.
That was a depressing day.

Then... then what's this Ah'm readin'?
That's a supplement for the Ghostbusters RPG.

You should invite your friends over and make some nachos.

Is tha' why th' dice don't work with mah Ouija board?

1145

Candy? We need to talk—
No we don't, George already told me.

Yes, we do. George doesn't know what I--

Wait, what did George tell you?
About the store closing.

We need to talk.

1146

I thought you said the recession would never affect the store?
It ain't. I'm retirin'.

You're retiring?
Shore! This runnin'-a-business thing's for th' birds.

Well-- then why don't you just sell the business?
What, an' let go 'all this porn? Then what'd ya s'pose I'd do with all that free time? Heh.

Candy, I need you to cut & paste all these dicks into the lady mags.
Woo, craft-time!
SURPRISE! COCKS

1147

The porn store's closing?
Yeah, so I really need to talk to your mom about jobs at the library.

Why don't you just make an offer to the guy and buy the store?
Did you miss the part where I've wanted to be a librarian all my life?

But--but where are we gonna buy our vibrators?
Hazel, I'd like to introduce you to my good friend, the Internet.

The Internet does not give me employee discounts.
But the Internet DOES give you, let's see... dildos shaped like Mister Rogers. "Please won't you be my neighboner."

1148

Um... hi, Ms. Tellington, I'm--
Oh hello, Clarice! How's the dancing going?

Uh--fine! Um... actually, not so well. I lost my job.
Ooh, honey I'm sorry!

Would it keep your mind off things if you helped me shelve these returned books?

1149

Hmm... did you see a large pile of musical compositions?
I hope you don't mind, I sorted them and put them back where they belonged.

Oh! Thank you, Clarice, that's my least favorite task of the day!
Well, if you'd like something else to do, the periodicals are always a--

I-- I kind of already--

VOLUNTEER of the WEEK

1150

Man, I'm gonna miss our trips to "the bookstore."
At least our grand finale was a going-out-of-business sale.

Alright, it's show & tell time. What'd you get?
I got a dozen vibrating eggs, massage oil, and THE GREATEST 1970'S PORNO TAPE EVER!

I can't believe you still own a VCR.
"Rebecca takes a load in the mouth from one stud, as she's poked in the--" AWW man, this is ANAL!

You've never even tried anal. How'd you know you don't like it?
Well, this one time, I was REALLY constipated, and
H'OKAY why don't we talk about what I got now?

1151

Our last "Chinese & Porn" fortune cookies.
They'd better be good!

"Pleasure yourself." ...in bed.
Haha, PERFECT! Mine's "Toys & novelty items"... in bed...
"126 North High Street... in... Bedford?"

1152

124, 128-- where's 126 North High?
This is right behind my old apartment.

We don't even know what we're looking for.
If there are "toys & novelty items" involved, I'm sure we'll find--

We have been waiting for you.
Come.

Heehee, "come."
Shh!

1153

What IS this place?
It is the Secret Cave.

Whoa! fancy vibes!
How did we not know about this place already?
Entry to the Secret Cave is by invitation only.

And you just sell vibrators?
All of your desires will be fulfilled within the Secret Cave.

Everything you say is an innuendo.
In YOUR end-o.
yes.

We sell more than just vibes here.
You have an entire wall of bondage gear...

Vibes and dildos are here, that's our bondage wall, lingerie rack, lotions & lubes...
And we do have porn as well.

What's behind the curtain?
Things that many women don't want to see.

Such as?
Anal fisting. facials.
Ron Jeremy.
Got it.

1154

Well, I guess we have a new porn store.
Heck yes!

Weekly visits?
I vote Tuesdays.
Done. See you guys later!

OH! Hello there, aren't you the girl who used to live in our apartment?

Your-- apart-- OOH, you're the people who moved into MY apartment.
Hah, it sure USED to be!
We've brightened it up with a little rose paint and a lot of Lysol!

1155

So, are you gonna pick up more hours here now that the porn store is gone?

Yeah, you?

Nah, I'm gonna get serious about finding a job at the library.
YAAAY, Sexy Librarian will finally become a reality!

You know, I get along with you a lot better when I'm not your boss.
Well, that makes two of us.

From now on let's only play dominant/submissive on the stage.
Deal.

1156

Hi, Carol.
Oh hello, Clarice! Are you here to volunteer again?

Ah, yes, but-- uh, I was hoping I could ask you some questions about the library?
Of course, dear! But first, why don't you join me in the events room for a little party.

A party?
It's a going-away party for one of our librarians - she's moving to France.

We'll mis
you so
much!
How... convenient.
Ooh
Mari
thank
you!
BON VOYAGE

1157

1158

Um, Carol, I don't want to get ahead of myself, but I wanted to ask you about positions at the library, and it looks like you have an opening--
Oh, Clarice!
We would love to have you, dear, but being a librarian requires more than a love of books!

You have to go to school for--

Well I'll be.

1159

A Master's in Library and Information Science! I thought you went to school for dancing?
Clarice
itzpatrick
ntials
ah University
y and Information Science
Well, I more or less "danced" my way through college, heh.
My, aren't you multitalented!

Clarice, I'm going to schedule you for an interview immediately.
Oh thank you, Carol!

And then we can discuss putting together a dance workshop for the community!
Oh. Thank you, Carol.

1160

POP!

To Clarice, the Librarian!
Woo!

So when the fuck did you get a master's degree, you ninja?
While you were stocking shelves and arranging the dildo displays.

And you paid for it how?
It's amazing what some people will pay to get whipped.

You lead a strange life, Clarice the Librarian.
Here's to your mother never finding out.

1161

Hey, thanks for coming out to celebrate, Thea. I wasn't sure you'd want to join us, since it's at the Meck and all...
You'll notice Angel doesn't work on Tuesdays.

Ahh, I see. So, I guess you guys never made amends?
Augh, no. I don't even care anymore. I'm just glad she isn't here tonight.

slurp
On an unrelated note, these drinks are awful.
Yeah, I'll give her that.

Hey, sweetie—WHOA, what happened to—
Tyler happened to me.

first it was water balloons with lemonade... then, Nerf guns with superglue... then he reprogrammed my phone to make fart noises.

Here's a towel, and here's the "help wanted" ads.
Th-thank you, Za
PRRRT

1162

Geez, it's been forever since I've looked at the classified ads. These jobs are all AWFUL.
Keep an open mind. Maybe they're not as bad as you think.

Truck drivers, housekeepers... bee nest removal?
Whoa, wait-$20/hr, 401k, and health insurance?

1163

So, I hear you're working with bees now-
No, I didn't pass the first evaluation.

They put me in a bee suit and made me stand in the middle of a swarm.
There may have been some screaming and flailing involved.

Ooo yeah, I could see that.
Hey, did you know the ice cream shop is hiring?

Chocolate fudge Ripple while you're at it!
ZOOM

1164

DING
Is there a job here?
Yep.

Oh--Candy, what are you doing here?
Applying for a job.

You are NOT taking this delicious ice cream job from me.
I was here first.

Like I care. I'm after that kid with the braces.
Over my dead fucking body.
Congratulations, kid, you're hired.
YAY!

1165

1166

We just got our asses handed to us by an eighth-grader.
Hardly. She just got there before we did.
JOSH

Is that all it takes? Getting there first?
Hazel, we are two highly employable women. Whichever of us applies to a job first is gonna land it.

RACE!

1167

NOW HIRING
UNG, MINE
HRG, NO MINE!

Hi, I'd like to apply for a job.
But, I-- was-- AUGH

Huh. Okay. Can you tell me why you feel you're more qualified than the other applicants to
I was here first.

Uh-- yeah, that's not--
Oh, hold the phone, this is a pawn shop? When did this town get a pawn shop?

You are SO bad at this.
Do I look like a badass?
NOW HIRING
BUY-SELL-TRADE

1168

So I understand you're competing with Candy for jobs.
And WINNING, I might add!
I almost got that last one...

Which one was that? The pawn shop or the gas station?
Judge all you want, Miss Dominatrix von Librarian. Not all of us can land our dream job.
Jobs. Plural.

Hazel, you may not get your dream job NOW, but you don't have to get a job you'll HATE.
Sigh...
I don't even know what kind of job that would be.

Think of something you'd like to be surrounded by every day.
BOOZE.
... wait, that's it! BOOZE!

1169

Hey, Charles.
Hazel! Where's our #1 customer been all month?

I moved to the other side of town.
Ahh, I see. Well, what brings you here tonight? The usual?

Actually... I was kind of wondering if you're hiring...
Whoa— Hazel, you realize fourSquare has upgraded you from Mayor to President, right?

So the REAL question is, would our PRESIDENT like to hire you?
HIRED!

That's it?
That's it.

Wow. I can't believe they hired you just like that.
Well, it's not like I needed much training. I know everything about this place.

Oh yeah? What's the best cognac you carry?
This one.

Why's the cap off?
Employee discount.
swig

1170

Maya, does this dress scream "oldest lesbian at the party?"
No, but that attitude does. Party at Mimi's?
mush mush

sigh Yeah, she wants her friends to meet me.
That hardly sounds like something to sigh over!

But, they're gonna think I'm OOOLD!
You're only as old as you feel, sis!

Can you just pity me for two seconds, please.
I'm a single mom. I pity no one.
MAKE IT WAIN!

1171

Hey, Mimi
Ooo, don't you look cute!

Yeah? You don't think I look too old?
Psht, if that's old then I'm hot for teacher.

Hey everyone, come meet my girlfriend Thea!
Hey Thea!
Hi Thea!

And this is my mom.

Oooh, why we could be twins!

1172

I done raised her all m'self holdin' down two jobs.
You're amazing, Ma.

--getting my PhD, but I also volunteer at the museum twice a week...

--used to be a model, but I wanted to make a difference in the world, so now I'm in med school--

So how do you feel about my friends?
inferior COUGH um, IN AWE, in FREQUENT AWE.

1173

1174

I do tend to surround myself with pretty amazing people.
Yeah, everyone in your living room.

And YOU, silly.
Sigh Sure, the amazing hot dog vendor.

Y'know, we're not defined by our jobs. If I told you what I do for a living, I'll bet you'd agree.
What do you do for a living?

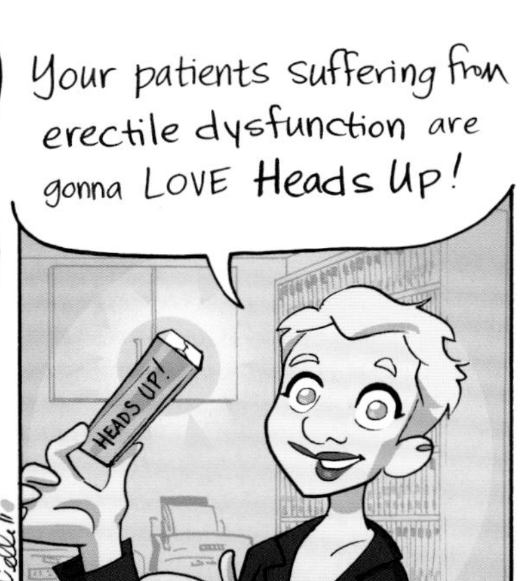

Your patients suffering from erectile dysfunction are gonna LOVE Heads Up!
HEADS UP!

1175

HAHAHA you rep for an erectile dysfunction medication?
Hehe, yeah, I guess we both work with a bunch of wieners!

Do you feel better now?
Yeah— I guess you're right about the job thing.

AND did you notice that MOST of my friends are in their thirties, just like you?
Sigh Mimi, every time I start to feel insecure, you mak
Mimi!

Ooh you have to come meet Angel!
Angel?

1176

Angel, this is my girlfriend Thea!
Thea?

Thea, this is-- uh, my ex-girlfriend--
Ex-girlfriend?

Do-- do you guys-- already--

I'll be in the room with the punch... having... Punch

1177

Thea.

Look, you don't have to like me, but I'm not gonna let you put Mimi in an uncomfortable position.
I cared about her more than I cared about any other woman I dated (no offense), and I still do. Besides, I hear she's crazy about you.

So, let's pull up our big-girl pants and drop the drama.

I'm not wearing pants!

Oh, don't worry 'bout her.

Angel's not a bad person, but she ain't terribly sen-sitive, huh?
No, she's like, the **opposite** of sensitive... y'know, like-- **in**sensitive.

Well, she was no good for my daughter. I can tell you're a much better girlfriend.

Aww, Mimi's mom really likes you!
HAHAHA Mimi's mom thinks Angel's a bitch!

1178

Hey, are you okay?
I'm okay. I'm sorry I made a scene.
Ooh, I wouldn't have invited her if I'd known the situation.
I can't believe we both dated Angel.
Really? I can! Angel's dated every lesbian in this zip code.
By "dated," do you mean "played Scrabble with"?
Oh, has she moved on to board games? When we were dating, she did "jigsaw puzzles."

1179

Hey, um... I'm also really sorry I've been so insecure lately.
Sometimes I don't know what you see in me. I'm such a mess these days. I used to be so confident in myself, passionate and determined, before the paper went under...
I know.

How do you know?
Because **that** is what I see in you.

1180

Hmmm
May I help you?
Oh, uh, I'm looking for a copy of Atlas Shrugged, but I can't seem to--
That's because you're looking in the over—sized art books.
Well-- I've always considered Atlas Shrugged to **be** an oversized art book, myself.

Oversized in **concept**, you see--
Let's see if we can find it in the oversized ego section.

1181

1182

Here, Atlas Shrugged, in the How to Attract Women who are Smarter Than You Section.
Say, do you like poetry?
That depends on who's asking me to a poetry reading.
'Tis the very gentleman before your beautiful eyes.

No.
I w--was that--blatant rejection?

Oooo I love it when a woman makes me feel EMOTIONS

1183

HAAAZEL!

Is this the Happy Booze Dance?
It's the Happy You're My friend Dance!

1184

Look at you, all dolled up!
Yeah, I fibbed a little. It's also the Erin's Coming Back from England Dance.
I was wondering when that was gonna happen.
TONIGHT! I guess the dress kinda gives it away.

So, are you guys, like, dating, or..
I... guess you could say that?

Are you taking her somewhere romantic?
Big Josie's Dinosaur Wonderland and Barbecue!

1185

NATIONAL

ERIN!

Ooh it's so good to see your face!

Heh, aww, you really missed me, huh?

Zzz

Big Josie's
DINOSAUR
WONDERLAND
& BBQ!

1186

Hi Jameson, hi Maureen!
Hey Sunshine! Here's your brew.

Do you need any... SUGAR with that?
GASP! SPECIAL K!
murr?

Aww, well I don't normally take sugar, but--
HURK

BLEAH
Black is fine.

1187

Yeeah, I didn't think that'd be sanitary.
I'll clean him up. C'mon, Spesh-K.

Okay, you are positively GLOWING. What's the deal.
Erin came home last night!

Ooo, so, was it Make-out City? Grope Central? Strap-on Headquarters?

We cuddled!
Aww, that's the best!

1188

1189

So, not to get too personal, but are you and Erin, like... dating?
Um, yeah, I mean, we don't have sex, but--hm, how do I explain it?

It's like, if you and Chris went out on dates and held hands and cuddled naked at night.

I'm pretty sure it's not like that.
Well yeah, there's less body hair.

1190

Booze b-booze booze booze, it's th' BOOZE SONG
Excuse me--

My wife and I are looking for--oh! You're the girl who used to live in
my apartment.

Right, you used to live in our apartment! My wife and I are looking for a wine--
Let me guess: It comes in a box.

Wow, you're very good!
That wasn't hard.
Do you-
YES, we also sell 7-Up.

1191

Well, you've been very helpful, Miss-
Hazel.

Hazel. A pleasure to formally meet you.
Oh, the pleasure's all mine, Mister-

0721
01/14
PERPHECT

...perfect.
It better suits my wife.

1192

A poem by E. E. Cummings.

WHAT
She walks in beauty, like the night
Of cloudless climes and starry skies
And all that's best of dark & bright
Meet in her aspect and her eyes

That was Byron!

GRR PSEUDOINTELLECTUAL MEN!
Ah, I see you've met Tucker.

What, does he hit on EVERY woman who works here?
Let's just say Tucker has a thing for librarians.

Who the fuck names their child Tucker, anyway?
Some people don't like children, Clarice.

1193

So, are there any other library scumbags I should know about?
Hm. Well, there's Homeless Dan, and then...

THAT GUY.

that guy?

What does that guy do?
HE READS.

1194

I'm pretty sure reading is allowed in the library, Beatrice. Encouraged, even.
But he just-- he just READS!

It's like he doesn't have a job, but he doesn't look homeless.
In fact, he looks like he still lives with his MOM, and she still dresses him.
Do you see how high up his pants are?

And he checks out EVERY SINGLE BOOK I want to read.

1195

Psht, Beatrice. There's nothing wrong with that guy.

1196

1197

Erin! The beach is calling us!

I'm almost ready!

Ready!

Say, do you burn easily?
Naw, I just REALLY like clothing.

1198

Here, the SPF on this is so high the sun will actually run away in fear.
Haha. okay.

I thought you were joking!
I was! I think it's hiding from the reflection, ow!

1199

KRA-KOW

EEE!
Run to the car!
We're going home!

Good thing we didn't bring books.
Word.

1200

This is the best.

I tried really hard to make friends in grad school, but everyone was too grown-up. Nobody had any imagination. Everyone hated the rain.

It's hard to find someone you can lie around with, cold and soaking wet, and still feel you're at your happiest.

I'm so glad you're home.

Girls with Slingshots
VOLUME SEVEN
by danielle corsetto
underwear!

VOLUME SEVEN

strips 1201-1400

1201

Hey, whoa, what're you doing with my graph paper? That stuff's expensive!

Ah need eht fehr mah research! Ahm tryin' t'connect th' frequency of th' kittehs sayin' "DOOOM" wit' occurances of actual doom.

Huh, that's pretty clever. What've you found?
Well, on Tuesdee Ah heard 'em say DOOM twice--

--an hour later, yeh lost yehr tampon in yehr cooch.
Stop reading my diary!

1202

Hazel, dear, I don't suppose you have any AA batteries?

I can't seem to find the ones I use in my BACK MASSAGER,
right right, let me check.

I don't know how I feel about lending my mom batteries that were inside something I've loved up and whispered naughty words to.

Unless... it's... empty?
Problem solved!

1203

What th-- they're all EMPTY!
Where do yeh even PUT this?

Good thing Jamie has that vault.

Jamie?
A-huh huh huh huh huh HAZEL they're GONE! The batteries are all--

Oh wait, there's one!

...it, it's just a Tootsie Roll, a-huh huh huh huh huh huh!

1204

Jamie! Huff puff I ran as fast as I could
Did you try the store?

I tried THREE stores. Nobody has batteries.
freak coincidence.

No... Jamie, have you looked outside?

It's not just us.
WHYYY

1205

What're we gonna do?
Use our hands, I guess.

But--I don't remember HOW.
Yeah, and our hands don't vibrate.

WAIT! You have a boyfriend!

He doesn't vibrate either, I know.

1206

What do we do, what do we do...
We could try calling the stores in New Brunswick.

Already did that, they're all out.
Hm. Can't we buy batteries online?

It'll take too long!
This mystery needs to get solved today.
The Romance Detective? Really?

If this isn't a crime against romance, then I don't know what is.

1207

Excuse me, I'd like to buy some... batteries.
Sorry "detective," Some guy bought us all out this morning.

I don't suppose you'd care to tell me about this BATTERY CAPER
four foot eight, Seventy-five pounds, used his Mother's credit card. Here's the address.

Could you make this a little more difficult for me? I've got a reputation to keep up.

1208

Diane Conrad. Huh, that name sounds familiar.
DING DONG

Mrs. Conrad? Romance Detective Jamie here. Could I have a word with your son?
Oh, dear!

He's in the basement. Oh I hope he hasn't caused any trouble!
So do I. ...NEITHER do I...

What I mean to say is, I hope your son hasn't caused any
EEP!

1209

What in the name of Romance is THAT?
MOOOM I told you not to let anyone down here!
It's the police, dear, I had to!
⁂Sigh⁂ This is my new invention, the Sex Bot 2000.
She's AWESOME! She can play video games, talk about comic books, and she's TOTALLY HOT!

I'm not a very good artist.
No, I'm afraid you're not.

1210

Do you know why I'm here, young Mister Conrad?
Uhh, because my Sex Bot is criminally sexy?
Just how many batteries does that thing take?
I'm just BORROWING them!
Borrowing! Do you know how many crimes you committed? Breaking & entering, credit card fraud, uhh Stealing Stuff

Fine, put me in jail or whatever.
Oh, I have a much more appropriate punishment in mind.

Hi I'm the Battery fairy I've come to return your batteries.
Louder!

1211

One for you...

and one for you.
There. Now you'll never have to rely on batteries again.
I can't believe you'd never heard of rechargeable vibes before.
bzzzz
These look... expensive.
Yeah, well I swiped all of the samplers when I worked at the porn store.

...EW.
kinky!
bzzz

1212

See ya, gals.
See ya.
Thanks, Clarice!

hi um I think we should date.
Do you see any books here? I don't, so that means I don't have to play nice with you

whoa wait stop!

I think you should, um, be nice to me. Because...
I know your secret.

8 o'clock, tonight, at the BlueMoon.
Mistress.

GASP!
You came!
Shh.
3 rules:
DON'T say my name. DON'T mention which club I work at. DON'T mention which library I work at.

Afraid someone's gonna recognize your secret identity, eh?

Afraid someone's gonna recognize me with you.

1213

Look, I don't want to lose my job at the library. I'm willing to negotiate with you.
click
click
I brought money. Lots of it.
Clari--uh, Mistress--

You don't have to pay me off. I don't want your money. All you have to do is go out with me, give me a chance.

Please take the money.

1214

But, I don't want--
FINE, let's play boyfriend and girlfriend. I'll be the boyfriend.

Come to the club tonight at ten. I'll show you what it's like to date a dominatrix.

O-- okay
Is this the wine you wanted, sir?
Dang, I should've grabbed a twenty!

1215

um, Hi! I'm here to--
AAAA
Your ID, please, and read and sign this form. First time?

Oh.. sure.. I mean.. yeah?
That'll be $15 please.
Hang on. Are you Tucker?

yeah?
Follow me. Miss Clarice is expecting you.

She is?
If you're smiling, you must have heard me wrong.

1216

1217

Clarice, you have a visitor.
oh WOW, you look--
SHUT UP

SNAPPA!
You will speak only when I prompt you. Did you read the waiver?
um yes?
I'll start you out easy. You shall address me as Miss Out Of My League. Any questions?

D-do I get a safeword?
Your safeword is "Pansy-Ass."

1218

Turn around.
Oh, ah, you don't have to tie me up, I'm not gonna run!

I'm tying you up for YOUR enjoyment.
oh but, uh what if I don't--

WHAT DID I SAY ABOUT TALKING?
Y-yes, Mistress!

NO! DO NOT CALL ME MISTRESS! I DID NOT GIVE YOU PERMISSION!
Y-yes, Miss Out Of My League!

Very good. Pants on or off?
ON VERY MUCH ON!

1219

You've been a bad boy, Tucker.
oh god oh god oh god oh god oh god ohg oh god oh

You harass me at work!
EEEE!

You miscredit famous poets!
AAAA!

You BLACKMAIL ME into going out with you!
AAA stopst- PANSY-ASS, PANSY-ASS!!

Tucker, I haven't even hit you yet.

1220

Here, have a seat.
whimper

Now, tell me honestly: Did you enjoy that?
N-not particularly.

See, Tucker, I'm looking for someone who ENJOYS being dominated. You're simply looking for a smart girlfriend.

See, unfortunately, a smart girl isn't gonna--

sigh
You were a good sport. I'll help you out.
pat pat

So, did you tame that little blackmailing twerp?
Candy, I think I'm gonna quit the club.

What?
I should've never used my real name on stage. Besides, I have plenty of clients for my private sessions, which are way more fulfilling.
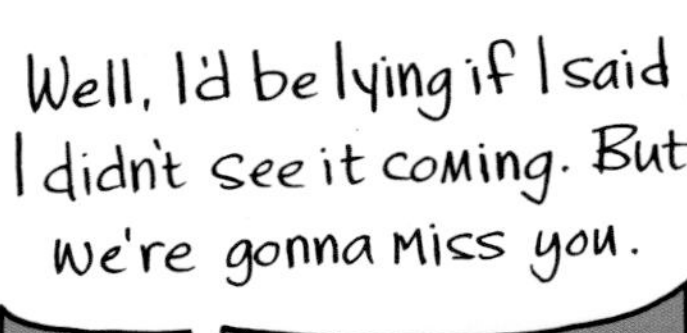
Well, I'd be lying if I said I didn't see it coming. But we're gonna miss you.

So, what about the twerp?
I made him cry and I never even touched him.
Champ.
clink

1221

I'm so glad we're finally talking about this.
Sweetie, I've wanted to expand our family as well.

I'm not sure I can create one myself--
No one expects you to do that, silly! And there are older ones that need a good home, too.

You're right, Jameson, let's do it.
You wanna look at some tonight? I know a place that displays 'em right in the window.

Oooo pretty.
I guess they only come in white?

1222

Ooo, my first Mac!
You've earned it!
You know, my mom still asks me about grandkids.
You know I'm not ready--
I know, sweetie. I just wish she'd drop it.
WE'RE not ready! We have enough on our hands-
Student loans, wedding debt--
We still haven't gone on our honey-moon yet, and--
SPECIAL KITTY!
mrow?

1223

I kind of like our life the way it is.
Me too.

We get so much time alone together.
And yet, somehow, we can't get enough of each other.

SNXXKTzzz
blog
blog
blog
blog

1224

1225

♩
Hey, Jameson.

Hey Chris! Uh--sleep much?
N-not really.

Heh, I'd ask if it's all Melody's fault, but you don't look too happy--

Unless it IS Melody's fault, and you're here to ask me for
HELP

1226

Nobody can hear us in here. Now, what's up.
Everything started out great!

She initiated it, which was AWESOME! But once we got in bed--
--she just didn't seem to respond to anything that I was--

Wait, isn't this the closet where you and Maureen—

Up high!

1227

Chris, can I ask you a question?
Shoot.

Lights on or off?
Off. Why?

Chris. She's DEAF.
She was probably going--

LIGHTS ON, LIGHTS ON!!

1228

Huh, maybe that's why she kept going for the lamp.
But why would she want to talk to me during sex?
Dude, seriously?

Look, if Melody is anything like Maureen, and I'm guessing she is, she's VERY SPECIFIC about what she wants.

Maureen practically NARRATES it.
Oh. Really? That sounds--

AWESOME

--oh, and NEXT time, bring your own lube. The stuff on the condoms doesn't last.
Ooh yeah, that'd help.

We--were just--
NOT talking about sex--
--in the closet.
forget it, boys, too easy. Just get me a latte.
1229

Hey honey! How was your day?
Pretty slow. But Chris stopped by--

Oh. Yeah? How's he doing?
Well he's--uh, I guess he's--

We're not supposed to talk about this, are
LET'S WATCH A MOVIE.
1230

--but we wouldn't have these problems if you would just LISTEN to me!
Psht, yeah Chris.

Chris? I thought his name was Rick?
uhh yeah I meant Rick.

Wait, is that it? Is that why Melody is upset with Chris?
Ooh look they both ended up back in Paris!

Maureen you're not listening to me.
Ohh this is so romantic!
1231

C'mon, do you really have to
YES Jameson, Melody asked me not to talk to you about Chris, so let it go.

Honey-bear!
Augh, I'm sorry, I'm just frustrated that my sister isn't having sex as good as ours.

1232

1233

the SIGNS of your love
INTIMATE ASL

boodle boop

Melody<3
I want you to come over.

hm!

Melody<3
want you to come over.
NOW

hm.

1234

Hey.

I think I know what I did wrong last night.
I forgot to keep the lights on for you.
I'm sorry.
LAST NIGHT
FORGET

Yes.
Yes!

Also...
Also?

1235

What else did I forget?

mouth..

oh..

OH

1236

'Morning Chris.
Hey, Jameson!

Ahh, see NOW you're glowing.
Yeeeeah.

I take it SOMEONE remembered to leave the lights on last night.
Someone ALSO remembered to eat a club sand-wich last night.

Um..
I don't-
FISH TACO.
I always mess that up.

Wait... so, what, you'd never gone down on her before?
I didn't think women liked that sort of thing.

Wuh-- buh, what kind of women did you date before Melody?
Oh... you know, the kind that didn't like that sort of thing?

How many women can POSSIBLY not enjoy being eaten out?

... one?

1237

One? I thought you'd—
I've gone out with a lot of women, but I've only dated one.

But, you told me--
I know, I know. I'm a recovering liar, remember?
I just hope Melody never finds out.

No offense, dude, but she's probably already—

--he's a NOOB.

1238

I thought he'd been with a lot of--
Yeah, me too.

But he's all--
BLEHH LEH LEH LEHH

LEH-LEH LEH LEHH
Pfft hahaha!

poke poke
BLEH BLEH LEH?
Uhh that means she likes the soup!

1239

Sooo, is this a deal-breaker?
Of course not!

We have chemistry...
He just has no skill.
I can't teach chemistry, but I can teach skill...

...with lots of practice.
That sign is filthy.

1240

1241

Chips ahoy, Bok Choy!
And hello to you, in English.

What're you up to today?
Clearing out some old high school junk.
PHOTOS

Ooo let's watch old episodes of "My So-Called Life!"
I still have those?
HOME VIDEO

"Hazel's poetry, 1995 to--"
BURN PILE

1242

Ooo, is this what I think it is?
what

SCOOORE senior yearbook!

Ugh. Pass.
where's me where's me where's me...

There I am!
WOW, I forgot how much you've changed since then!

And you've-- uh, gotten a haircut since then!
THANKS.

1243

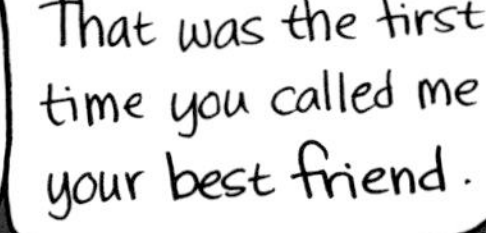
Aww look what I wrote to you!
That was the first time you called me your best friend.

It's like a legal document.
And now I know where it is in case I ever catch you cheating on me.

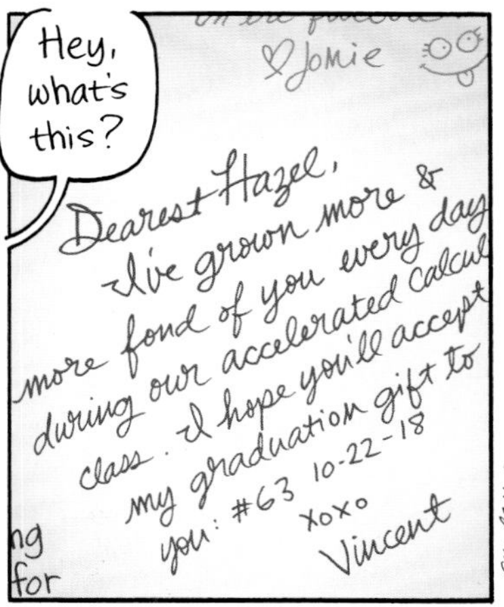
Hey, what's this?
♡Jomie
Dearest Hazel,
I've grown more &
more fond of you every day
during our accelerated calcul
class. I hope you'll accept
my graduation gift to
you: #63 10-22-18
xoxo
Vincent

VINCENT??
You took accelerated calculus??

1244

Who the hell is Vincent?
I have no fuckin' idea.

Vincent, Vincent, Vincent... there's only ONE, but--
NO PHOTO AVAILABLE

Mysterious.
What are these numbers?
I don't know..

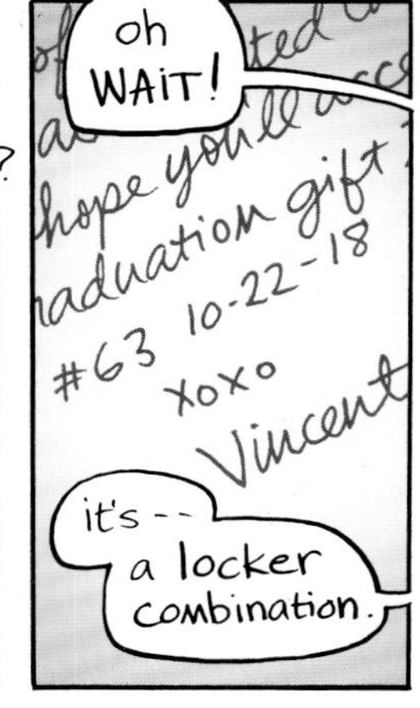
oh WAIT!
#63 10-22-18
xoxo
Vincent
it's -- a locker combination.

NO
YESSS

Jamie, what the fuck.
You can't just break into a school these days, Hazel. We have to look like students.
UFHS

But it's a Saturday.
Were you aware that high school sports existed when we were in high school?
UFHS

Cheerleading is not a sport, it's -- ah, it's an ART. Hello.

Do you want to use some of my wrinkle cream?
Bitch I will cut you.

1245

...-22-18. Do you think it still works?
POP!
Aha!

I bet it's just a bunch of
PORN?

Holy gangbang! Uh -- I guess my gift is porn?
LOVE IS ALL OVER
Wait a minute...

"Love is all over."
I don't think that's love, I think that's semen.

1246

See?
Love is all over.

It's the same thing that was scratched into the back of the locker.
Okay. Sooo, now what?
UFHS

Hm. I dunno, but this ivy wasn't here when we graduated, so --

gasp
YES!

Come on!
225 High Street You've got MAIL

1247

This is it!
This is what?
NO TRESPASSI
The Alexander Mansion at 225 High Street. Old Man Alexander died years ago, but his family's in a battle over the estate, so it just SITS here.

Great. So, we have to search the whole house for this mystery gift, or just talk to his ghost?
Neither; we have to check his MAIL.
creeak

gasp!
what?

"Did you know that it's cookie season?"
Woo Thin Mints!

1248

1249

Okay, well, this has been a nice excuse to take a walk, but I think that gift is long gon
WAIT

Hazel LOOK
Hazel

Oh my god.
Open it!

Two free sundaes from Jimmie Cone.
YAAAY!

1250

Jamie, these probably expired years ago.
It doesn't hurt to try!

Hi, um, we have these gift certificates, but they're super-old--
That's okay!

That's okay, we'll still take them. Two sundaes?

Oh. Yeah.
Coming right up. Choose any toppings you'd like.

Oooo, butter-scotch please!
Uh, just chocolate fudge, I guess.

Here you are, ladies. Heh, didn't know you were a cheerleader.

Oh, I'm — uh, I'm not.
Yeah, I guess that's not likely. You gals come back anytime.

Anytime.

1251

Hey guys, there's a free table over here.

Yeah, but you can't see the game from there.
I thought you guys didn't like sports?

I never said that.
Just baseball.
Same here.

but--

Oh you know why I'm watching it.
Bend over and pick up that ball, honey.

Hey, guys.
Hey!
Hey Clarice!

Uh, so I have a favor to ask of you. I have this guy named Tucker who REALLY needs to learn how to talk to women--

AUGH
Clarice, we would, but-- we kind of have our hands full already.
With whom?

Hey guys, I got a girl's number!
What town has the area code 555?
1252

Wow, he's just as bad as Tucker.
Is Tucker that guy from the library?

Yeah, I promised I'd help him understand women, but I thought it might be nice to find him a male support group first.

Ahh. I'm sorry, Clarice.
It's okay. Huh, I wonder what'd happen if I got Tucker and Jim together.

DON'T CROSS the STREAMS.
It would be bad.
1253

Tucker? It looks like I'm gonna be your professor for Women 101.
Oh.. good!

Beatrice is generously donating her time to the greater good.
I hate you.

Now pretend you've just seen Beatrice for the first time. What do you do.
I-- invite her to open mic night.

Okay Tucker, every time you're wrong I'm going to throw a book at your head. Ready?
Nooo not a sports & recreation book!
1254

I don't understand— what's wrong with asking her out on a date?
Tucker, you just saw her! There are other ways to get to know a girl.

I'll give you a hint: it rhymes with "STALK," but it IS NOT "STALK."
Oh-talk?
Right.

Oh.. okay...
Hi. My name is Tucker. What's yours?

Okay, see that look she's giving you? That means
I have to try harder.

NO!
OW!
1255

1256

What did I do wrong this time? You told me to talk to her--
Yeah, but if she gives you a "fuck off" look, you fuck off. You don't "try harder."

That was a "fuck off" look?
YES! God, how hard is it to read somebody's body language?

How hard is it to just say "fuck off" instead of assuming that I can read a vague expression?
That-- that would just be--

Easier?
Boring!

1257

I wish women would just say what they mean.
Wait--WAIT. I flat-out told you "no" the first time you asked me out.

You did?
YES. I did. And what did you do? You "tried harder."

Bu-- um, I thought--
You thought I didn't mean it. You thought if you were persistent enough, I'd change my mind about you.

But-- that's how it works in romantic comedies
AAUGH

1258

I don't EVEN believe that you watch romantic comedies. You're at least above THAT.
Well, not for FUN. It's more like... research..

RESEA--AUGH! Okay, you know what? I'm giving you homework.
You are to watch three movies that depict healthy romantic relationships.
Ready?

Number one...

...
Lion King.

1259

I guess romantic movies aren't entertaining unless they're a little fucked up.
Sigh
I give up.

It's no wonder you're so confused, Tucker. The most celebrated "romantic" stories would probably get you a restraining order.
Or, at the very least, slapped in the face.

Well, at least now I have someone to teach me what's romantic and what's not.

Oh! That reminds me, I have a 3:00 appointment with a client who wants to be punched in the taint.
I've gotta go!

Hey, Clarice? Thanks again for helping me with this.
Oh, it's nothing. You're a good listener and you're willing to improve. I'll bet with a little work you'll make some girl very happy.
THE LIBR

Well.. you know, if you ever change your mind about me, and you want to be a very happy girl--

That wasn't a "fuck off" look, Tucker.
It was a "fuck no."
pat pat

1260

So, are you going to hand out candy with me on Halloween?

Uh, yeah, I guess I can, but I'll probably be at somebody's party that night.
Well, I hope you'll come to MY party—I just invited you over the face Books.
the what?

I still don't understand why it took so long for you to accept my friendship.
Well, the Internet is still new, Mom, Sometimes it takes awhile to process things.

Until now, my only friend was your cousin Robyn. It was very lonely--
MOM, it's the INTERNET, it's not REAL

1261

Hey guys, who's throwing the Halloween party this year?
Your mom!

YOUR mom.
No, seriously, your mom. She just invited me using the Face Books.

Oh yeah! I just Booked my Face for your mom's party, too.

I DON'T UNDERSTAAAND
Haha, "Like!"
Comment: ROFL

1262

Is EVERYONE friends with my mom?
Your mom is the best!

Better than me?
Ooh, don't be like that. Did you even read her invitation?

No
Well, she's really going all out. She's got a pumpkin piñata, prizes, and that thing where you-

OOH, where you put your hand in the bag and it's --
--spaghetti brains and peeled grape eyes-
EWWW YAAAY!

1263

1264

Trick or Treat!
Ohh you all look so great!

Did you dress up like your childhood heroes?
I am BATMAN
Brain, we've got to help Uncle Gadget!

COWABUNGA, dude!
ha ha!

We didn't get the memo.

1265

Okay, now that Jamie's broken the piñata, it's time for cookies and cider!
YAAAY!

I get the feeling my mom thinks we're still in grade school.
Nah, we're just having so much fun that we feel like kids again.

Naptime!
But I'm not sleepy...zzz
ZZZZ
ZZZZ
ZZZ
ZZZ

1266

THUMK
Woo!
Yeah!
mmm, I should take naps more often!
I'm so glad Mom's party ended at 8:30. This is like double Halloween!

We should do this every year.
What, go to my mom's house and then crash a college party? I'm in. Let's never grow old.

Are they bobbing for apples--
In a bucket of vodka.
GROSS! I'm next.

1267

So you changed your costume from Care Bear tooo what, exactly?
You'll get it when you see-- oh! ERIN!

Nnnyeah, still don't get it.
We're Bert and Ernie!

What.
SEXY Bert & Ernie.
Sexy Bert and Ernie, holding hands.

Let's go ruin people's childhoods.
My childhood is gonna kick you both in the puppet nuts.

Ooh, you're so cute when you're homophobic.

I'm **not** being homo-phobic.
Well, then you're cute when you're uncomfortable.

What are you doing here, any way?
You're seriously asking that when I can see two, three, four shirt-less jocks without turning my head.

But, they're idiots. And probably straight.
I'll bet **your** mouth still waters when you see some-one else's delicious steak dinner.

Not when it's college cafeteria steak dinner.
I'm only a foodie when it comes to **food**.

1268

So, who'd you think is the catcher? I'd always guessed Bert--
I'm **NOT** being homophobic!

Of **COURSE** you're not, honey! That's why you're being so defensive about it.

It doesn't bother me that Jamie's seeing a woman. It's just--

--I thought **I** was the Bert to her Ernie.

1269

The cat is **finally** out of the bag. Hazel is--
I'm not **gay**, you moron.

I just-- don't wanna be **replaced**.
Honey, Jamie's never going to **replace** you. You and Erin fulfill her in com-pletely different ways.

Well yeah, they're all kissy an' shit.
Not like that. Erin is her sunshine and rainbows.

And I'm--
Her cold, miserable rainy day.

1270

OOooooOOoOOO

OOOoOOO
Gotcha!

DOOOoooo
Dooo
Do
Doo
Doo
Dooo
DOOOoo

1271

1272

I noticed a net on the counter. Did you catch any ghosts last night?
Shut eht.

I'll take that as a big "no." Did you try your Ouija board?
Eht's broken. Server error or somethin'.
Have you considered just TALKING to Ghost Kitty?
Well, Ah--

Brring Brring!
Hello? Oh, McPedro! He's on the Ghost Phone, do you want me to
SHUT EHT!

1273

Ghost Kitteh? Are yeh there, Ghost Kitteh? Eht's meh, McPedro.
Ah-Ah'm sorreh Ah've been chasin' yeh wit' a net, but Ah jes' wanna know what yeh're tryin' t'say--

DOOOOOM
But, what does eht mea--

Splch.

Well, Ah was not aware tha' ghosts get hairballs, too.

1274

ACH! This book is garbage!
How To Clean ANYTH
What're you trying to clean?
Ghost hair ball.

...
Riiight.
Ah think Ghost Kitteh's been sayin' "DOOM" 'cause of all his super-nat'ral furballs.

McPedro, he's a ghost. He doesn't HAVE fur.
Oh Ah see yehr an expert on this subject.

Look under "unicorn blood," it should be in that section.
Ooo, good thinkin'.

1275

Hairball Relief
for all cats young & old
Heeeeere kitteh kitteh kitteh kitteh

DOOOOOO

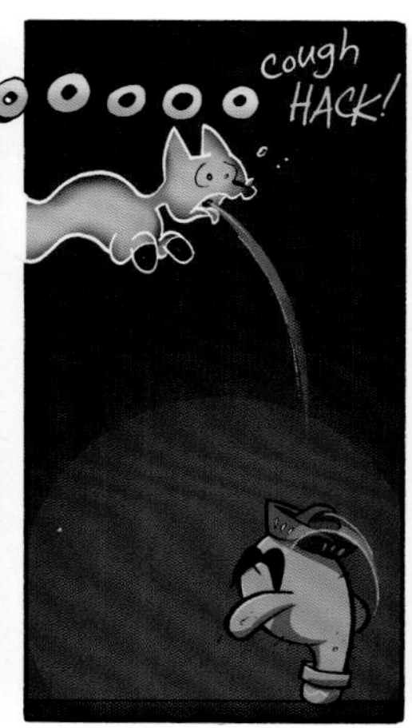

OOOOO
cough HACK!

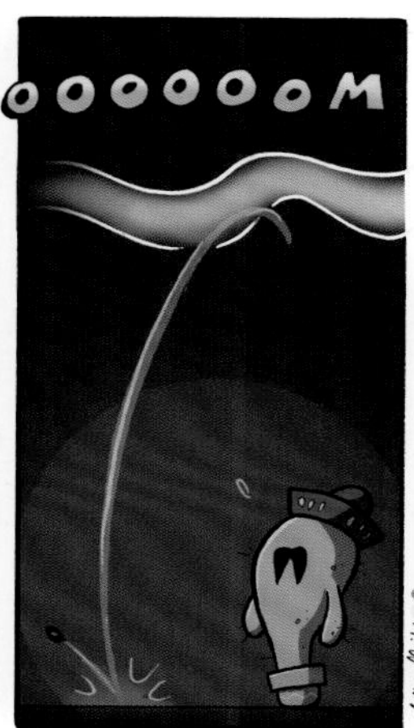

OOOOOOM

Tha's a trickeh digestive system yeh've got there.

Hey Chris! Wow, you look like you really need this.
Huh? oh. Yeah.

Is somebody having too much bedtime fun?

Heh, umm... a gentleman doesn't kiss an' te--
Hi-FiVE

1276

So I take it you remembered how to "ride a bicycle."
Like a pro cyclist!

Well, now that you're "eatin'" the fish taco"
Ooh man, her "fish taco" is so good!

Y'know my favorite part? The "sour cream." Hers is all thick and tasty and you can taste the cilantro—.
CHRIS, Chris..

This is my sister-in-law we're talking about, let's leave the condiments out of it.
Are tortillas condiments? 'Cause her "tortillas--"

1277

Hey, boys.
Hey, Angel.
Hey!

Wow, YOU sound happy.
The sex is AMAZING!
AND that's all you ever need to know about Chris & Melody's private life.

I'm gonna hit the john.

Details.
Two words: nipple.

1278

Hey, Chris.
Hi, Jim. You look, um--

Rejected? Because that's what I just was. Rejected through an automated phone service.
You have reached the Rejection Hotline!
Ooh uhh
Hey, Zach!
Hey guys, what's up?

?
Oh nothing, just getting MAD LAID
Nice

1279

1280

Welcome to the Getting Laid Club, Chris.
I'm the president of the club, especially after last night.
Haha

AUGH! Why is EVERYONE getting laid except ME? I'm ALWAYS nice to girls! I listen to them talk about their feelings, I buy them drinks... but I'm always just "a nice guy." And nice guys NEVER get laid!

Wow. You're right, Jim. We must be getting laid because we're such assholes.

1281

Guys, I--
You don't want to hang out with not-nice guys like us. We can take a hint. We'll get out of your hair.
Oo, there's a free table.

Guys--

There's a HOLE in the BRO-ZONE guys!

1282

How was your night out with the boys, Muffin?
Mmnnghh.

Well that doesn't sound good.
It's just JIM. He was being whiny and annoying, so we ditched him.

So... you didn't have to hang out with Jim tonight?
Nope.

But... you don't like Jim.
Huh... you're right, I guess it wasn't such a bad night after all.

1283

So, you had a good time, then?
:Sigh: I can't lie to you, honey cake.

It's not JIM that's bothering me, it's CHRIS. The way he talks about his sex life with Melody is -- I think it'd really upset her.
I doubt it.

Really? Why do you say that?

Melody: it was like riding an Italian sausage, minus the peppery sensation
Maureen: MELODY. TMI.
Melody: He likes it when I suck on his "meatballs."
Maureen: GAH MELODY

oh! Hey, uh, hey Jim!

Oh--hey, I mean--uh, why are you talking to me? You guys aren't my friends any
No, that's not true!

Look, I invited you to hang out with us in the first place. I have nothing against you.

Well... yeah, but, the other guys--
OH. yeah, no, those guys totally hate you.

1284

Why are you friends with those assholes, anyway?
Uh, because they're not assholes?

Are you kidding? They treated me like I was a PLAGUE!
Jim, just because they didn't like you doesn't make them assholes.

If they were decent they would've at least tried to like me.
I think I'm beginning to understand your problems with women.

1285

HAZEL! c'mere c'mere c'mere

'mere, what.
Do you have twenty bucks?

I won't know until you tell me what it's for.
There's this Group Pawn that my little sister and I wanna do, but we need one more person.

What is it
Just hit "Buy Now," it's gonna expire in like ten seconds, hurry!

click
Okay. What did I just buy?

HALF-OFF LINGERIE!
BACK BUTTON

1286

Wait.. lingerie for your Sister? She's like, FIVE
fiona's NINETEEN, Hazel.

Still, it's your SISTER. Won't that be weird?
Why would it be weird?

Because she's related to you, and you're gonna know what she's wearing under her clothes!
Spoken like a true only child.

I used to feel weird seeing underwear on my BARBIES.
You also used to hide their disembodied heads around the house to scare your mom, so I'd say that's a little different than having a sister.

1287

1288

Ooh, Cups of Love, I am home.
y'know, there's a sale at the As Seen on TV store, maybe I'll just go in there while you guys--
HAZEL!

oh
WHUMP
Hey, fiona, you got, um--

...BIG.
Haha, you haven't changed a bit!
C'mon, let's try on some panties!

What does your mother FEED her?
Everything that didn't fit in me!

1289

Ooo, Hazel, what do you think of these?

Haaah yeah, I'm not really a thong girl.
Oh! What kind of panties do you like to wear?

Underwear.
Well yeah, but what kind of panties-

Underwear.

1290

Jamie, do you like this bra on me?
oh my god, YES! show Hazel!
Hazel, c'mere!
FITTING ROOMS
SOCKS

What do you think?
Uh, I don't--

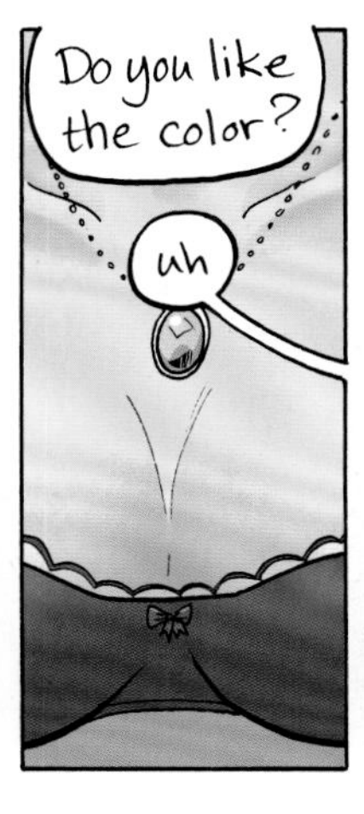
Do you like the color?
uh

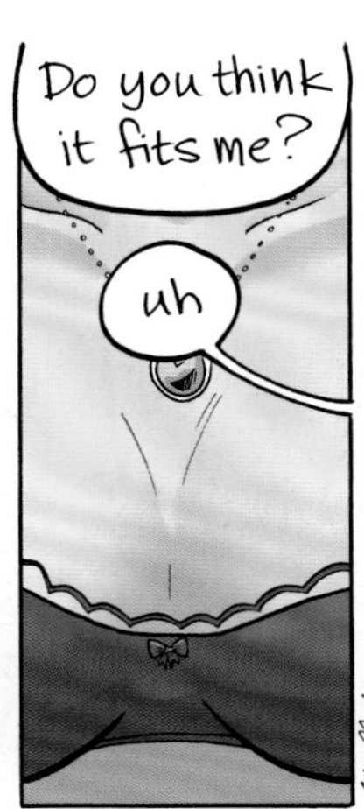
Do you think it fits me?
uh

Okay, thanks!
h--
help

1291

what -- what just happened?
Hee hee!

What?
I think Hazel likes my boobs!
NUH UH
she couldn't stop staring!

oh my god, did you break her?
I think I broke her!
no-- no, I don't LIKE boobs--

I don't LIKE boobs!
EVERYBODY likes boobs, honey.

Hey, you seem a little tense—
No no, I like looking at people in their underwear, it's my favorite thing.

Here, reach down my shirt. It'll take the edge off.
WHAT?! That will NOT take the edge--

It's BOOZE

glug
glug
glug
glug

1292

See? All better.
glug
glug

Haha, I knew that would work.
You've just touched some boobs, Hazel. How do you feel?
I-- I feel--

LIKE A CHAMPION!
HOORAY!

LET'S GO BUY SOME PANTIES!
WHOA, she had too much.

1293

LOOK
LOOKIT THIS it's SOOO PRETTY
WOW.

What was in that flask?
Water.

Just water?
Sis, I'm nineteen!

BLOOOLOOLOOLOOLOOO
Then... your boobs did this?
They're kind of like the invincible star in Mario, aren't they!

1294

Hey.
Hey, babe. What were you up to all afternoon?

I honestly have no idea. I vaguely recall Jamie laughing at me. Everything else is a blur.
And I've had the WORST wedgie for the past 20 minutes!
What the fuck is--
zip!

What the fuck am I wearing?
Something I want to remove with my teeth.

1295

1296

Hey.

Don't tell anyone I said this, but thank you for sending me to Zach's place in those lacy underthings.
Me?

Hazel, I didn't pick those out, you did!
I did?

But, I would **never** pick out something like that!
Clearly your Inner Hazel would.

Huh, I guess I should give this thank-you card from Zach to Inner Hazel, then.
As Inner Hazel's representative, I'll take that.

1297

So... why didn't Erin come underwear shop-ping with us?
Oh, it's really not her thing.

Oh yes, because it's really MY thing.
Haha, apparently it is!

No, Seriously...
Haze, I invited YOU because you're my best friend.

Oh.

Okay
And because I LOVE making you uncomfortable.

1298

WIENERS!

I know you want my fresh, hot wiener in your mouth!
Good grief!

How has he NOT been sued for sexual harassment?
Why am I still working this shit-ass job?
When will the stupid economy pick back up?
Hey!

Stay after the game, I've got a surprise for you.

What was I saying?

1299

Hey, what's the surpri
Shh!
c'mere

Um, are we allowed in here?
Nope! We're breaking all the rules tonight.

How long are we staying in here?
Until the janitor leaves.

Whatever will we do while we wait?

You make me feel like I'm 16 and hiding girls from my parents.
Hee hee. Well, keep that teenage mentality when you open your Christmas gift.

But it's not Christmas yet!
I know, but I'm impatient. Open it!

gasp! Roller skates?

Uh... Mimi, I really suck at skating.
That's why they come with free lessons from your girlfriend.

1300

You ready?
No.

Sure you are.
You're doing fine.

Okay, let go of my arms.

1301

Oh man, you're doing sooo well!
This isn't as hard as I'd expected!

So, you planned all of this just to give me private skating lessons?
Well... also...

I want you to move in with me.
HUP!

Wow, I should try that move in derby!
WHUMP

1302

Hee hee, I guess you had to learn how to brake somehow.
Oo, my thigh.

You don't have to answer my question right away if you don't.
Yes.

Wow. Really?
Yes. I'm sick of telling myself no. I'm in love with you, and I'm not getting any younger.

Mimi, have you ever made out on the floor of an empty roller rink?
Umm, no..
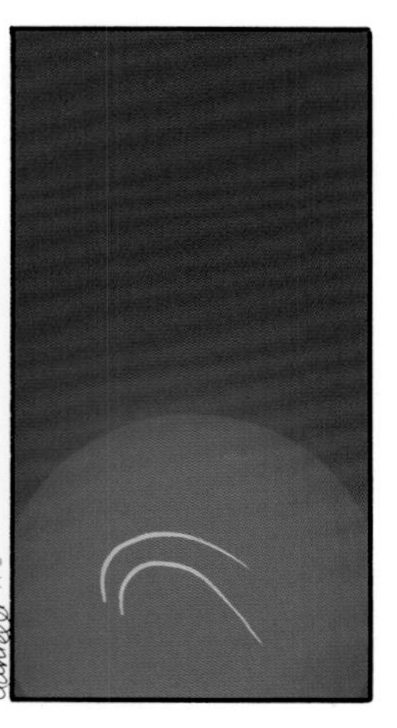

1303

1304

MAYA! I'm in love with Mimi and we're moving in together!

Sis, that's great news! Why are you cringing?

I don't get it. Nothing bad happened.

The last time I felt this good, you got breast cancer.
The great thing about losing both breasts to breast cancer is that you can't lose any more breasts to breast cancer.

1305

Hey guys, I have big news! Let me get a drink first so we can toast.
Ooo!

I hear you're moving in with Mimi.

I thought you didn't work on Fridays.
Emmett went home for Christmas. I'm filling in for him.

How'd you find out about me & Mimi?
Lesbian grapevine. Chill out, I'm just trying to congratulate you.

Psh.
What is it?
Okay, fine. Just take this drink and I'll fuck off.

It's an "I'm Sorry for Everything But I Don't Like Saying I'm Sorry" cocktail.
Merry Christmas.

1306

ding!
Hi, Hazel.
Hey, Bob. The usual?
Yep, the usual.
Say, have you had anything published lately? I used to love your column in the paper.

Nah, I mean-- I got this job at the booze shop, and I still live with my mom, so... maybe when the economy picks back up.
But, Hazel... you're so OLD

HH'EEEEEE

1307

HAAAY, booze princess!
Jamie, how old do you feel?
Mm, I'd say about twelve.

Yeah, me too. But, y'know, we're NOT twelve.
Good thing, too, 'cause I still get carded at bars sometimes.

Well yeah, but I meant more like... do you ever feel like life is passing you by?
Yeah, totally.

Which is why you should hurry up and close so we can get to the Meck!

1308

Hey Angel, the usual.
And what do YOU do?

Oh, I'm a musician.
Wow, professionally?

Yeah, I'm pretty lucky. I've wanted to do this all my life, and now I'm living my dream.

Angel, can you make that to go?
I'd like you to consider the legal ramifications of "to-go beer," and then answer that question yourself.

1309

bing bing

Text from: Jamie
Hey, where did you go?

Home. I want to work on my writing portfolio.

KNOCK
KNOCK
KNOCK

What have you done with Hazel?
How did you get a to-go cup??

1310

So, this is all because of a dream you had?
Yeah, I guess. It just felt so... REAL.

Well, I think it's a great way to start the new year. Lemme get outta your hair so you can work.

Hey, when do you suppose you'll dream that you give me back my noise-canceling he
can't hear youu

1311

Good morning, Beautiful.
HUAH you're up before me!

And you made coffee!
And I made a list of publishers I'm going to send my work to today.

Thea! What's gotten into you?
You've gotten into me.

I didn't get into you enough last night.
Well I'll just be sitting here typing with my pants off all day if you need a fix.

1312

Oh Pussy Whipped Magazine, please need new writers.
beep boop beep

...
Hello?
Hi, Esther? This is Hazel Tellington..
HAZEL! How've you been?

BROKE.
I mean, good! How've you been? How's the magazine?
Oh Hazel, the magazine's been dead for years. I'm making a fortune selling apps now.

Oh— really? What does your app do?
It coordinates your customer database and inventory records between employee devices using a handy scheduling tool over a secure application.

What does that mean?
Hazel I have no fucking idea.

1313

How's the writing goin', Lois Lane?
The writing's fine, the climate is NOT.

Yeah, I wish it would snow.
Every publication I've ever worked for is dead.

All two of them?
Y-- yes.

Maybe you should try other publications.
Maybe you should.. ...let me do that and think it was my idea.

1314

HAZEL!! What are you up to??
Yikes, Megaphone! Just quietly trying to reboot my writing career.

YOU ARE? Hazel that's FANTASTIC!!
Aa--
Thea. c'mere sweetie.

BREATHE
H'YEEE

Oh that's MUCH better.
What--
Decaffeinator machine. I know a coffee overdose when I see one.

1315

What had you drinking coffee all day, Shake 'n Bake?

Well, I'm trying to get back into the publishing world...

Wow, we both caught the bug!
...wait, does that make us competitors?
Not if we work together.

Oh!
...how would that work?
Well, I could use some writers, and you could use an editor...

Ah, excuse me, what are you saying about my grammer?
Hold still...

Wait... you need writers? Are you starting your own publication?
I, I think so!

WOW! Thea, that's... risky?
Not if it's online. I'm taking a free course on website development and social media--

Whoa whoa, slow down, Jane Jetson. You lost me at "website."
Hazel, we've gotta face facts. It's smarter to self-publish on the web these days.

So... do we... charge by the pixel, or--?
We haven't covered that in class yet, but... yes, yes I think so.

1316

So, what's this digital online pixel publication gonna be about?
I'm not sure yet. They say "write what you know..."

So: booze, coffee, and being a terrible lesbian?
HEY! Mimi asked me to MOVE IN with her. I am a GREAT lesbian.

Still, you have all that EXPERIENCE.
Whatever. At least mine's not booze, coffee, and being a DICK.

We could devote the entire publication to friends who are assholes to each other.
That's kind of inevitable, Hazel.

1317

Hi, Mom.
HAZEL! Are you getting back into writing?

Yeah! How did you--
I read some of the stories you left on your bed. They're good, but--

MOM! Those aren't--
Well, I was washing your sheets, so I thought I'd proofread them. But this one about "riding Zach bare back--"

OH GOD OH GOD
Young lady. I hope you two are being safe.

this isn't happening..
I don't care HOW well he drives, you should ALWAYS wear a seatbelt.

1318

Mom, I promise Zach and I are BOTH wearing seatbelts. This was just, ah, a silly fantasy piece.
Well, that's a relief.

I would like it if you would PLEASE ASK before you read my stories from now on.
Okay, honey, I'll try.
I didn't really understand them anyway.

Thank GOD.
Do you think maybe you'll write a children's book?

I think that would be a bad idea.
You're right, you should wait until you have your own children.
MOM.

1319

1320

Thea, your decorating crew has arrived!

Wow, nice place!
Mimi, you have this whole house to yourself?
Until now!

Lucky for you she doesn't take up much space, but lemme tell ya, she doesn't know how to hang toilet paper correctly.

It looks nicer hanging from behind!
Do you know how it looks to a drunk person?
"I can't find the end, guess I'll just shake dry."

1321

We brought all the important stuff– wine, board games...
You do realize we're just helping Thea move in.

Yeah, but did you see the weather forecast?
Looks pretty nice out to me.

WHUMP

Flash blizzard.
Hope you brought a sleeping bag!
I call the couch!

1322

WOOOO, Operation Snowed-In Sleepover is GO!
I'll get my overnight bag!
Can everyone eat pork chops? I have enough to feed five.

Did you guys plan this?
Emergency candle for you...

I'd ask who sucked the weather's dick for such a convenient blizzard, but seeing as you all date women--
Don't be quick to assume that the weather's a dude.
The weather's a big happy clam in the sky and it tastes like sunshine!

1323

Hoo, those pork chops were amazing, baby.
thanks!
What do we do now?

Scrabble!
Strip Drunk Scrabble!
DRUNK Scrabble.

But, Strip Drunk Scrabble--
As your Token Hetero, I veto all stripping.
Would this change your mind?

Double word score AND triple letter score! Drink, drink, drink, and I'm OUT.

Holy BALLS, Thea.
Were all three of those drinks for me?
Yup.

You do realize that ALL of your drink commands have gone to Hazel.
glug glug glug

WOOOOO let's play any game you lesbos wanna play!
Thea, you're smarter than you look, and you look really smart.
Thank you.

1324

Hazel, how do you feel about Truth or Dare?
Wh'ever, le's play it!

She's sloshed.
HAY, hay Thea, truth or dare?
Ee, uhh, d-- truth.

Go outside and make a butt angel in the snow, with your butt.
I said truth.

The truth is, you're gonna make a butt angel in the snow, with your butt.
I only know how to draw angels that look like middle fingers.

1325

WOOO lookit those butt angels!
hee hee
Ha ha!

Hahaha oooooo my butt's gonna fall off!
Here baby, lemme warm it up.
Hey Mimi, truth or dare?
Hazel, it's not your turn.

uh—
Did you know Thea has Restless Leg Syndrome?
HAZEL!

THUMP...
THUMP
THUMP
THUMP
THUMP

1326

Heh... you can imagine my relief when I found out Thea had it, too.
Wait wait-- have you ALWAYS had it?

Since I was 19. I wasn't a very smart lesbian back then.
So-- YOU gave it to Angel?

No no, I made her use protection when we were dating.
You can guess how THAT went over.
Hold on, how-- do lesbians-- protect--??

Truth or dare, 'cause I dare you to look in my medicine cabinet.
Only if I can visit your liquor cabinet afterwards.

1327

1328

Whoa, are those dental dams?
Yup!
But--why do you have rubber gloves in here?

Take a wild guess.
five little penises?

fingering, silly.
Wow... I feel really bad for all this stuff you lesbians have to do to be safe.

Uh... if oral and fingering are things only lesbians do, then I feel REALLY bad for you straight people.
Oh, wait--
OH.

1329

So wait, what are all these condoms for?
Also guess.

Uhh... you have...

GASP!
oh my god you- do you have a penis??
giggle
You are the straightest person in the world.

I don't, I don't know how to act right now
Calm down. I have a penis. It's teal, it vibrates, and it's shaped like a porpoise.

Your penis is a porpoise?
My penis is a dildo.

1330

Ladies, Hazel has successfully graduated from the Community College of Lesbian Sex Ed.

You guys do a lot of the same stuff we do!
Well yeah, what'd you THINK we did for sex?

Let's call over some boys and not tell anyone we fucked them.
Okay!

I probably shouldn't answer that.
You're probably right.

1331

Thea, we skipped your turn after the butt angels.
Ooo, you're right! Hazel, truth or
DARE.

Hmm, you have to--oh! Call Zach and tell him you got in a fight with one of the 300 women he slept with.
Ooh, brutal!

Wait--how did you know about--
The walls in our old apartment were paper-thin.

Wait--does that mean--
I heard every naughty thing you ever called him in bed.
Aren't you glad you didn't choose truth?

Hehe, okay, it's ringing.
giggle
sh!

Hey, Sweetie!
Hey, HONEY. Do you remember old Mrs. uhh, Robinson?
snrk

Uh--
Well I just bumped into her, and she was all "your boyfriend Zach was the best lay I ever had--"

So I smacked her bifocals off her face and punched her wrinkly old mouth
click

Haha, he hung up!

1332

Uh, Hazel--
Call him back RIGHT NOW

But--
Here, it's dialing.

Hazel?
Hey Zach, uh... you knew that was just a prank, right?

NO. How would I have known that was a prank?
Uh, well, because...

I mean, why would I ever do something that stupid?
What, like prank your boyfriend?

1333

I--I'm sorry, it was just a stupid prank.
sigh
It's okay. Where are you? Did you get my texts?

No, I'm hanging out with the girls at Thea's.
Ah, okay. I don't want you to drive out here, then. It's too dangerous.

Well... yeah, why would I leave?
Because-- of our date? Valentine's Day?

...
Ooohh.
Riiight.

If you were the boyfriend, I'd be cutting you off from sex for a week.
If it makes you feel any better, I'm technically sleeping on the couch tonight.

1334

Well, I'm an idiot.
No, I am. That was a really stupid prank.

No, I mean-- well YEAH, it was, but-- I forgot that Zach and I planned a date tonight, since he was working on Valentine's Day.

Oh.
Uh.
Well, it's not like you would've made it anyway, what with the snow.
I know. But I still forgot.

Hey, guys? Can we stop being grown-ups now and play Bubble Bobble?
YES!

1335

1336

Post-Valentine's Day Date Take Two, and this time I remembered! Aren't you proud of me?
Well-- I'm glad you're here

You're not proud of me?
Hazel, you're thirty minutes late.

What? No--
You don't own a watch.

Well... maybe I just wanted you to have all the bread.
More bread?

1337

Well, on the bright side, there's no prank involved this time.
The prank didn't bother me that much.

You hung up on me.
I was frustrated. I'd been worrying about you all night.

And then, when I finally hear from you, you drunkenly tell me you beat up a nice old lady.

You didn't believe me, did you?
Of course not.

Mrs. Robinson passed away years ago.
More bread?

1338

Let's--change the subject, okay? I don't wanna bicker on our night out.
Yeah, me neither.

So... what've you been up to all week?
Well, I've got some big news. I found a good van for under $10k--

Why do you want a van?
Because--I want to expand my business? We talked about this last week--

So, if I get a van, I can--
mhmm you can do me in a van yeeaahh

1339

Oh. Sorry, I didn't remember.
sigh Yeah. Hazel--

The bigger news is, I found an apartment I really like. I was looking for a place big enough for both of us, but--

But?
I-- I need you to grow up. I can't be the only responsible one-

More brea
NO

The ONLY responsible one?
Well, I mean--

If I'd known you were just gonna berate me all night, I would've stayed at home.
Oh come on, we haven't even eaten yet.

I can cook my own dinner.
Y'know, like a grown-up.

DAMN!

1340

cough cough
Sweetie!

I'm surprised the smoke alarm didn't go off!
That's :cough: because I took the batteries out.

Oh Hazel, you shouldn't do that!
I know, but-- it went off every time I cooked something.

Cooking was never really your thing.
I wasn't even cooking this time! I just wanted to microwave some water in a cast iron saucepan!

1341

Here, let me heat you up some leftovers instead.
Thanks, Mom.

Mom...
when Dad was still around, did you fight a lot?

:sigh:
...we did.
Well-- I mean... when two people fight, if they really love each other...

Well, Hazel, he left us.
So, you're saying I should ask Aunt Barb.

1342

Psst! Hazel!

Not now, McPedro.
But Hazel, look!

Ah got th' cutest kitteh photo!

Oooh.
I guess kitty photos DO make everything better.

What's THIS one?
THA'S NOT FEHR YEHR EYES!!

1343

1344

I didn't know there was a flower under your hat!
What'd yeh think I was, a eunuch?
I prefer to believe that, actually.
Anyway-- what's got yehr face in th' shape of a cat's arse, princess?

Oh, McPedro. I don't wanna talk about it.
Ach, there there, lass.
pat pat

Ah'll just read yehr diary t'morrow.
BAD CACTUS

1345

DING!
Hey! You're only ten minutes late!
I wasn't expecting you for at least half an hour
I GET IT, OKAY? I'M IRRESPONSIBLE!!
MIMI

Just a little prick..
MIMI

fzzz
zzss
sss
twitch

There y'go.
I'm sorry I yelled.
MIMI

1346

Are you all coffeed up now?
Hoo, yeah, I think I can take this off.
I have some news. Guess who wants to fund our publication?
Uhh, nobody?

Esther Thomas.
from Pussy Whipped? I thought she was too busy filling her pool with gold coins.

I think she's gotten bored with the apps industry.
What makes you think that?

Esther? Are you in a car?
Nope, just stepping away from a ledge.

1347

Wait, how do you know Esther?
I used to write for Pussy Whipped Magazine.

WHAT? Thea, I used to write for Pussy Whipped!
I know.

Unlike you, I used a pen name to avoid breaching the Tribune's no-compete policy.
Oh, I-- kinda skimmed that part of the contract.

I used to write under "Lipstick Vixen."
Putting the "pseudo" in "pseudonym."
MIMI

So we're gonna bring back Pussy Whipped Magazine.
Woo hoo!

Esther's gonna have a website designed with a custom-coded back-end.
Subscribers can view the entire magazine in their browser or on their smartphone/ tablet PC...
We already have a facebook fan page and Twitter account live...
We'll give away free content on the front page to entice people to subscribe.

So... then... do we roll the wax onto the backs of our articles and stick them to the modem?
Yes, Hazel. Yes... I think so.

1348

Boy, the magazine world sure has changed.
No kidding.

Well, the good news is, all **you** have to do is write, and write well.

You remember how to do that, right?

I thought you were working tonight?
What does it **look** like I'm doing?

1349

Well, here we are: the quirkiest café I could find.
Wooow.

Wait, I thought you **hated** quirky cafés?
I do, but you need some real-life girl practice, and this is your crowd.

I'm a little worried— all these girls are **really** pretty.
Well, I'm a little worried too, Tucker...

Worried I'm gonna try to kill them all.
Ooh don't you just LOVE Hemingway?

1350

Okay, if you're gonna get a date, we can't look like we're together. I'll be over here in this corner, avoiding EVERY-BODY. Wave if you need me.

Well -- why don't you sit over there, near the book-shelves? They're **your** crowd too, y'know. Look at all those people with books!

Tucker, these are **not** my people. I read **alone**. I don't consider reading to be a spectator sport
Ladies & gentlemen--

--open mic poetry night will begin in five minutes.
Yes!
CURSES

1351

1352

...could've sworn open mic night was on Tuesdays..
first up, let's hear it for Autumn Rose!
SNAP SNAP SNAP
SNAP SNAP SNAP

This is a poem about my life without you.

Thank you.
SNAP SNAP SNAP SNAP SNAP

Easy, Trigger.
I'M IN LOVE

1353

I'm gonna go talk to her.
'Atta boy. I'll stay here and cringe, I mean watch.

Excuse me..

We have a date friday night!

1354

That's it? You barely said two words to her and you have a date?

We speak the same language-- the language of our souls--

Spare me. That-- was not what I was expecting to happen at all.

You said it yourself— I just needed to find a girl who would say "yes."

Did she actually SAY yes?
She didn't have to. Her soul--

Nevermind. Tucker, you two deserve each other.
Aww, Clarice
No no, I mean it.

1355

Angel, can I get, uh-- something alcoholic?

Well that narrows it down.

I just need something to get my mind off things.

How 'bout a "Clarice You'll Meet the Right Man Someday?"

That's not what I meant.
Oh really? How long have I been a bartender?

too long
That's right.

You're a terrible oral surgeon, Joey!
Arugula!
You like that safeword too much.

Nah, you're just too good at your job.

Mistress...
do you enjoy our sessions as much as I do?

Well, technically, you're paying me to beat you, and I enjoy beating you AND paying my bills...
But I think you enjoy it enough for the both of us.
Oh! I guess I can take off the cock ring now.

1356

Um... so, what I meant to ask you is--

I've grown fond of you, Mistress, and... if you're looking for a more perm-anent slave, I'd--

Ooh... Joey, I have a wonderful time playing with you, but I don't feel that way about you.
I'm sorry.

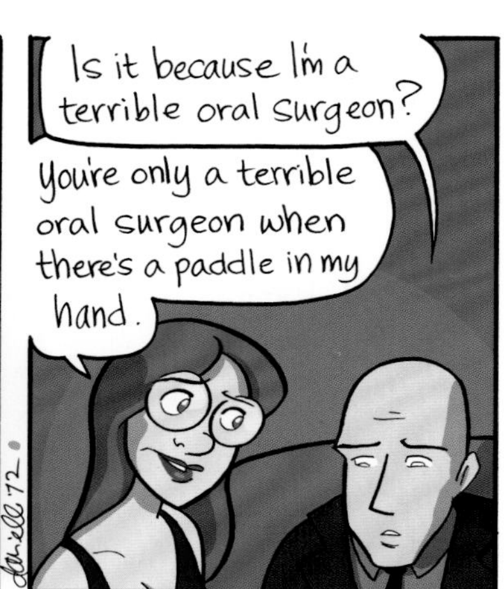

Is it because I'm a terrible oral surgeon?
You're only a terrible oral surgeon when there's a paddle in my hand.

1357

And you turned him down? I thought you were looking for a permanent slave?
I'm looking for a boyfriend.

Well that's boring.
What, falling in love with someone I can dominate?

Yeah. Boring.
Oh whatever Ice Queen.

I bet you cry at romantic comedies.
I do! I cry because there's never enough spanking!

1358

You know, I could always hook you up with someone—
UGH. No thank you.

How else are you gonna meet men? You won't do Internet dating...
I want to meet them the old-fashioned way.

What, like kick 'im in the nuts and see if he likes it, then ask him out?
That's not a terrible idea..

Clarice, your dream man isn't gonna just fall into your lap.
Oh, but if only he would, so that I could love him with my paddle.

1359

1360

Yay! It's been FOREVER since we had a Jamie-Hazel night at the bar!
We need to ditch the S.O.'s more often!
CLINK!

Aww... yeah, but... Erin's really great.
Yeah, I mean... Zach is--

Yeah.
Hmm.

HAZEL JAMIE I NEED YOUR HELP!

1361

Wait, why do YOU need help? You and Zach--
are... maybe not dating?

YOU BROKE UP??
I don't know! I can't tell. We had a fight last week and we haven't talked since then.

A fight about what?
How irresponsible I am.

OOH okay.
oh THANKS!

1362

Well... do you think you guys can work it out?
I don't know. He's talking about moving into his own apartment, alone.
That doesn't mean you can't work on becoming more responsible.
Jamie, if I could become more responsible overnight, don't you think I'd have done it by now?

I know it won't happen overnight, but you can work on it. Trouble is, people only change when they want to. Do you want to become more responsible?

Hm? I'm sorry, I couldn't hear you over the sound of my sixth beer.

1363

Wait, wait--why did you say YOU needed help? You and Erin are all hearts an' stars an' gay-ass unicorns.

We are! She's WONDERFUL, but...
But...

HAZEL I'M HORNY AS SHIT
So? Get Erin a strap-on.

Erin is COMPLETELY asexual. It's official.
Okay. Get Erin a strap-on and tell her to close her eyes and pretend to be a jackhammer.

It occurs to me that we have very different definitions for "satisfaction."
Satisfaction: noun to be jackhammered.

I don't know what to do. I love Erin, but--
You need some sexin'.

These boobs won't grope themselves!
Things you don't shout at a bar.
But yeah, I get it.

That, and I miss BOYS. Those big hard lumps in their pants--
Jamie stop.

I JUST WANT SOMEONE TO RAVAGE MY BODY!!
NOooo Jamie I can't hold them, run!

1364

Hey, Jamie.
Oh, hey Clarice.

So, I hear you're having troubles with Erin?

OOOH Hazel, you have such a big mouth!

Actually, you were kinda shouting about it at the bar. EVERYONE heard you.
SHIT! NO!
Well the good news is, now you have to talk to Erin, before she hears it elsewhere.
How is that GOOD news?

Because if you hurry, you'll reach her before the YouTube video does.
...RAVAGE MY BODY!
Haha, classic!

1365

ERIN? Erin, are you home?

I'm in my room!

Erin, we have to talk--
...RAVAGE MY BODY!

Did you know that you're a meme?

1366

I'm so sorry, I'm SO sorry!
Why? What is this, anyway?

I don't-- I can't--
Oh, duh, I could just read the description..
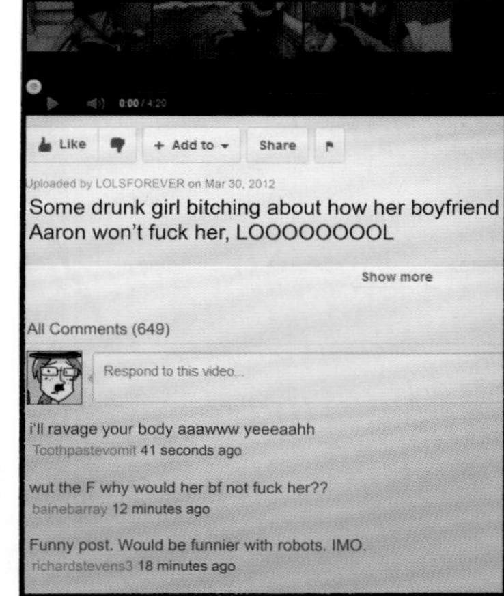
0:00 / 4:20
Like
+ Add to
Share
Uploaded by LOLSFOREVER on Mar 30, 2012
Some drunk girl bitching about how her boyfriend Aaron won't fuck her, LOOOOOOOOL
Show more
All Comments (649)
Respond to this video...
i'll ravage your body aaawww yeeeaahh
Toothpastevomit 41 seconds ago
wut the F why would her bf not fuck her??
bainebarray 12 minutes ago
Funny post. Would be funnier with robots. IMO.
richardstevens3 18 minutes ago

...oh.

1367

1368

I--I never even said that!
Jamie--

Um-- I can-- DO that for you, y'know. I'm not into it, but I want to make you happy--

Oh Erin, I'd never want to put you in that position.
It wouldn't be that bad. I could just close my eyes.

TOLD YOU

1369

Erin, you're so sweet to offer that, but-- I---
oh, I can't say it!
You HAVE to, Jamie. I love you and I wanna know what to do.

I--
I just--
Spit it out--

I MISS GETTIN' IT ON WITH BOYS I'M SORRY!!

Why are you sorry? That makes my job WAY easier!

1370

I guess-- we never DID talk about the rules of our relationship...

Pfft, WHAT rules?

I just wanna love you. And even more than that, I want you to be happy.

I can still love you while you get your freak on with other people, y'know.

You mean--
OH! Not in the same room. That would make for a REALLY awkward threesome.

1371

KNOCK
KNOCK
KNOCK
Zach?

Zach?

click

um, hi.
yYAH!

Man, you're jumpy.
I didn't know you were here! I didn't see your car.

You didn't see the new van?
Oh. I guess I did.

I just assumed it belonged to a pedophile.
Thanks. Thanks a lot.

1372

So, you got a van.
Yep.

...and you got the apartment.

Yeah.
A lot of good things are happening for me, Haze.
I don't like change.

You sound like the Internet.
DISLIKE.
poke

1373

Nothing's really CHANGING, anyway. You'll just visit me at my new place instead of my parents'.
Are we even still together?

WHAT? Of COURSE we're still--

I mean, we're still together, right?
I haven't heard from you in over a week, Zach.

Well it's not like you've tried to contact me, either.
I was--afraid you didn't want me to.

Wha--who do you think you're dating?
Ummm, hopefully the same guy who wants to do me in his new van?

1374

Mmm, is new car smell an aphrodisiac?
Heh.

So, tomorrow: Same time, same van?
Well, I was thinking, maybe we should keep taking some time apart--

WHAT? But, you just--
I didn't say I want to break up! Just, y'know, give each other some breathing room.

I CAN BREATHE JUST FINE
You sure?

1375

1376

Why do we need "breathing room?"
Well, I mean-- I got a lot done last week--
oh WHAT, am I getting in the way of your career?
I didn't SAY that, Hazel.
But-- y'know, you're trying to focus on your career, too, and you kind of stopped writing when we started dating.
Well DUH, that's because fucking you is more fun.
That's not--
okay, actually that's a pretty good reason.

1377

Look, I'm just suggesting we give each other some time to focus on ourselves.

You're too talented to spend all your spare time on the couch with me.

Besides, maybe the break in our routine will inspire a new direction in your writing!

Stupid stupid stupid Zach is a stupidhead.

1378

RRIiiiiNG

mm what
Hazel? It's Thea.

whatup
Dude, what's with the poem? It's hilarious, but--

what po'm
The one you just sent me. "Ode to a Dumb Boyfriend." You don't want me to publi--

publ'sh it
Are you even awake?

zzzz
Hazel it's 9:30 on a Friday night

1379

Ahem.

"Ode to a Dumb Boyfriend"
[sic]

HAMMUMFFMM WAMANAMMUMM RRUMMUFFAMM

SNAP SNAP SNAPS
Thank you.

Hi, Clarice.
Well, if it isn't Mister Hot Date with a Poet!

So? How was it?
Oh, it was... good. She's... good...

Uh oh.
No no! It was... good! She's really...

Terrible?
But she likes me!

1380

Tucker, "she likes me" isn't a very good reason to date someone.
I know, but it's better than being alone.

Oh do not EVEN get me started on how wrong that is.
But-- you're ALWAYS alone. Don't you ever get lonely?

That's-- none of your-- it doesn't matter, it's still better than dating some-one you're not 100% into.

Clarice, do you ever fear you'll die al
ANYWAY BACK TO YOU

1381

So lemme guess. You guys spent the entire date in silence.
I wish.

Oh?
At first, we were content to stare lovingly into each others' eyes--

Eyes, like windows into our souls,
staring so hard I could feel her starting to undress for me--
until the curtains of her lips finally parted, and --

Turns out she's a REALLY bad poet.
You don't say.

1382

But, I mean, she speaks FRENCH– maybe she could just speak in french to me? I'd only understand the articles
Tucker.

Sigh
You'll meet other women. Let this one go. It's insulting to mislead someone you're not interested in.

Besides, I discovered a place where you're sure to find women who will date you!
Really? Where?

Stay right here.
SELF-HELP

1383

1384

Are you sure you're okay with this?

Of course I am, silly!
I picked this place SPECIFICALLY because it's a good place for hookups.
H-how did you find that out?

Hazel let me browse some of her old reviews. I assumed her "friend" who took "five numbers and one lucky guy" home was you, right?

I-I didn't think you'd wanna know about that--

Jamie, your girlfriend is taking you boy shopping. Enjoy it.

1385

So... do you see any boys you think are cute?
Umm, a few...
Which ones?

Mm, that guy in blue..
Nice!

That guy..
Not bad!

Aaand that one, on the right.
Ooo, yes!

Are you even attracted to men?
Nah, I just judge 'em by what they're drinking.

1386

Why don't you go flirt with one of those guys?
Well, I don't wanna leave you alon

Excuse me--
Do you like dancing? Because my buddies and I just put on this song--
Oh!
She LOVES dancing!

BZZT
bing bing

Text From: Erin
I love you.
Go get 'im!!!

1387

...+?

1¢

...+?

Ooh!

Doughnuts for me?
mm-hm

Did you have fun last night?
um-- I--

Pretend I'm Hazel.
um-- he-- had a nice body and made me come four times!

See? That wasn't so bad.
I missed you.
Also his dick was HUGE.

1388

Well if it isn't the Mistress of the Library.

How do you keep all these books in line without your riding crop?
DARREN. Ix-nay on the istress-may.
you were always so good at languages.

What're you doing in a library, anyway?
I hear reading makes your dick bigger. Is that true?

You're here to torment me.
Does this book make my ass look fat??

1389

What are you REALLY here for.
I was wait-listed for a new release for three months. I'm here to pick it up.

Three months? WAIT- are you checking out that saucy romance book everyone's talking about?
'Deed I am.

But-- it's such a chick book.
And you know what they talk about in chick books? WANG.

But-- it's so hetero.
Not if you pretend all the women are drag queens.
Try it with Twilight. Such a better story!

1390

Is that "50 Shades of #888888"?
That it is. Looks like I was the last one on the wait list.

Does that mean--
Nope.
But we have two copies!

Sorry, Beatrice. Someone snagged the other copy just ten minutes ago.

?
THAT GUY

1391

1392

Wow, he really does check out all the books you want.
SEETHE

How does he know?
I dunno, breaks into my house and reads my diary?

Do you really have a diary?
N-NO.
And I don't use it to write about the books I want to read.

Do you really want to read that romance novel?
N-NO! forget everything I ever said!

1393

Hey! Hazel! Guess what happened today.
Uhh, bowel movement?
That, AND the first issue of Pussy Whipped went live!

Oh! Hey, that's-- wait, did you publish that poem I sent you?
Duh, of course I did.

Thea! Are you serious??
Of course I am!

Thea I can't BELIEVE--
Quick, which hand?

Uh, right?
Just fuckin' with ya!

1394

So, how'd it turn out?
Have a look.

Wow, it looks so professional!
PUSSY Whipped
Esther's got good people working for us.

What's this story, "How to Trick your Bartender into Pouring Stronger Drinks?"
You wrote that.

I don't remember writing that.
That's why it's on the front page.

1395

Thanks for not printing that stupid poem I wrote.
Dude, I'm not an idiot.

What was that all about, anyway? Are you and Zach fighting?
Augh, I dunno.

He's changing, and I don't like it. He got a place to himself, he thinks I'm too irresponsible to live with him, he wants space--

It's like he thinks he's a grown-up or something.
Weird.

Hey, Charles.
Heya, Haze! Ready to take over?

Yup yup.
They gave us an extra case of that seasonal cider you like, so just give 'em out to the regulars, okay?

Uh-huh, uh-huh...

Do I still count as a regular?
Only after close.

1396

Oh, hey, some guy came in here looking for you.
Oh—uh, was his name Zach?

No, he said his name was John, but his nametag said "Vincent."
Vincent?

Vincent...

Why does that name sound familiar?

Oh! It's the name of my neighbor's dog.
Haha, Woof!
Well, he probably had the wrong Hazel. See ya!

1397

Thank you.

OOOH, "50 shades of #888888"
Hold up, Clarice. Beatrice is next in line.

I don't believe you. You'll simply have to show me the holds list.
Here, look.

Dalilah Johnson
Joshua Krzesk
Be ce Motte
Hmm, I see.

Welp, guess you were right! I'll hand-deliver this to Beatrice
Hey!
SWIPE

1398

♪

Hey Beatrice, I've got that romance book you wanted.

WHAT ROMANCE BOOK
Y'know, that ROOOOOOMANCE--

Uh-- I mean, that book on advanced physics you wanted.
thank you.
SNATCH

Nobody's even HERE
I DON'T CARE!

1399

1400

Hey, Carol.
Hello, Clarice!

Hey, how long have you known Beatrice?
Oh, a long time now. She started coming here when she was in high school.

Do you know if she's ever dated anyone?
Oh-- well, I don't know her that well, but--
...not that I'm aware of.
Why do you ask?

Just curious.
Beatrice—
It appears we have similar tastes in books. Perhaps we can discuss them sometime.
Yours,
Joshua

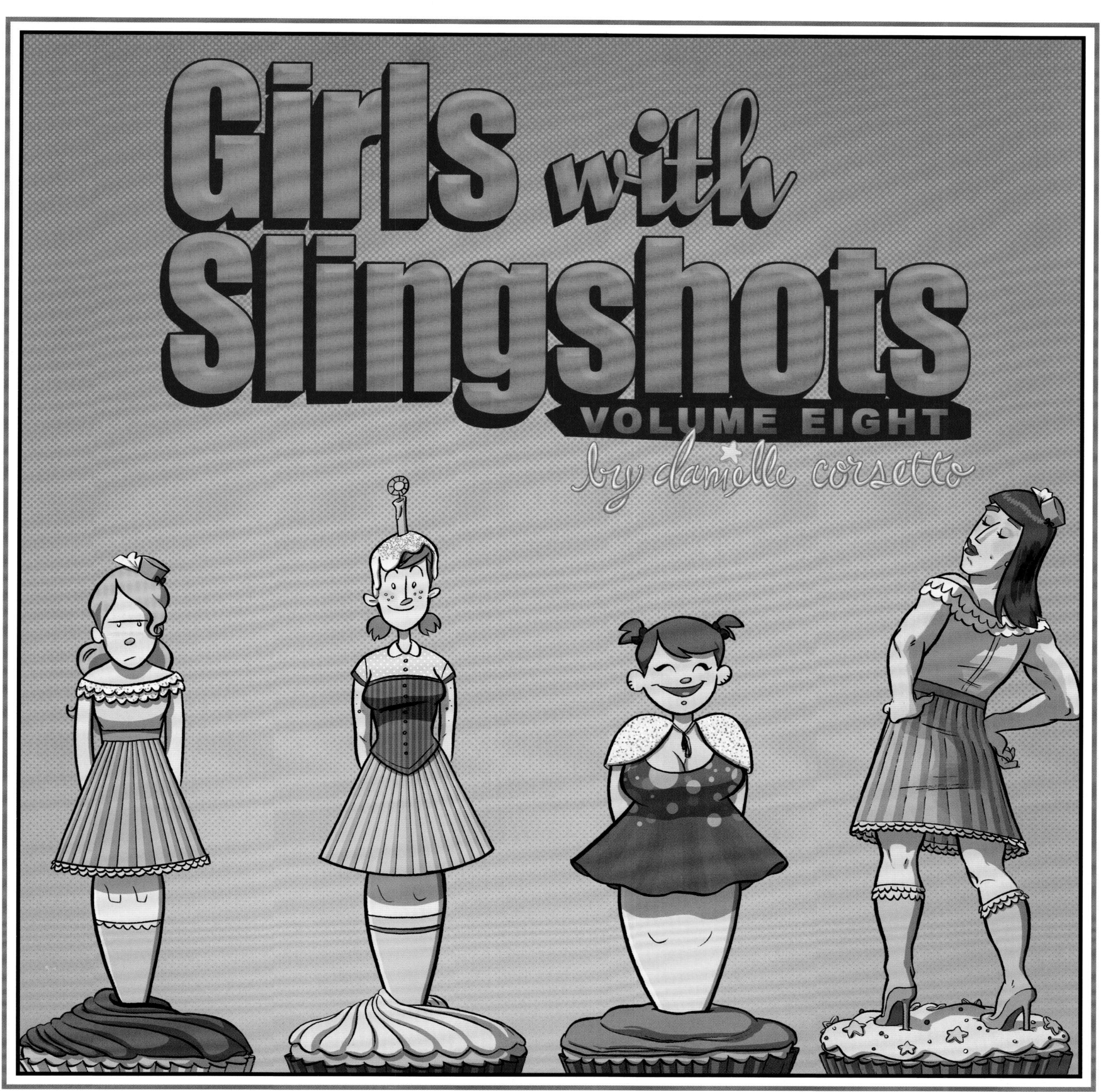
Girls with Slingshots
VOLUME EIGHT
by danielle corsetto

VOLUME EIGHT

strips 1401-1599

1401

That's the last box.
Nice!
I guess I officially live here.

Now you've just gotta make it feel like home.
Yeah.
Thanks for your help, man.

WUMP

1402

KNOCK KNOCK KNOCK

Hey!
Hi.

You got me a plant.
It's a forget-me-not.

Y'know, like how you forgot about me when you picked this apartment.

1403

Can we PLEASE just enjoy the new apartment together?
Does this place even have a bathroom?

It's not THAT small.
Not for one person, I guess.
SHUFFLE SHUFFLE

Well, that's what it is, for now.
Yeah.
bup bup bup bup

McPEDRO!
bup bup

1404

What are you-- how are you even --
Y'can't tempt meh wit' that fine blue piece o'ass an' NOT expect meh t' chase it!

I thought you were in love with the spiderplant?
Yeh, but-- her petals are so small!

Dude, that is a REALLY shitty reason to cheat on someone.

By the way, I'm really glad I'm not the only one who can hear him.

Well, I guess I'll take my flower-molesting cactus home.
What, you're not staying?
grumble

I thought you wanted space?
Well yeah, but I didn't mean we should NEVER see each other.

Okay, then I'll see you next week.
But--

I'm on my man-period and I wanna cuddle!

1405

Hey, I haven't seen your face in awhile!
Yeah, I was hoping I might find Jameson here. Have you seen him?

No.
Oh.

Do you wanna talk about your FEEEELINGS?
As much as I wanna talk about my nosy bartender.

1406

Hey! Angel called and told me you could use a drinking buddy.
Oh! Hey, yeah, that'd be nice.

So, you all moved in now?
Yeah, just about. Just a few more things to, uh.. sort out.

So, uh, how're you and Maureen?

Dude, you know you can just skip it and talk about your feelings.
HOW DO YOU ALL KNOW??

1407

So, are you and Hazel okay?
Man, I dunno.

I love her, y'know? She's a pain in the ass, but I like that about her. She's a really fun girlfriend.

But-- I'm reaching the end of my girl-friend phase. And I can't picture Hazel in a real, adult relationship.

Like the one you and Maureen have.

K.O.
OOH Chun Li kick yo ASS!
Voldo vill seek ASS VENGEANCE vith his ASSLESS CHAPSSSS!

1408

1409

Wow— so, you wanna get married?

Yeah, I mean, that's how I've always seen myself.
I can't even **imagine** Hazel married. No offense.
None taken! That's the whole problem.

Does she want to get married?
Oh right, like **that** conversation has ever happened.
It generally goes like:

Aw, that married couple is so sweet. I hope we're that happy if we ever—
DID YOU KNOW MOST KOALAS HAVE CHLAMYDIA, TRUE FACT!

1410

So, do you have a plan of action?
Pft, no. I'm terrible at breakups.

Ironically, this has been my longest and most serious relationship.
I can't just **end** it, but I can't keep waiting for something to change.

I don't envy you, man.
You don't have any advice, do you?

Well yeah, "break up with Hazel," but she'd punch me in the dick for saying that.
Why'd you think I'm so scared to break up with her?

1411

SLAM

Um, good book?
Read this.

"... similar taste in books... discuss them sometime... Yours, Joshua."

Aww, Beatrice, you have a not-so-secret admirer!
I hope he not-so-secret admires my fists.

1412

You have crossed the line.

I am **not** interested in the contents of this book. I am **not** interested in discussing it with you.

Stay away from me.

What?

What, what did you do?
I told him to fuck off.

Beatrice, he was just trying to get to kn
Do you have any idea what this book is about?

It's about some twisted sub/dom relationship. That's not **romance**, it's **abuse**.

I'm not interested in "getting to know" anyone who thinks that **physical violence** is the same as **love**.
swipe
I'm--just gonna return this book for you.

1413

Hey, um.

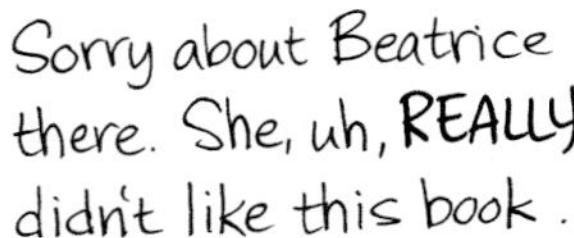
Sorry about Beatrice there. She, uh, **REALLY** didn't like this book.

I understand. The writing was terrible.
Oh— yeah, that was probably it. The writing.

Anyway, **REALLY** sorry about that!
That's okay. You didn't do anything.

That's right, I didn't do **anything**!
Sorry!

1414

Hey. Romance Detective.
Oh! Do you need my services?

I need your **advice**. Have you ever **seriously botched** a well-intentioned matchmaking project?
Ooh, yeah. I try not to do those anymore. They **always** end badly.

Yeah. That's the advice I expected.
Do you need **help** with a failed project?

YES! How do I fix it?
Oh, you don't fix it. You just sit back and watch it implode.
But I can get us some popcorn!

1415

POP

1416

bzzzt
bzzzt

Uncle.

Uncle who?
I give in. I don't want to fight anymore. Can I come over?

You're on your period, aren't you.
...

How did you know?
You're always horny on the first day of your period.
Can you please just invite me over and fuck me.

1417

Hello, I have a 9:45 appointment for an internal massage?

You know this isn't going to fix anything.
Sure it is. It's makeup sex.

You have to make up to have makeup sex.
Let's streamline the process and skip that part.

HAZEL.
If you sex me now, you'll have one less thing to make up for later.

1418

How's that feel?
Mmmm morrre

How about -- this?
GASP!

Ooh, Zach, you haven't done that to me in so long.

You want me to keep going?
YES

Let's talk about our future.
NO!

1419

If we don't talk about this now, we never will.
but I hate the future.

Can't we talk after we're done?
Hazel, every time I bring it up, you fall aslee--

WH-- what is that
Little trick I learned. You like?

Y-- Yeh--
Talk later?
Talk later

It's times like this I wish I could smoke a cigarette without coughing.
Holy GOD that was good.

Wanna go again?
I-- body says yes, brain says...
also yes?
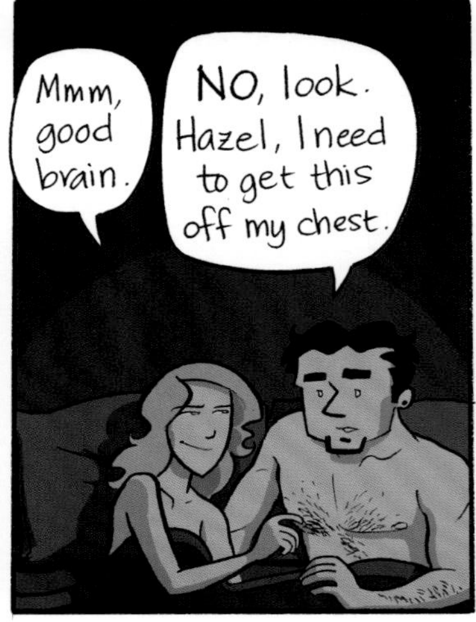
Mmm, good brain.
NO, look. Hazel, I need to get this off my chest.

Mmm, good chest.
What do you want from this relationship?

1420

UGH
Boner killer.
I know what I want. I want someone to spend the rest of their life with me.
FWUMP

Ehh, so, you want I should get you a puppy?
I want YOU. But... I don't know what you want.

I want-- to not talk about this.
You want to NEVER talk about this. And I can't stay with you if we never talk about it.

Welp, I guess that settles it.
HAZEL.

Call me when you're content just having a girlfriend.
That's not gonna--

HAZEL
SLAM

You forgot your--

Damn!
1421

1422

1423

NAKED?
Well, I didn't want my last words to be "could you please pass me my underwear."

Wow.
So you guys actually broke up.
What? No. He just knows where I stand now.

I'm heading over to his place as we speak, before I go to work. He'll probably hand me my clothes WHILE he apologizes, and everything will be--

1424

Dear Hazel— Here are your clothes, and everything else you've left at my place.

I'm sorry I couldn't say this in person, but: I've loved and admired you more than anyone in my life. Which is why this breakup is going to be so hard for me.

What?
I don't think I can handle seeing you for awhile. It's going to take a lot of time for me to get over you. I hope you'll take this as a compliment, rather than a cop-out.
Good luck with your future.
Z

DOOOOOOOOOM
Stop that!

1425

Hey, Hazel!
Hey.

Are you okay?
Allergies. I'll be fine.

Okay.
If you need any help with the kegs, call Jeremy.
Later!

pop

swig

RIIING

H-hello, Grapes & Grains.
Hello, Betty. May I speak to Edward? I miss him.

Um...
I think you have the wrong number.
Oh.
Yes, okay. I'm sorry, I always forget.

Edward used to work at the hardware store. But that was 20 years ago, before the stroke.

He was a very good man. He loved me very much. You understand.

...yeah.

What did you think of the book?

Oh— um, you were right. The writing was terrible.

But the Spanking scenes were really fucking hot.

But the--

--apartment sounded nice!
That's exactly how I felt!

1426

Psht. Don't encourage him.

Don't encourage him to what? Discuss books in a library?
Yes.

Beatrice, let it GO. He didn't even write that "love note" to you, I--

--/////I think it was meant for Nadja.
He's a bad speller!
It said "Beatrice."

1427

BOOKFACE
Welcome, Clarice. logout
1 friend request
Beatrice reviewed a book!
"Hated it."
Read more.
New suggestions for you!

Joshua wants to be your Book Friend!
Oh!
click
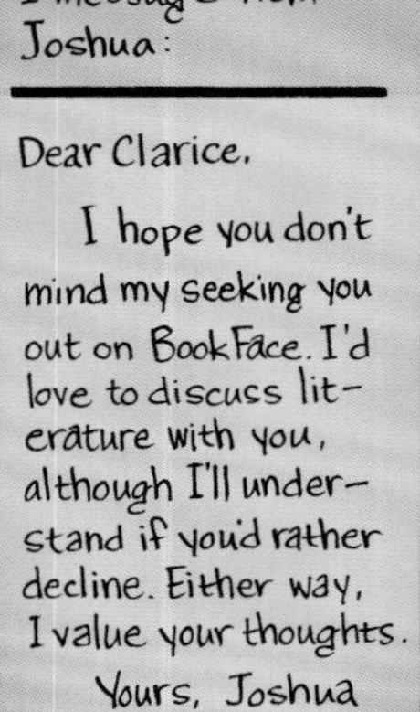
1 message from Joshua:
Dear Clarice,
I hope you don't mind my seeking you out on BookFace. I'd love to discuss literature with you, although I'll understand if you'd rather decline. Either way, I value your thoughts.
Yours, Joshua

Weird! He writes exactly the way I thought he would.
Accept.
click

CLARICE, would you be interested in
NO
CONGRATULATIONS You just won a new
AAUGH
click click click click click click

1428

Hey Clarice, have you seen Hazel lately?

No, not at all.
I'm really worried about her. She's not answering my calls, my texts, singing telegrams--
Are you talking about Hazel?

Yeah! Have you seen her?
I haven't SEEN her, but she's been sending me TONS of articles for the magazine.

Are they angry?
VERY angry.

Breakup Central.
I'm going to her house.

1429

1430

Hazel?
--ooh.

That's a lot of Vlad.
M'old friend Vlad.

Hazel, Vlad is your enemy.
FRENEMY.

How did you even get this much Vlad?
Mom got it.

How did you get your Mom to get you Vlad.
Told 'er, "I'm sick, get me th' Russian cough syrup from 7-11." hic!

1431

Okay, obviously I'm not gonna let you do this to yourself.
NOooooooo

C'mere.
-ooooo

-Mmmff

Is this hug therapy?
No, I'm restraining you until I come up with a better idea.

1432

nng

whu-- why am I at your place?
I carried you here.

nnng owWw need booze
You can't have booze. I took all the booze away.

But-- if I don't have booze, then I'm gonna--
I'm gonna have--

FEELINGS!

1433

Sob
It's okay. You can have feelings with Mama Jamie.

we broke up
I know, baby.

it hurts
I know it hurts, honey.

No, you're sitting on my foot.
oh!

Hey! Jamie! Did you ever find Hazel?

Yeah, she was stuck in a bottle.
Oo, yeah, I kinda figured that. Is she okay?

She will be. I'm locking her in my place until she sobers up.
Oh.
Uh... but isn't your apartment filled with booze?

One guess as to what's in the bag.
Ooh, a vanilla vodka for me please, Santa Liquor!

1434

Hey baby, I brought home some vanilla vodka!
Oh yay, I just bought orange juice!

Ooo, like a Creamsicle?
Like a Creamsicle.

Wanna watch Adventure Time with me?
Duh!

♫ with Jake the dog ♪
♪ and Finn the human

I feel like such an adult right now.
We should play "doctor" after this.

1435

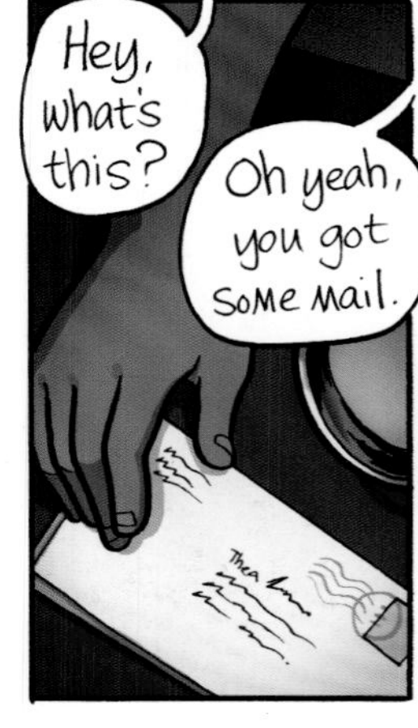
Hey, what's this?
Oh yeah, you got some mail.

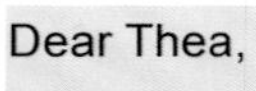
Dear Thea,
Enclosed please find your share of the ad revenue fro our first online issue of Pus Whipped Magazine.
If you have any question

WHOA.

Mimi--
HOLY CRAP! Do you have any idea how many My Little Ponies you could buy with that??

Mimi.
You can quit your job!

1436

ALRIGHT, WIENER GIRL! ARE YOU READY TO SELL SOME BIG, FAT, FULFILLING WIENERS?

um, boss--
Oh Thea, you know you can call me Dick.

Can I PLEASE call you Richard.

1437

1438

Boss, I need to give you my two weeks' notice.
I don't under-stand...
I have another job, and it's going really well, so I don't need this job any-more.

I still don't understand.
um...
This other job... it's my passion. I don't really have a passion for selling wieners.

Well, now I REALLY don't understand!
The job is selling Italian Sausages.
Ooh, I see. I suppose I'd leave for a bigger wiener, too.

1439

Please welcome Thea the Editor, née Thea the Wiener Girl.
I thought you were giving your two weeks' notice?
I did, but he said I could just go. Some teenager wants the job.
Well check you out! How's it feel to be back in the editor's saddle?
It feels like I'll never have to touch an-other hot dog for as long as I live.

oh!
un..
It's nice that you feel that way, but--
I still smell like hot dogs. Right.

1440

All clean an' ready to eat your--

cuuuppcaaaakess

oh-- WAIT!
GULP

If you're gonna eat a deviled egg, you probably shouldn't expect it to be a cupcake.
MF.
GUK.

1441

How's my favorite red-head doin'?
fine.

I just wanted to check up on you.
I'm okay.

Sniff Sniff

It's water.

OH I'm so proud of you!
That's my bladder.

So, you've been able to restrain yourself?
Every time I want a drink, I pour myself more water, just like you told me to.
EMPLOYEE ONLY

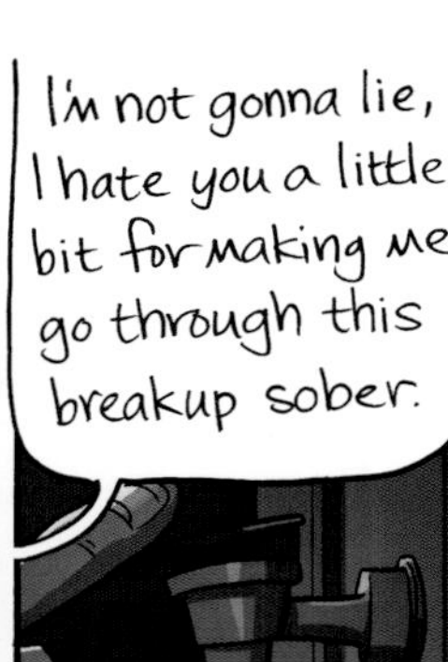
I'm not gonna lie, I hate you a little bit for making me go through this breakup sober.

Well... the good news is, you're REALLY hydrated now!
The bad news is, I cry all the time.

The good news is, my tears no longer burn like vodka.
The bad news is, vodka tears are like, the best organic glass cleaner EVER.

1442

So, whatcha doin' after work?
Oh, I dunno, CRYING.
CLOSED!

Let me take you out, get your mind off Zach.
And how do you plan to do that without drowning me in alcohol?

I found a place that's really fun and doesn't have any booze.
Liar.

LIAR.

1443

C'mon, let's do the Space Whirl ride!
nng.

Remember, you used to LOVE this ride in high school!
tickets
hmm, yeah, it WAS pretty cool...

I bet it'll be way less scary now that we're adults.

K-CHUNK
K-CHUNK
K-CHK

1444

Do you ever consider that a 17-year-old kid is responsible for locking people into what is essentially a death trap?

I don't think this is locked.

ALL ABOARD!
oh my god
I don't think this is locked!!

AAAAAAAAAAAAAAAAAAAAAAA
WHRRRRRRRRRRRRRRRRRRRRRRRRRRRRRR

AAAA
WE'RE GONNA DIE
WE'RE GONNA DIE
WE'RE GONNA DIE
WE'RE GONNA DIE
WE'RE GONNA DIE
AAAAAA
RRRRRRRRRRRRRRRRRRRRRRRRRRRRRRRR

AAAAAAA

See? Told ya it wasn't scary!

1445

Let's -- let's do something a little more low-key.
YES.
PLEASE.

Look! It's the ping-pong goldfish game. That's a nice game.
That's a very nice game.

tic
tic
PLOP

You won a goldfish!
GOD DAMMIT.

Why did I play that stupid goldfish game.
At least you won something!

No, I lost something. I lost the freedom of not being responsible for a goldfish.

Do you wanna trade me the fish for the banana?

I'll keep the gold fish.
yesssss

1446

Okay, Goldfish, all I could find was this wine glass. I hope you like your new ho—

splish

NOOOOOOO

oooo
GULP

eh.

1447

Hewwoooo! I'm here to see how the WIDDLE FISHY is doing!
Yeeeah, about that..

Uh, did you know that cats like to eat fish?
GASp! Did Sprinkles eat him?
Well, I put him in this wine glass, and the next thing I knew...

DOOOOOOOOOM

1448

1449

I guess she didn't like the taste and spat it back out?
WHYYY do I always get the magical fucked-up pets??
Hey, so... I'm also here to see how you're feeling--
HRRGH AUGHH don't wanna talk about FEELINGS
You don't have to talk about it NOW, but--
Don't wanna talk about it EVER! GAAH, must-- drink-- something--

HAZEL, NO!

You--
GLUG
GLUG
GLUG
GLUG

Is that-- water?
gulp
Yeah, turns out I never really needed ALCOHOL, I just need to drink SOMETHING.

Oh.
Like-- a pacifier?
THUCK
THUCK
THUCK

Well that's-- better, I think.
THUCK
THUCK
THUCK

1450

Oh my stars, is that my little sourpuss Hazel?

Since when do you work here?
Since last year.

Oh, well that makes sense, it's so close to your
I moved in with my mom, remember?

Oh, I thought you moved in with that hot piece of meat you call
Zach and I broke up.

You should really update your face-
OR YOU COULD LOG OUT OF FACEBOOK AND USE YOUR PHONE LIKE A PHONE.

1451

So, does this mean you're single?
Do I LOOK like I'm getting laid? Of COURSE I'm single.

You know what THAT means.
I cry all the time?

We can go REBOUND SHOPPING together.
Pass. I'm still recovering from buyer's remorse.

Oh c'mon, you don't have to keep it, just take it home and return it in the morning.
But what if it gives me a raaash?

Here we go, rebound central.
Darren, this is a gay bar.

So? You're not interested in touching anybody, why not look?

Here, dear, have a beer.
Oh, uhh-- Jamie's making me stay sober during my, y'know, recovery.

Is ONE BEER gonna make you not-sober?
Well, no--
Then you should—

KEGSTAND!
I said ONE!

1452

BLAARGH

Jesus, when was the last time you drank?
two weeks

Wow, you must be really broken up about Zach.
No, I was just-- thirsty--

Are you crying?
No, it was just-- onions--

In the toilet?
GODDAMMIT I'M HAVING FEELINGS

1453

A-and he wanted to talk about our FUTURE-- like, marriage--
EW.

I fucked up.
What? No you didn't!

You're not thinking about marriage right now, and perhaps you never will. So what? You'll figure it out when you're ready.

B-but, everybody else--
Do not EVEN start a sentence like that.

1454

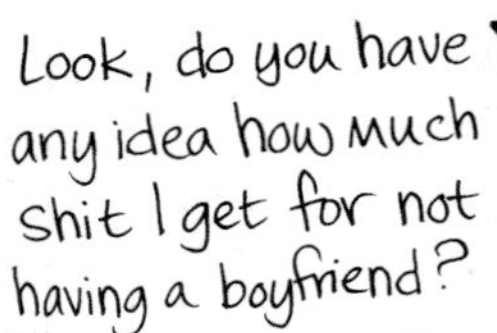
Look, do you have any idea how much shit I get for not having a boyfriend?

Especially now that we have the right to marry!

People are constantly telling me to "stop perpetuating the gay stereotype".
They want me to stop being the promiscuous fag that I am, as if I represent the ENTIRE gay population.

But y'know who doesn't talk to me like that?
N-no.
The men I choose to be with.

And y'know why?
N--
Because my dick is in their mouth.

1455

So, did you and Zach break up SOLELY because your future plans don't mesh?
Yes.
...um, I think..

That's not a bad reason to break up, y'know.
Then why does it hurt so bad?

Because you broke up for a logical reason that makes sense to your brain, but not to your heart. Of course it hurts; your heart didn't have any say in the matter.

You know an awful lot about love for a gigantic slut.
That's because I collect people's souls by sucking them out through their dicks.

1456

CREEEEAAK

Hazel, is that you? I left you some dinner, Sweetie.
click

Aww, Mom.

flip

I'LL JUST GET A HOT POCKET!
flop
flop

1457

What was that, deaOH!

oh gracious!
GET IN THE BOWL GET IN THE BOWL

sploosh

Now what happened to that meatloaf I left out?
WHAT HAPPENED TO MY FISH?!!

1458

Is that the little goldfish you put in the wine glass?
Yes! What did you feed it?!
bloop

Well, I suppose I fed it meatloaf, but it was intended for you.
Ugh, stupid weird animals.

You'll need a bigger bowl.
Oh I've got a bowl for it.

Tha's not gonna fit.
DAMMIT.

Hey Jamie.
Hey sweetie! Oooh, you look rough.

I shall not tell a lie: I drank last night.
So that's what Darren's text was about.

What'd he say?
"Not my fault bitch can't count."

Charming.
He also said "she needs a Jamie hug." Aww, c'mere.

HURK

1459

Clarice.

Oh, hi Joshua, what's up?
I believe I've found a book you'd really enjoy.

Ooo, I've been meaning to read this one! You've really nailed my taste!

Your Bookface profile is quite telling.
Clarice!

Dear, our 5:00 speaker just canceled. I don't suppose you could whip up that dance workshop?

uh–
Great! Thank you, dear!

Dance? I would've never guessed you were a dancer!
Neither would I.

1460

Ring♪
Yo.
Hazel, I need your help.

Remember how you told your mom I was a dancer?
yeah..
Well, now she wants me to do a dance workshop.

When?!
In an hour!
Okay, I'll be right over.

Hey, I brought Darren to help.
Great, thank you.
So what's the plan?

Uhh, to watch you make an ass of yourself?
I'm taking video.
You are the worst friends.

1461

Guys, you've gotta help me. I don't know ANYTHING about dance.
Which is why we're taking video.
This is gonna be hilarious.

Oh, nice, I suppose you're here to mock me too.

What? No, I'm here because I want to learn about dance.
Then why do you have that smug look on your face?

This is my "interested" face.
Oh. What's your smug face?

1462

1463

Clarice, dear, there's a room full of people ready to listen to you!
Ah, right, okay..

Um.. do these people **know** that they're learning about **DANCE?**
I mean, what was the original event supposed to be?

Oh, originally it was going to be about **karate**, but I figured that's basically the same thing as dance.
Uh..

Change of plans, kids! Today we have a **PROFESSIONAL DANCER!**
Is she gonna **professional-dance** a block of wood in half?
KARATE

1464

Is everyone in this room under **ten**? I can fake the entire lesson!

Hello, kids! I'm Miss Clarice and today we're going to learn about
DANCE!

This is--
this is a **pirouette**
No it isn't.

That's a **plie**.
How would **you** know?
I took three years of ballet, **duh!**

She's not a very good dancer, is she?
Yeah, you basically saved her career, Mom.

1465

Uh, okay. let's try-- a waltz, perhaps?

Hiiiiiii YAH!
Alright, Fancy Feet Jamie wants everyone to get up and try..
DANCE KARATE!
YAAAAY!
KARATE

CHOP
SLICE
HAW!

Oh my god, they love it.
What, were you **BORN** an adult? Of **COURSE** they love it!

1466

That was **AWESOME!**
KUNG FU DANCING!
Hiiiii— YAH!

Jamie, I owe you.
Oh whatever, dude, I had a **BLAST!**

Clarice, um..
I know, the cat's out of the bag. Carol, I'm actually—

A **dancer**, but not a **teacher**.
Yyyes, that's exactly what I was going to say.

Hello sweeeeetie
Wow, someone's in a good mood! What'd you do today?
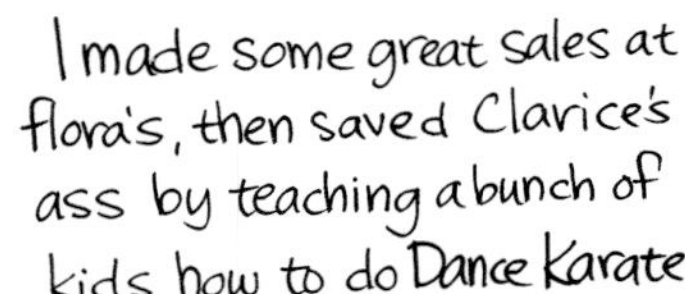
I made some great sales at flora's, then saved Clarice's ass by teaching a bunch of kids how to do Dance Karate.

Sweet!

What'd YOU do?
Applied for jobs that have nothing to do with my Master's degree.

oh.

And made cookies!
YAY!

1467

mmph oh my GAW what even IS this?
Pear and ginger cookies with golden raisins.

Erin, I know you wanna be a scientist, but..
I mean, your baking is off the hook, dude.

Aww, thanks, but-- it's just a hobby, y'know? I wanna make a difference in the world.

Like, what if I could cure cancer?
I think you just DID.

1468

Seriously, though, why not sell your baked goods while you're waiting for your career to start?
Hm...

Ooh! We could do a joint photography show and bake sale!
Ooh!

I'll photograph everything you bake--
Can we make balloon animals?
And dress up like cupcakes!
And throw confetti!

Man, being an adult is so much better when you forget that you're supposed to be boring.
WORD.

1469

Hey, Hazel!
Hi, Hazel!

Hey, do you guys ever do art shows here?
We have this idea..
Uh

Oo! We can hang my art in front of the wine racks--
I can set up my table right here--
Uh--

How's the 22nd?
Make it the 21st and 22nd.
Uh!

Great, we'll send out invitations tomorrow.
Thanks, Hazel!
I just work here!

1470

1471

Hey Hazel! Did you know we're having an art show this weekend?
AUGH
I'm sorry, Charles, my best friend doesn't know how to ask permission.
I think it's a GREAT idea.

She just picked a date and made postcards-
If you work that night, I'll give you Commission on anything you sell.

God DAMMIT. I can never stay mad at her.
Great, I'll put you on the schedule

1472

BEEP
BOOP
BIP
RIIIIING
Are you seriously doing this.
Yeah! I talked to Charles on the face Books, he loves my work.
What's the big deal?

Jamie, you're a GREAT photographer. But--
"Cupcakes & Costumes?"

Erin came up with it.
Of course she did.

You're just trying to make Halloween into a career, aren't you.
Well DUH!

1473

How are you gonna get this show together in a week?
I can do it. I'm making all of the costumes right now.

"All of the costumes?" How many are you making?
Just three, one for each of us.

NO.
YESSSSS

1474

NO.
Oh come OONNNN I made that dress just for you!
EMPLOYEES ONLY

No, you made this dress just for YOU.
No, she made it just for US.

Darren?
TADAAAA

Well, this has just gone from unbearable to ridiculous.
I'm in.
YAY!

Under one condition: I get to drink.
Well, I guess you're not drinking to mourn, so...

Oh, make no mistake, I'm mourning.
Mourning my dignity.
Pop

Ah, dignity. I remember when I had that.
No you don't.

1475

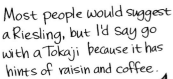

Are we ready to open the doors?
Just a moment.
What goes with carrot cake?

Most people would suggest a Riesling, but I'd say go with a Tokaji because it has hints of raisin and coffee.

You already look better than me in this dress, you don't need to win at everything.
Did I mention my 6-inch heels are 2 inches smaller than my dick?

1476

Alright, let's start this party!
Whoa, where'd all these people come from?

Welcome to Cupcakes & Costumes!
I am NOT cleaning this up.
POP!

AN HOUR LATER...

Okay, I'll clean up some of it.

1477

Excuse me, to whom do I inquire about purchasing the--
oh, hello Haley!

HAZEL.
My wife and I are interested in that photo right there, the cupcakes one.

They're ALL cupcakes.
We're going to hang it between the first two big windows—you remember.

YES, I REMEMBER.
I still can't believe you LEFT that place!
?

1478

1479

Jamie, please help this EXTREMELY nice man before I do.
Oh..
OH

Wow, what'd that guy do to piss you off?
Stole my apartment.

He stole the apartment you were evicted from?
CAN'T HEAR YOU LA LA LA LA LA

I bet he has a nice dick.
I bet you're making predictable comments about his dick now LA LA LA LA LA LA

1480

Well, that was downright SUCCESSFUL
MONEEEEY!

Hey, there you are!
Is he gone?

Who, that guy who moved into your apartment? He was nice!
You just like him because he bought something.

No, I
MONEEEEY!

Pop!

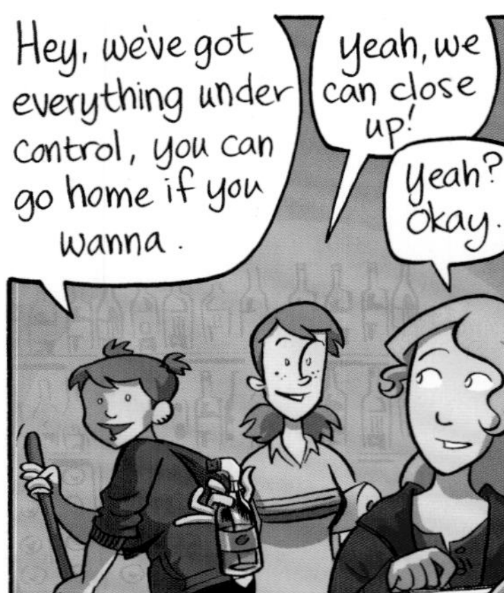
Hey, we've got everything under control, you can go home if you wanna.
Yeah, we can close up!
Yeah? Okay.

Man, I miss being able to walk home.

I guess there are a lot of things I miss.

1481

Hi--
Uh-- hey, I was just--

I miss this place.
I miss it, too.

What've you How've been up-- you--

1482

Heh.
Look, uh, I know this goes against my own rules, but, I just dropped off my last fare--

I just got off work--
Can we talk? Like, catch up? I mean, would you be okay with that?

I would be really okay with that.
Okay, good.

It turns out I don't have very many friends.
I coulda told you that.

bloop
HAAAAAAAZELLL
AAAAHH!
I need to feed the fish!

1483

1484

OH--
OH--

WHOA
okAY
STILL DRUNK
FWUMP

How did I get drunk?

At least I'm not naked this time.

HURk

BLUURRRGH

1485

My car! How did my car get there?

OH GOD
STAIRS

beep boop bip

mmN hey
Jamie I need you to drive me home I'm drunk

Hazel it's 7:30 in the morning.
Also I puked on my car.

1486

You slept with Zach.

No, thiz' just a friend's place..
Zach lives here.

You don' know tha--
ZACH'S
taxi service
AIRPORT • NORTHERN

oh, then.
Move over.

1487

I--I don't think I slept with Zach.
Do you REMEMBER not sleeping with him?

N-no, but-- I'm wearing clothes
You're wearing HIS clothes.

Oh.
That still doesn't mean--
There's a condom in your hair.

AAAAAAiiii
You slept with Zach.

Holy shit
There's seriously a condom in my hair

But it's empty.
Do you remember using it?

Why do we have to use a condom? I'm still on birth control.

Ah.. to be safe?
What, y'think I've gotten laid in the past month?

Nnoo, I--
What, 've YOU slept with someone else?

1488

No, but-- Hazel, I just-- we're not TOGETHER anymore, so-

HAZEL

Are you covering your mouth because you're afraid the truth will fall out?
NOD
NOD
NOD
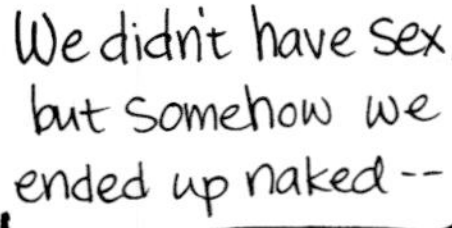

We didn't have sex, but somehow we ended up naked--
Have you checked your pockets?

Why would I-- How did you change your--
All Romance Detectives take a Hangover Detective class and a Classic Super-hero Costume Changing class.
Check your pockets.

Huh.

the Crowing Cock

Y'want another one of those?
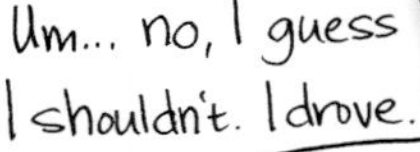
1489

Um... no, I guess I shouldn't. I drove.
Yeah, I feel like we can't really... talk here, anyway.

Would it be too forward-
No.
okay.

So, I guess we went to his place..
Bottlecap, left pocket.

Holy shit, you're good.
Elementary, my dear.

1490

So, we had a few beers, and then...

I've missed this. I miss hanging out with you.
Yeah, me too.

I feel like we didn't end on-- well, actually, I feel like we didn't END.
I know...
Do you think, maybe, just tonight, we could--

Pretend we didn't?
Exactly.

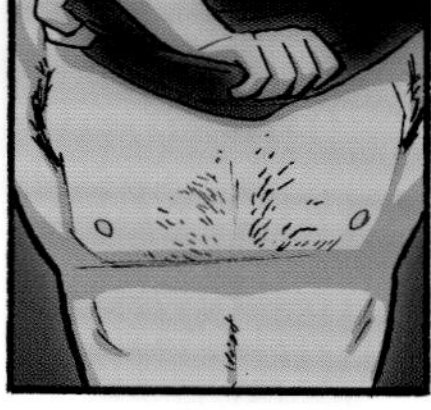

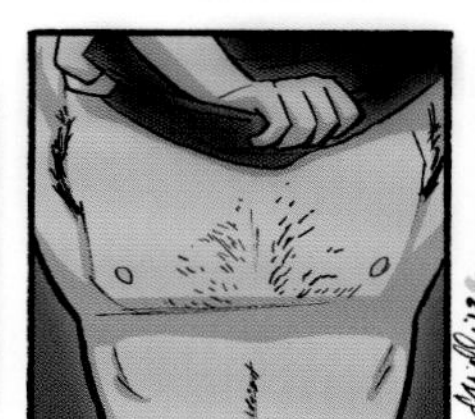

And then?
Shh, don't rush it.

1491

But then you didn't have sex, and you stormed out of his room...

Yeah, I don't remember what happened after
ding ding

8:02
1 msg from
Darren:
GET IT GURL

HAZEL...

Darren
I'm at Zach's, I dunno what I shoulddo
should do

SEND

2:52

4:17

I still love you.

Where are we going, anyway?
I have to go to work. What are you doing today?

Uhh, eating aspirin with a spoon and crying?
Good, you can do both of those here.

You're not taking me home?
Nope. You're officially on Best friend Watch.

Do I have to sit in the corner?
No, you have to water all the plants and not drink any alcohol.

1492

H'EEE!
McPedro! What're you doing here?

Hey! Don't you play dumb with me. How'd you get here?

SILLY WILLY CACTUS FRIENDS
$5.99

This is the worst hangover.

1493

ding ding ♪

12:14
1 msg from Zach:
Don't remember much from last night. Are you okay?

I'm okay.
Wanna grab lunch and talk?
I'd really

I'd really like

tap tap tap
return

talk?
I think we should take some time apart.

apart.
apart.
...
apart.

This is the worst hangover.

1494

Haaaaaazel, it's time to --

...ooooh

Let's get that off your face, sweetie.
whu-- whut is it?

That's chicken poooop.
nooooooo

And here's a sluuuuugg.
This is the worst hango-wuh huh huh huh

1495

1496

Sweetie, is that you?
Good gracious, what happened?
Everything.

Ooh sweetie. Why don't you curl up on the couch, and I'll make you some soup.

And we can watch reruns of "Murder, She Wrote."
I love Angela Lansbury.

siiiiiigh

Yehr face smells like poo.

1497

I VANNN TO SAAHCK YOUR BLAAAHD
mow?

Hee hee! Aww, who's a good kitty, WHO'S A GOOD KITTYYY
prrrrr rrrrrrr

aaa
AAAA
purrrrr rrrrr

1498

Honey, do you think it's time to have Spesh-K's headgear removed?

Ooh-- I dunno. Don't you think it's too early?
It's been well over a year.

Yeah, but -- I just can't imagine him without it. It really SUITS him.

Jameson, it's a dental apparatus, not an accessory.
BUT IT'S JUST SO CUTE

1499

Open wide
RRRRR

Well, it looks like his headgear isn't working anyway. Might as well take it off and try something else.
Like what?
RRRRR

Well, we could just REMOVE those teeth-
CHOMP

In fact, I strongly recommend removing those teeth.
RRRRR

Oh, I hope we made the right choice.
If removing his teeth is the best thing for Special Kitty, then it's the best for us, too.
Ah, folks?
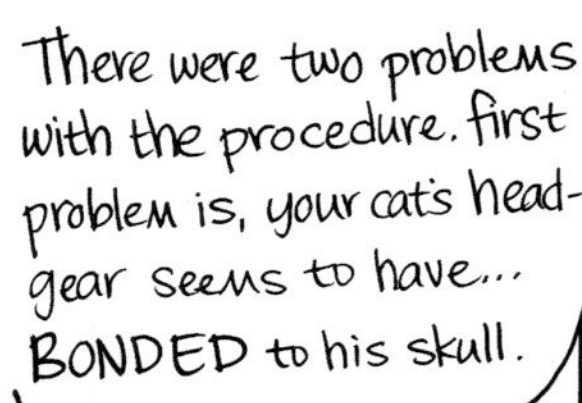

There were two problems with the procedure. First problem is, your cat's head-gear seems to have... BONDED to his skull.
I've never seen anything like it before.

WHOA.
What's this part?
That's the second problem.

1500

Y'know, maybe it's better that Special K's headgear bonded to his skull.
He seems so much happier with it.
Like I said, it SUITS him!

Yeah, I think it makes him even SPECIALER.

Plus, we finally found a toy he'll play with.
That was so nice of the vet to let us make a mold of his arm!
RRRRRRRR

1501

TRICK or TREAT!
AAA!

I'm gonna go with TRICK, 'cause that is NOT a costume.
Sure it is! Zombie Lingerie Model!

Ooh, you are NOT gonna like your sister's costume, then.
Why? What'd she--

Sis!
What? I thought it was cool before you did.

1502

I can't believe your mom rented the rec center for her party!
I can't believe you brought a backup costume.
...sexy-zombie butterfly.

The only problem with the rec center is: no booze.
That's the opposite of a problem.

You're still on Best Friend Watch. I don't want you to even SMELL alcohol for at least a month.
Buuuut... we can mix fruit juices together to make MOCKTAILS!
Which is the beverage equivalent of dry-humping, so I'll be over here at the water fountain.

1503

1504

Oh, there you are, dear! Enjoying the party?

°cough°
Ah, yes, the water is particularly... chlorinated.
Dorothy Gale! And you're a--
Are you--

Uhh, Puppy Cow? All they had left at the store was a dog costume and udders.
Oh, honey...

...you know I kept your old Toto costume...
MoM...
We could match!
MOM.

1505

I hope your friends like me...
Don't worry, Tucker, my friends are very nice. A few of them are single, too!
NUDGE

Y'know what? I don't even care. Im just here to have fun.
That's what I like to hear.

So much... fun...
Tsk, and you almost beat your record.

1506

Okay, picture yourself going up to that girl.

Picture her rejecting you.

Picture yourself being okay with that.

Hi!
I AM TOTALLY OKAY WITH THAT!

Im Tucker.
fiona.

1507

I LOVE Doctor Who!
Oh! Uh... actually, this isn't a costume, I just--

Wait, you like Doctor Who?
Yeah!
I LOVED that show when I was a kid!

Hah! When were you a kid, like, five years ago?
Haha, uh, nnooo, Doctor Who started in the 60's and ran through the 80's..

Are you seeing this.
I cannot even FATHOM what kind of irrelevant shit he's boring her with.

1508

Is that your romantically-challenged library friend?
Yep.

Dude's mackin' on mah sister!
That's your sister?

Yep! Good choice, she's a huge nerd.

What're you dancing to?
Thriller.

There's no music.
There is in my head.

1509

Are you, Alice, menstruating right now?
I knew you'd get my costume.

So I hear you're abstaining from booze.
No, I just really like-- "Boo-berry Blue" juice.

And you threw up on your car--
Hey, I've got an idea, why don't we talk about everything I hate?

Oh Hazel, I just want you to know that I'm here for you.
nng thank you.

And that if I catch you drinking, I'm telling Jamie.
nnNNng nng nng

1510

Well hello, Mister Social!
Hehe, yeeaahh.

So, did you ask her out?
Who, fiona? Nah, she's really cool, though! We're gonna watch Dr. Who together on friday night.

Did she give you her number?
Well yeah, we need to make plans.

Are you going to dinner first?
Well yeah, we need to eat--

1511

Oh my heart, I've got a date!
What do I do? What'll I wear?
Whoa, hang on there, buddy.

Let's recap. What'd you do tonight?
You were yourself.
You wore clothes that you like.
You weren't trying to impress anyone.
And you got a date.

Wow. You're right.
So, on friday, you need to--

Try twice as hard.
NO!

1512

five minutes late... perfect, won't look too eager...

Huh, actually, I'm not even that nervous!
Hey!
clap

you came!

WHUMP

almost
I hope you like full-body hugs, they're my specialty! Haha
shift

1513

I hope you like wings! This place has the BEST wings.
Hmm...

Oh! They have vegetarian wings!
GASP!
Tucker, I didn't know you were a vegetarian!

I'll bet it's because you don't want to hurt little animals, isn't it?

B-bb-b-b-big ones, too.
Ooh, that's so sweet!

1514

Sir, it is finally time to introduce you to... the NEW Doctor Who.
Ready?
I'm ready!

Oh, by the way, I'm not sure if I told you, but I live with my MOM.
Oh! That's--

fiiiiiiiiiiine
RUUUUUBB

Hello! Is this Tucker?
Yep! Tucker, this is my MOM!
Hi!
SWIPE

Every boy she bring over LOVES that pillow!
It's a very nice pillow.

1515

Aw, Tucker, you can sit over here! I don't bite.
Ha! It's okay, I-- I like this couch.
PAT PAT
PAT PAT

Suit yourself!
click
WOOOOEEEOOOOO
DOCTOR·WHO

...it's more like a big ball of... wibbly-wobbly... timey-wimey... stuff...
Heh

Wooow, that was a really good one.

So, you like the new Doctor Who?
Yeah!

And...
do you like--
me?

Yyyyyyyyyyyyyyyy ee I gotta go!
That's not your pillow!

1516

Soooooo
I don't want to talk about it.

Ooh. Hey, look, Tucker, just because fiona isn't interested--
She IS! She is TOTALLY INTERESTED!

She kept HUGGING me... and TOUCHING me...
And she's so BEAUTIFUL...
And new Doctor Who IS really good!

And I stole her PILLOW..
Okay, let's take you to the kiddie section.

1517

So, fiona likes you, you like fiona, and the problem is--?
Clarice, I felt like a twelve-year-old boy the ENTIRE DATE.

Aw, that's sweet.
WHAT? Have you ever BEEN twelve?

Well yeah, but I wasn't a bo--
oh.
OH.

Tent city?
In khakis.

Here, hug this penguin.
whimper

1518

I uhh, I'm afraid this goes beyond my expertise.
I know. That's why I didn't even want to talk about it.

Ah Tucker, you know I'll do whatever I can to help.
Do you have, like, the OPPOSITE of an erectile dysfunction pill?

YES.
Yes I do.
Meet me at the Meck tonight at eight.

Hi! I hear your cock gets hard all the time.
CLARICE!

1519

1520

So, what's the problem? Poppin' boners in front of your lady-friend?
C-can we find a table?

I say flaunt it if you've got it! I LOVE it when a guy gets--
With all due respect, I believe there's a difference between trying to impress a gay man, and trying to impress a straight woman.
What, don't straight women like a nice, turgid wang? It's like a compliment!
I-- I don't--
For example, if you'll look down for a moment, you'll notice that I'm saying some VERY nice things about you
AAAAAAA

1521

Excuse me, are you boys talking about boner problems?
no

Because I'm off the clock, but I rep for a company that makes a VERY good ED drug.
Actually, Woody McGee here has the OTHER kind of boner problem.
Awww, I understand, buddy.
I get a turgid wang every time I see a girl giggle, and I have a HUGE
CLARICE!

1522

Man, some people get so squicked out about chicks with wangs.
Don't I know it. So, are you a chick with a wang?
Nah. I have a soft pack, but I haven't worn it in years.
I never got lesbians who pack. Aren't penises like your Kryptonite?

Mine hardly looks like a penis. It's hot pink with sparkles!
So, you're actually cos-playing a unicorn.

But with less whinnying.
Unicorns don't whinny, they just open their mouths and Enya falls out.

1523

Hey.

Sorry I was a dick to you, pun intended.
I don't wanna talk about it.

Well, you know the belt trick, right? Stick it under your belt
I know the belt trick. I'm just... scared.

I haven't felt this way about a girl since I was twelve, and when she found out I liked her, she never talked to me again.
I don't want that to happen with Fiona.

Sooo you're saying you haven't had a hard-on since you were twelve?
This is the end of our conversation.

Hey Sis! How was your date with Library Boy?
UNNGH

Oooh, no fun?
TOO fun. We had SUCH a good time.

So what's wrong?
I asked him if he liked me, and he just stammered and ran out the door!

With a pillow?
YES! How'd you know?

Sis, we need to talk about your boobs.
Don't change the subject, how'd you know about the pillow?

1524

Fiona, the McJack girls have been blessed – and sometimes burdened – with magical sweater puppies.
But, with great cleavage comes great responsibility.

Some men just can't handle these lumps!
But -- men LOVE boobs!

They DO, but ours are particularly potent – we must release them in small doses.
(Unless we really, really want something.)

Keep the brochure. I drew it by hand!
I see.
OUR BOOBIES ARE MAGIC

1525

But -- I didn't think my outfit was too provocative for Tucker.
OUR BOOBIES ARE

What did you wear?
Actually, this exact same shirt, only in mauve.

Buttoned up to --
um, here?

Why not button it up to --

Oh! I thought those were just for decoration.
Nevermind, they are. Wear a hoodie.

1526

Fiona

I feel maybe I was a bit forward the other night... can we have a do-over? 8:00 at Thai Not, Doctor Who to follow. ...?

I wouldn't miss it for all the world. :)

I hope I wasn't too forward...
Tucker!

Hi!
Hi!

um...
can we --

1527

1528

CALL FROM: Tucker

beep
Clarice! The second date was Stellar!
Ooh good! Why are you calling me, then? Shouldn't you be exploring her mouth with your tongue or something?

No, we're taking it really slow. No kissing yet, but she LOVES to cuddle!
Awww.

I read some poetry I wrote about her, and she LOVED it! She wants me to write more!
Awww.

You realize you're on video chat...
Just stretching my face!

So THIS is why their date went so well?
I drew it by hand!

Yes, I noticed.
thank you!
Jamie, it's not your sister's responsibility to hide her cleavage just because she's got bodacious boobs.

Oh, you don't understand.
McJack racks are LEGIT magical. Our great-grandmother Maria lived next-door to a WITCH!

She used to look after the witch's cat when she was away.

When the cat grew old and died, the witch told Maria:
You always took such good care of old Barnabus.
What can I give you to thank you?

Maria was 16 and a late bloomer, and she said:
I would like some magical titties, please.
The witch laughed and replied:

I will give you titties so magical, if you expose just an INCH of cleavage, you will receive ANYTHING you desire!

Waaait a minute-- is this why I always waive your late fee when you bring in overdue books?
nooooooooo

1529

Hey sweetie, y'wanna start decorating the tree?
Meh, sure.

YAH!
mow

FLIP
FLIP
FLIP
I GOTCHA, FISHEH

FLIP
FLIP
WHAP
WHAP
DONE.

sigh
C'mere, fish.
PLUCK

I don't understand how you're still alive, but I intend to keep you that way.
FLIP

Mom, where do we keep the fish?
In the freezer, dear!

No, the LIVE fish.
In the bathtub, dear!

1530

Did you seriously give up your bathtub for a goldfish?
Oh I hardly "gave it up"— watch what she does!

How do you know it's a she?
I'm a librarian, dear, I know a lot of things.

Hee hee!

It nibbles your toes.
You know what would go well with this? A neck massage.

Bye, I'm going somewhere very far away.
Ooh, you need to try this, Hazel!
BZZZZ

1531

sigh
It still doesn't feel like Christmas to me.
Ooh, it NEVER seems to feel like Christmas to you.

Does it feel like Christmas to you?
It ALWAYS feels like Christmas to me!

Of COURSE it does.
Here, this will help.

What's "Christmas Shoes?"
It's something that'll make everything ELSE feel like Christmas to you.
Please wear earbuds.

1532

I hate you.
Oh c'mon, if I hadn't made you listen to "Christmas Shoes," someone else would've.

Does Christmas get harder as we get older?
No, Christmas gets harder when you've had a bad breakup and your best friend won't let you have any booze.

Because my best friend hates me.
Because she LOVES you.

Will next Christmas be even worse?
Perhaps.
But at least it'll never be as bad as "Christmas Shoes."

1533

1534

Yaaaaay you're here!
WHUMP
Haha, this is the exact opposite of how my last five hours went!
Oh! Did you visit Hazel?

Yep! We made cookies and had hot cocoa.
Did you have fun?

Um-- a different kind of fun...

The kind of fun that--
--makes you really depressed?

Bing Crosby Christmas Songs?
And cuddles, yes please!

1535

You and Hazel-- how did you guys ever, uh--
I know, we're not the most likely friends.
Merry Christmas

Most of the time, she's overly sour and I'm overly bubbly--

But she needs a lot of love, and I love giving it to her. So we fit together like puzzle pieces.

Oh.
But then-- how do WE fit together?
Like spoons.

1536

Wooooooow

That is the gayest tree I have ever seen.
Hee hee, I love it.

I love you.
mmm

gasp!
Thea, what if Santa sees us?

I don't think Santa's into lesbians.
THAT guy? Yeah he is.

We'll just tell him there's a cookie jar in the kitchen.
Eww, then we'd have to watch HIM get off!

1537

Happy Almost-New Year!
Yaaay you came!

Where are your guests?
Guests?
That was the whole point of the "Bring a Guest" party; you're supposed to bring someone new to the group.

um..

Hey little lady, what's YOUR name?
Wouldn't you like to know.
ACK you two are so cute I'm gonna puke.

Yo.
YAAAY Hazel's here!

I don't know anybody new, so I invited Mall Santa.
Ho-Ho hello!
Oh! Welcome!

Uh-- wait, but-- isn't Christmas over?

Not Mall Santa 2012, Mall Santa 2013.
They're starting earlier this year.
Woooo Christmas forever!

1538

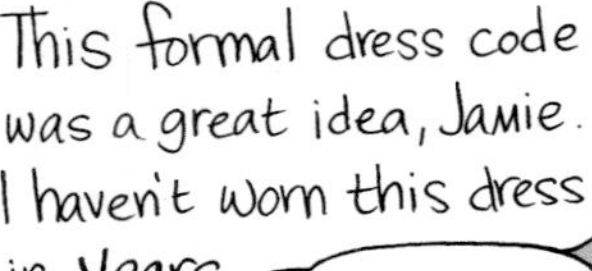
This formal dress code was a great idea, Jamie. I haven't worn this dress in years.

DAAAMN, you wear it well, girl!

Same to you, Vanna.
So who's your guest?

Oh, that's Beatrice. She works with me at the library.
oh.
...is she okay?

Yeah, that's her happy face.
What's her unhappy face?

She doesn't have one. She just starts throwing things.
I'm gonna put away the crystalware.

1539

Hey, way to dress up that cueball, Jameson!
Doesn't he look sexy?

Yeah!
That was rhetorical, Hazel.

Wh-- I'm not trying t'steal your man!
Well, but you didn't have to answer-

11:59 COUNTDOWN!
Wooo!
Whewww

1540

I put some ginger ale in here for you.
Thanks, mom.
Do you have any resolutions?
It's not a resolution, per se--

Well, I have one. Mimi, I want to love and support you even more this year than I ever have...

But in order to do that--
You have to answer a question for me first--
10 9 8 7 6 5 4 3 2 1

Will you--

HAPPY NEW YEAR!

1541

1542

WHOA!
WOOo!
yeah!
clap clap clap clap clap clap clap clap clap clap clap clap clap clap clap

Did you know about this?
I knew about Thea, but not Mimi!

Get a room, you two!
Alright, alright, just don't stuff us into any closets!

1543

Well, I believe this calls for a toast!

May today be remembered as the day you loved each other the least, for the garden of your love is merely budding.

aww

aw

clap

clap

clink!

Aww, that was really sweet, um--
Mall Santa 2013

oh!
Yeah, you wouldn't believe what I have to do to fit these into a Santa hat.

1544

wakey wakey
mmn

oh damn, did I fall asleep here?
Apparently.

mmn I'm still in a dress
m-hm.

AAAA my dress hiked up in my sleep!
I took pictures.

Oh wow, my ass looks amazing.
Yeah, I applied the "Great Ass" filter to it.
Let's see what "Great Tits" does!

1545

Haha "Great Mustache" filter

You're in a way better mood than I'd expected.

It's New Year's Day and I'm not hungover, you're here, coffee's here, my ass looks amazing, my ass has a mustache...

Did you make a resolution?

I wanna be happy again. I'm just gonna focus on all the things that make me happy.

So... does that mean you're over Za
HAPPY THINGS
Haha Puppy face filter

Oh hey, speaking of happy things, thanks for bringing Mall Santa to the party.
Oh yeah, Sorry I brought a total stranger instead of some-one I knew.

Uh, did you miss the part where I said "thank you?"
Yeah, I missed that. Why are you thanking me?

I wanna sit on his lap an' tell him to give me a Pony, if y'know what I mean.

Do you mean you want a horse cock?
No!!
not really

1546

Hey Maaaaya

Notice anything different about me?
GASP! Sis! Oh my god!!

AAAAA I'm so happy for you!!
Mommy, why?

Aunt Thea's getting married! You're gonna be a flower girl!
Well, we kinda GOT married..

1547

You GOT married?
Yeah, we just wanted to get it over with, y'know?

But--you're still going to have a wedding, right?
Well, we hadn't really PLANNED on it--
Aunt Thea?

Can I REALLY be a flower girl?

I'll talk to Mimi.
YAAAAAAAAY!

1548

Is it the cost? Because I can help--
Nooo no no, that's not it, it's just--
I never pictured myself having a wedding, y'know?
flower girrrrl!

Well of COURSE you didn't, Sis. The only images of weddings we saw growing up were of men and women.

We should look up videos of lesbian weddings—
—and count how many of their parents showed up.

Oooh I'm an idiot.
Yeah, kinda. This was an easy one.

1549

1550

I can talk to Mom an' Dad—
UGH, no, that's the last thing I want.

Or actually--
Yeah, talk to Mom and Dad. AFTER the wedding. Let 'em know they were cordially NOT invited.

There's nothing CORDIAL about that.
It's been over a decade, sis, maybe it's time to bury the hatchet.
Hmm. hatchets..

SIS
What? It's not murder if I just lop off a finger or two and make them beg for mercy.

1551

It's not like Mom and Dad ever "buried the hatchet" over you getting pregnant.

Well, not out loud, but...
It's amazing what a baby will do to a heart of stone.

In fact, I bet if you introduced them to Mimi--
Are you about to compare my wife to a baby?

She does watch My Little Pony.
AND I finger-bang her, new metaphor.

1552

Hello, wife.
Oh! Hello, wife!

Hehe, it's so weird calling you my WIFE
Like, I'm trying to picture you in an apron, making me a meatloaf.

In JUST an apron?

If I get you an apron, will you please do that?
Of course not. I've no idea how to make a meatloaf.

1553

So, how'd your sister feel about the news?
Ecstatic, then disappointed.

Ooh we should've invited her to come to the courthouse..
Well, it's not that, she just really wants us to have a wedding.

Aww, we're gonna have the BEST wedding. It'll be worth the wait!

When did you want to start planning that, anyway?
Uh, n-now? Now would be good!

We ARE having a wedding, right?
Uh-- so, when you said we could "do something special" after the courthouse, that wasn't about strap-ons?

No-- I mean-- that too, but--
You want a wedding.

I've dreamed of having a wedding since I was a little girl, Thea...
Me too, but--

I now pronounce you... Seahorse and wife!
muah muah muah

And then, GODZILLA TOOK BACK HIS BRIDE!
MOOOOM!

1554

Wait, is this about your parents?
Amazing, you guessed it before my own SISTER did.

Aww, sweetie. You know you could have Maya or someone else stand in for them--
Yeah, but it'd just be salt in the wound.

Well-- I mean, it's been a decade, right? Maybe we should meet up with them, see how it goes?

SIIIIGH, you're probably right.
Mm, I'm RIGHT. Just what a wife likes to hear.

1555

jingle jingle

gasp!
jingle jingle

Mall Santa 2013?
Naw, he's on break. I'm just subbing for him.

I'm back, thanks Reggie.
Anytime, man, your fans are way nicer than mine.

1556

Hey, aren't you--
Jamie.

Of course you are.
I like your hat.
Hee hee.

Do you do this all year long?
Yep, pretty much!
jingle jingle

Is Santa SUPPOSED to be seen all year long?
OH yeah.
You tell a kid that Santa works full-time for a non-profit, they will actually STEAL their parents' wallet for you.

1557

1558

Well, I've got some spare change--
HOLD ON. I need to tell you the truth--

--about this charity--
before you donate.

We are not associated with any religious sect...
We don't discriminate according to race, gender sex, or sexual preference...
We just give money to well-researched homeless shelters that share these values with us.

Wow.
I never thought a charity could get my panties wet.
Ah, I see you're familiar with our motto.

1559

So, ... do you have a REAL name, Mall Santa?
Hmm, yes, but I don't give it out to just anyone.

Well, I'm NOT just anyone.
No, indeed you're not.
But I don't share personal information while I'm at work.

Are you asking me out?
Nope!

You mean I have to do it??
Oh! Are you asking me out?

1560

Alright. Okay.
Will you go out with me?
Eight o'clock tonight at O'Brien's Tavern.

Oh, I see you haven't given this any thought at all.
I haven't. It's just my favorite pub.
See you there.
If you're lucky.

GEEZ, what HAPPENED back there?
I don't know! I just felt so-- POWERLESS!

Jamie--
OHMYGOD how long have these been covered up??

1561

Haaaazulll
Jaaamieeee

I need to complaaain.
So you came here, because I'm at work and can't leave.

How long are you here?
five more hours.

I guess that's long enough.
Two California and a Rainbow roll.
you can buy my time, but it won't be cheap.

I went on a date last night.
With who, Mall Santa?

Mm-hm.
WHOA, seriously? I was just joking!
Did he give you a "Pony Ride"?
No! He didn't even try to KISS me! We flirted ALL NIGHT, but he never made a move, and he hasn't texted me all day and now I'm CONFUSED

Oh, so like, how NORMAL people date.
YES!
It's stupid!!

1562

Lemme tell you something about normal dating, Jamie.

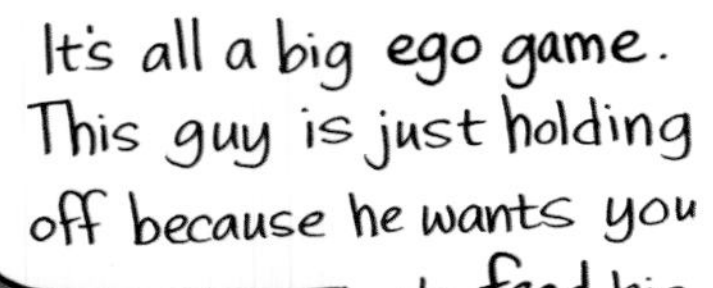
It's all a big ego game. This guy is just holding off because he wants you

to feed his ego some more before he lets you cash out with a kiss.

I don't think that's it, Haze. He acts like something's holding him back--
Yeah, his EGO!

Where are you getting your "dating tips" from?
The Internet.
Like, on Web Sites.

1563

How does Erin feel about the whole thing?
Oh, um..

I mean, I'm sure she'd be fine with it--
What, you haven't told her yet?

Well, she's visiting her dad up north, so--
And I mean, she WANTS me to see other people, so--

Y'know, your Instagram-facebook Machine has this other option, it's called a phone--
siiigh

1564

I just don't know if it's worth telling her about it yet, y'know?
I mean, maybe he doesn't even LIKE me that way.
Ehh, I guess.

Thanks for listening to me whine.
Thanks for sushi!

And don't let Santa Claus get you down!
His name is Keith!
boodle boot!

1 msg from:
Keith

1565

1566

KNOCK
KNOCK
KNOCK

Ooo for me?
Very funny. Come in!

Listen up, kids! Today we're all gonna be PROFESSIONAL FLORISTS!
YAAAAAAAY!!
YAAAAAAAY!!
YAAAAAAAAAAY!!
But I wanna be a DOCTOR!

1567

Ooo, that looks really nice!
Who're you gonna give it to?
My mommy.
MY PARAKEET!!

Thanks for doing this so last-minute, Jamie.
You're letting me play with kids all day, how could I turn you down?

You really like kids, huh?
If I could fill my apartment with kids like a ballpit, I would.
('cept that'd be pretty irresponsible.)

Speaking of irresponsible, y'know what I like to do after spending a day with kids?
Go to a seedy bar and get hammered?
Bingo.
Done.

1568

Order whatever you'd like, it's all on me.
Ooh, you're like a real-life Santa Claus!

Hey, it's the least I could do! The kids LOVED you today.
How long have you been doing the after-school program?
tap tap

Off & on since I was a teen. My mom started the program. Technically, it was my first job.

If you'd told me then that someday I'd have to force six-year-olds to put away their cordless, mobile, picture-taking game-phone devices, I'd have never believed it.
I'll bet!
HAPPY HOUR!

1569

So I told him to Google "fluffer," and THEN decide if it's a good nickname for his daughter.
pfft hahaha!

Hehe, I'm a little drunk.
I'm feelin' pretty bold, m'self.

Haha, bold? How "bold" ya feelin'?
This bold

That's a little too bold.
I can do it softer!

Jamie, believe me, I've wanted to kiss you since the moment I met you, but...
I don't wanna make this into some kind of Chasing Amy drama.
Huh?

Jamie, you have a girlfriend--
Oh! Yeah, no, but it's-- we have an open relationship!

And... I take it you're not a lesbian?
I'm kind of a whatever-sexual.

I don't suppose you could've told me all this BEFORE you kissed me.
Oh! Huh, yeah, I bet that was confusing for you.

1570

I think I need some time to process all of this.
I understand, Keith.

Thank you for walking me home. I guess I shouldn't invite you inside, huh?
Jamie, there is a VERY big part of me that wants to come inside, but-

pfft
snort!
Oh my-- I didn't mean it like that!!

How BIG is this PART you
NO SPOILERS

1571

mmmm

mmm
you feel so... small.

That's funny, I gained like, ten pounds on my trip!

1572

When did you get in?
Really late last night! I thought you might like to wake up to some company.

Aw, that was sweet of you.
Well, it was half-selfish.

Um-- you might wanna, y'know, give me a heads-up when you're coming over...
next time...
oh-- OH!

Did you find a PLAYMATE while I was away?
NO! nononono noooooo

1573

1574

Heh, Jamie, you're the worst liar.
Look, if we wanna keep our relationship open, we've got to be able to talk.

Here, close your eyes.

Pretend I'm someone you can say ANYTHING to.
It doesn't have to be a person.

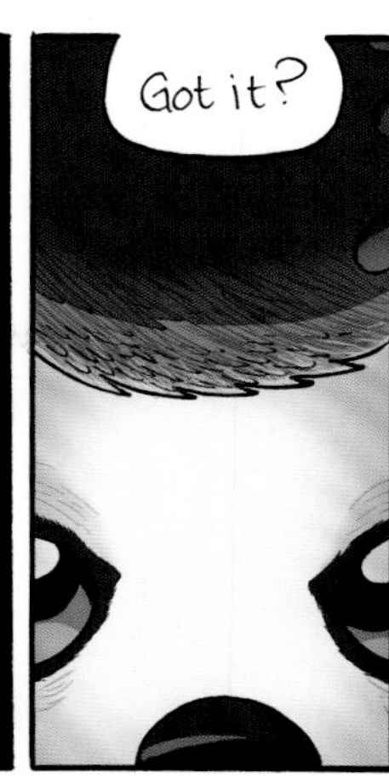
Got it?

nod nod nod nod
Okay.
Now, let's talk about your sex life.

1575

There's not much to report, just-- remember Mall Santa?
from the New Year's party?

Yeah. Well, I kinda bumped into him, and we went out, and...
nothing happened.

He says he needs time to process, y'know... US.
Well, we have a pretty unconventional relationship.

You're petting my face.
I turned you into a sloth.
AWESOME.

1576

Ta da!

How do I look? Conventional enough for your parents?
There's no such thing.

How much am I allowed to drink before we go?
NONE. You need to be sober for this.

Oh...
I meant, how much on top of what I've already had?
THEA

1577

Thanks for letting me take that shot.
You looked like you needed it.

oh god..
..there they are.

Honey, it's SO good to see-
Mom, this is my WIFE, Mimi.

Ha
haha
Where's the bar?

Well, Mimi, it's VERY nice to meet a friend of Thea's.
WIFE, Mom.

Thea, it's been SO long. I was afraid I wouldn't recognize you!
That's funny, YOU haven't changed a bit.

Honey, don't you want to get a table?
I believe the lady asked for the BAR.
OH, HA HA, YES THANK YOU SIR

1578

Can I get you folks some—
Whiskey, straight.
Oh! Dear, I didn't know you drank!

Y'know what, Mom, let's cut to the chase. There's a LOT you don't know about me, but the one thing you DO know is that I'm a lesbian.
And here I am trying to introduce you to my WIFE, and you can't step out of your bubble of make-believe long enough to even congratulate us.

Just married.
Drinks on the house!!

1579

Theadora, you can't MARRY your friend.
YES, actually, I can and I have. I'm on her health insurance, we have a joint bank account–

Honey, that's NOT all a marriage IS--
Oh, really? Because according to the STELLAR example you and Dad set for me--

I made up a drinking game.
We drink every time we want to leave.
Ha ha, IIIIII don't think I should--

Ah, what the heck, it's REALLY good health insurance.
Bottoms up.
clink

1580

Well, I'm afraid I just can't accept what you have as a marriage.
Good to know. Maybe we'll try this again in another ten years.

Thea
Mimi, let's go get dinner somewhere else.
Oh.. yeah, okay.
Cheers, kid

I may need to get my stomach pumped.
Me too.

1581

1582

Dammit.
Mimi, I'm sorry, I shouldn't have put you in that position.
NO, I'm glad you did. I wanna be a part of your whole life, not just all the good stuff.

Well, congratulations, you just saw the WORST of it.
Ooh, sweetie. Let's go back home.

Shit.
We're both drunk.
This is the Mondayest Tuesday ever.

1583

Wait — sniff! — why are YOU so drunk?
Your dad challenged me to a drinking game.

My dad?
Yeah--
uh, that WAS your dad, right?

Oh my god.
I didn't even say hello. I ignored him.

GASP!
I'M JUST LIKE MY MOTHER
BLAARGH

1584

Oh! Mimi!
BLURGH

Shit!
I should find my dad before he leaves. I should--
BLURF

um, I should--
BLURK

I should stay right here.
You should move your f
BLARGH
n'rmind

1585

Best friend Sushi Time, ♪ Best friend Sushi Time! ♫
I see we have a theme song.
This is my favorite part of the day! Why did it take us so long to start taking lunch breaks together?
Well, this isn't really a break-
We're just hiding behind the counter and eating.

ding ding ♫
SH!
Here comes someone!

May I interest you in one of our SEA-sonal wines?
Stop that!!

lookit that! He's checkin' out the seasonal wine rack!
You're a natural.

Hey. So.
How are you FEELING.
I HATE it when you ask me that.

But... I dunno, I'm doing okay?
I've just been trying to focus on the magazine... So...

So you don't even have TIME to think about sex and drinking!
What? All I WRITE about is sex and drinking!

1586

Speaking of sex and drinking...
well, just drinking...
I've been sober for over a month now, so--

OH! Wow, that went by fast!
Says you.

Well, I suppose you could start with one drink today, as long as it's with me.
I wouldn't have it any other way.

Okay!
Go ahead, I'll watch.
Not HERE!

1587

Cheers!
clink!

Aahh, I've missed this.
What, beer?
That too, but mostly hanging out with you at the bar.
Aww.

Hey Hazel, lemme make you a "Welcome Home" drink once you're finished with that one.
Aww, thanks Angel, but I'm on a one-drink limit tonight.

Ah, I see. Then how 'bout an "I'm the Responsible One" for your parole officer?
Yay!
Welcome home.

1588

So what else is exciting in your life, aside from the magazine?

One word: nothing. Now, distract me with your tales of wild debauchery.
Ooh, but I don't have any of those.

What, Secret Santa hasn't invited you over to sit on his lap and by "lap" I mean "face"?

HAZEL!
What?
You're smiling, does that mean yes?
We have a date tomorrow.
And by "date" you mean "fuckplans."

1589

1590

So, did you finally talk to Erin about Keith Kringle?
Yep! She's a-okay with it.

But... I don't wanna get my hopes up about starting a relationship with him. What if he's not okay with me having a girlfriend after all?

Wait-- so, you're not just trying to sleep with this guy?
I like him too much!

If Keith was my boyfriend, I could have a sex life with him, and keep my domestic life with Erin...
And still have time to ride your unicorn and slay the dragon.

1591

Dude, if you really want this guy to be your boyfriend, couldn't you just DOWNGRADE Erin to, like, "cuddle buddy" or something?
DOWNGRADE?!

Hazel, she's my GIRLFRIEND!
Is she? I mean, I never really got why you call each other that..

I know we don't fit everyone's definition, but "girlfriend" just feels right to us. It describes our devotion to one another.

Like, what if I "downgraded" you from my best friend to just a friend?
And give up my half of our yin-yang necklace? NEVAR!

1592

Either way, it WOULD be nice just to have some sex in my life again.
You're telling ME.

I guess it's been awhile for you
Last SUMMER

WHOA. Has it really been that
YES.

But, I mean, you have all those nice, attractive—
cold, heartless, predictable—

—coworkers?
—sex toys

1593

What about your coworkers, though?
Jamie, I don't have many rules, but "don't fuck where you eat" is one of them.

Bummer, that Charles is a cutie!
Not cute enough to lose my job over.

What if you met someone here at the bar?
At the Meck? NEVER!
Don't fuck where you drink, either!
haha!

I'll have the check, please.

sigh

e-mail ♫
What the--

to: Hazel
Adam&Eve&Steve.com
Are you tired of your cold, heartless, predictable toys? Do you long for a more HUMAN experience?
introducing THE LOVE DONG
"Who needs a boyfriend?"
BUY

That is the most RIDICULOUS sex toy I've ever seen.

BUY

1594

ZZZZZZZ

ding-DONG
zZ zZk??

H-hullo?

VROOOOM

What the..
clunk

huh?

aaa
AAAAA
LOVE DONG

1595

SHUT.
LOVE DONG
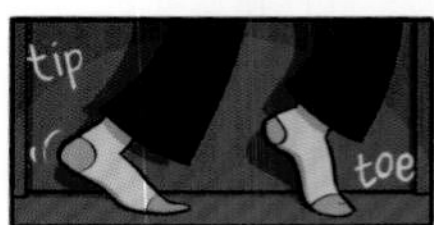
tip
toe

beep ♪
boop
bip ♪

Hello, Adam & Eve & Steve.com, Jarrod speaking...
JARROD. Hi. I just received this—
GIFT I ordered like, twenty minutes ago--

Ah yes, that's our signature Desperate NOW™ service.
Our system indicated that you hadn't placed an order with us in several months, so you qualified for our Emergency Relief instant shipping.

I want to return it.
Our system indicates that you feel that way NOW, but within 24 hours of involuntary celibacy, you'll change your mind.

1596

GAH this was the WORST idea.
Dear? Who was that at the door?
LOVE DONG

Uh, Jehovah's Witness, Mom!
Oh.
Did you let him in?

N-- no, it's like, eleven-thirty.

Mom, you know it's not okay to let strange men in the house, right?

1597

1598

Alright, if we're gonna be stuck with each other, we might as well get this show on the—
LOVE

AAAA!
Whatever happened to discreet packaging?
LOVE DONG

"Needs air pump"?
Huh.
LOVE

AAAA!!
flop
LOVE

1599

I can't. I can't do this.

"Desperate Now."
feh! I'm not DESPERATE. It was just a moment of weakness.
A $75 non-refundable moment of weakness.

I can find PLENTY of other ways to fulfill my needs.

DOOOOOOM
LOVE
SCRABBLE

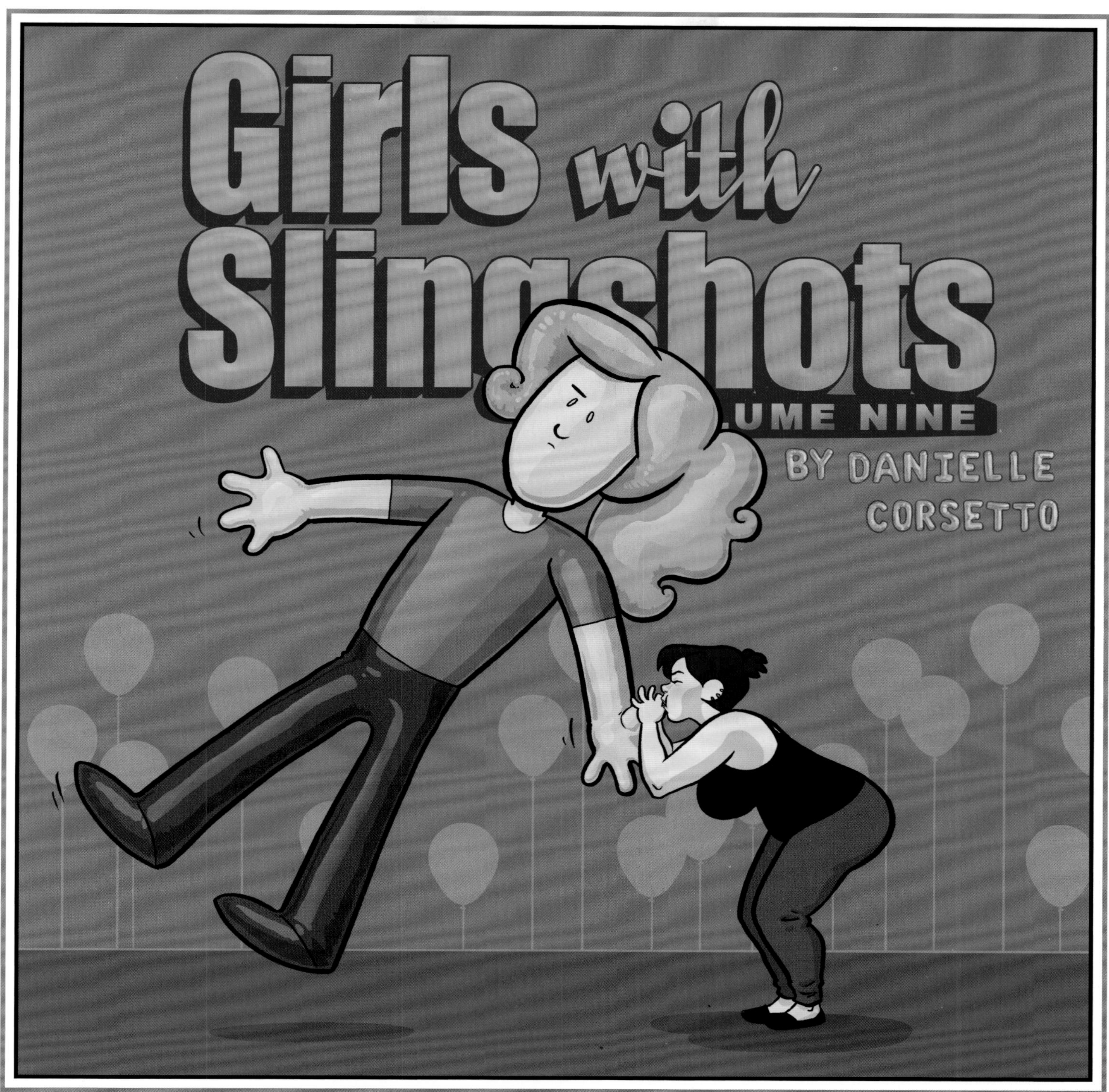
Girls with Slingshots
UME NINE
BY DANIELLE CORSETTO

VOLUME NINE

strips 1600-1798

1600

hmmm...
purrrr purrrr

What do you think, kitty?
floral, or straight-up little black dress?

mrow
You like the black one?

mow
Ooh, you REALLY like the black one!
okay.

You're right, I look better in dark colors.
POOF

1601

Oh noooo, kitty!

AUGH, I'm gonna have to lint-roll the HELL outta this–

POOF!

mrrow?

Did you just shed your--
eyeballs?
PLOOP PLOOP

1602

Fluffy, you've gotta behave yourself now. I'm going out for a fancy dinner.
moooww

I'll be home soon! And then we can cuddle all night.
mroooow

But I can't touch you until AFTER dinner.
It's FANCY.

Tickets?
I'm on the guest list.
FANCY DINNER
TONIGHT
5-7

1603

Oooh, Miss Jamie, you look as beautiful as one of your floral arrangements.
Oh you.

Here, let me get your seat.
oh!

That's a lovely dress. Let's cover it up entirely.
Oh?
Salad?

SQUiiiRT
OH.

That was the fanciest meal I've had all year.
You guys did a GREAT job!
Thanks, Miss J.

Thank YOU!
Alright, so, Miss Crenshaw is going to help you all clean up, and
Are you going on a DATE?!
Awwww

We're getting DESSERT.
Aww man, I want dessert!
Yeah!

GROWN-UP dessert.
The last time my parents had grown-up dessert I got a brother.
1604

So, did the kids raise tons of money with their fancy Dinner?
Enough for the basketball hoop they wanted.
Yay!
Fancy Desserts

Thank you for buying my ticket, by the way.
Thank YOU for accepting! I know it wasn't exactly a date-

Aw, that was kind of a date!
Well... not really--

But-- THIS part's really a date--
Well--
1605

Oh-- um- I thought-
Well, I guess it's KIND of a date, I just--

I don't know WHAT to call it.
If you'd told me you had a BOYfriend, I would've backed off entirely...
Just because you have a GIRLfriend doesn't mean I should treat the situation any differently.

So... why did you invite me out?
Well, I figured we could talk about it while we—

EAT ALL THE CHOCOLATE
Bingo.
1606

mmph
You're right, I'm feeling better already.
Good.

So...
um...
what ARE we doing?
Eating dessert together?
As friends?

And nothing more?
And nothing more. I'm sorry, Jamie, It just doesn't seem right to me.

...
What if I got Erin to sign a permission slip?
Jamie.
1607

1608

Look, I've been down this road before.
I tried to date a girl who was seeing someone, and--
...it got messy.

But, I'm not that girl--
I know you're not, but-- put yourself in my shoes.

I really can't convince you, can I.

More chocolate?
YES

1609

So, is it okay if we stay friends? Because I really do like you.
I'd be hurt if you DIDN'T wanna be friends!

Imagine if we'd done this WITHOUT the chocolate.
GOD, that would've SUUUUCKED!

Heh. Yeah.
Hey, hugs not drugs.
Pft, dork.
Good-night, Keith.

click
augh.

AAAUGH!!

1610

AUGH

I should've never bought you.
I don't NEED you.

If I wanted a dildo with a heart, I'd just go find a one-night stand.

What was that, dear?

I want a banjo and guitar
... and a music stand
oh, okay!

1611

Why am I talking to a dildo in a closet?
I'm gonna go get laid.

See ya, Mom.
Are you getting a banjo and guitar?

N-- no, just a--
music stand
from the department store?

Nnnnnnsure
Could you pick up a tub of Vaseline while you're there?

Nnnnnnsure
Thank you, dear.

"TUB" of Vaseline?
Maybe she needs it for--
NON-gross reasons.

Man, I'm rusty at this.
Where do people find one-night stands?

Hi

Uh
Hi.
How've you been?

Um
During what time period?

1612

Oh. You don't remember me.
I-I'm really bad with names.

Two ice cream sundaes?

See, I've had a LOT of ice cream over the years, so--
Jimmie Cone?

Oh--
OH
And-- senior year of high school?

I lost it in the Great Memory Purge of College.
Ah, I backed mine up on floppies.
The $5\frac{1}{4}$" kind.

1613

Well, I'd love to catch up, but--
man... I REALLY don't remember you. I'm sorry.

Wow, Hazel, I'm actually a little hurt.
I helped you with almost ALL of your Advanced Calc homework.

Wait--
are you..
Vincent?
Yes!

You wrote in my yearbook!
We were also friends!

1614

Well hey, I'm just out here looking for, uh, something to do, so--
do you wanna go get a drink and talk?
That would be incredible.

Heh, I'm not sure I can live up to "incredible," but--
Oh, you will. You always have.

HOW well do you remember me?

1615

1616

The Meck is my favorite bar.
Oh-- funny you'd take me here.

Why? Do you come here, too?
Ah, no, not really. I've only been here once-
Hey stranger!

Hey Angel! This is-- Vincent? We went to-- high school together?

I can't decide what kind of drink I'm gonna make you, but it's gonna have a whole lotta ginkgo biloba in it.
thanks.

1617

Ugh, is there ACTUALLY ginkgo in this?
Yup!
And that's the only drink you get tonight.

I was only gonna ORDER one drink, you don't hafta police me.
Just one?

Yeah, I'm-- weaning myself off of a booze sabbatical.
Oh. Why were you on Sabbatical?

Because-- FEELINGS--
Let's change the topic!

1618

It's not BAD it's just... it was a breakup.
Oh!

I mean, I guess it WAS bad. I was so heart-broken I drank myself NUMB.
oh.

But, my best friend knew I'd never get over him if I didn't deal with it sober, so I stopped.
Oh!

... but I'm still not over him.
oh.

1619

I'll get over him at some point. It'll just take time.
Ah... time doesn't ALWAYS help you get over someone you love...

Maybe you just need to... move on...
find someone new?

You know what, Vincent? You're right.

I'm going home.

But--
Your drink?
It tastes gross any-way.

SHUT.

Alright, motherfucker.
Shit's about to get real.

Let's see how much "human experience" you've got.
LOVE

Where the fuck am I supposed to find an air pump?

1620

beep boop bip ♪
Dialing Jamie

Hi, Sugar Poops!
Hey, I need a favor.
EW.
Do you have an air pump?

Heh.
What?

Inflatable sex toy?
BALLOONS.

1621

It's an inflatable sex toy, isn't it.
AUGH. Fine. Yes. Do you have an air pump or what?

Oh my god-- is it, like, a whole SEX DOLL??
NO, it's-- AUGH, I don't wanna talk about it!
I just need an air pump..

Okay, okay. Bring it over and I'll see what I can do..
N-no, I-- n-nevermind, I'll just do it myself.

WOW, you're afraid to let your BEST FRIEND see it?? This thing must be RIDIC-
GOOD NIGHT

1622

I don't need a stupid air pump, I'll just blow it up myself.
I guess.

HAAAAAAH

FFFFFFFFFFFFFFFfffffff
thud

SNAP

1623

1624

Huuhh--
Huh--?
nngg

I will NOT be defeated by an inflatable love dong!

Enjoy your current state of FLACCIDITY
Tomorrow, we're going shopping for an air pump.

What're you doing with my old phone?
Jus' updating mah face Book status!

1625

Oh, hello! I don't suppose you sell air pumps here?
uhh

Not for anything bad, just... it's like, a balloon, about-- this big?
uhh

Nevermind, forget I said that. Just ring up this giant tub of Vaseline.
uh
Vaseline

It's for my mom.
Vaseline

for her FEET
Would you like a bag to hide, I mean carry that?

1626

AIR

DAMMIT!
C'n I help ya?

NOPE, no, just -- nozzle doesn't fit my spare tire, haha THANK YOU!
SLAM

1627

ahem

Hello, do you blow up balloons?
Oh, yes sir, we do!

Can you blow up MY balloon?
Um... I'm sorry, sir, you have to buy one of OUR balloons.

Hm. Okay, how 'bout I buy--
THIS balloon--

--and you just blow up my secret balloon, in this pillowcase?
Security.

bzzzrvt
Call from: Jamie
bzzzzrvt

Hey, are you still looking for an air pump?
NO.
...yes.
yes, we sell Helium Tank

I got one for you. Come over and I'll let you borrow it.
You HAVE one?

Dude, it's not THAT hard to find an air pump!

Where did you find it?
I borrowed one from a clown making balloon animals, duh!

1628

Hey, Boopie! Where's your blow-up boy-friend?
In the car. I don't want you to—

No need to explain. I'm sorry I teased you about it.
Thank you. I'm just gonna take this and go, if that's okay.

Yeah, sure! Go, go!
Thanks.
Oh by the way, I bumped into Vincent, tell you about it late-

STAY.

1629

You saw VINCENT? THE Vincent?
It's not that big of a deal. He's just some guy--

Some guy who quietly pined after you in high school, whom neither of us remembers!

Yeah, it's weird, we hung out for an hour and I STILL don't re-member him.

Really?
Yeah, like, AT ALL. I don't even think he went to our high school.
WHAT IF-- Vincent was actually your CALCULATOR, and the man you saw was an incarna-tion of the lovelorn soul of a kind, but unappreciated, device?
You can't just let this story be boring, can you.

1630

What does he look like?
Huh... normal? OH—actually, remember the ice cream guy at Jimmie Cone? That was him.

VINCENT IS THE ICE CREAM GUY??
Yeah, in hindsight, I guess that was pretty obvious.

Let's go get some ice cream!
Nooo, c'mon, it was weird enough hanging out with him last night.

But, I'm already dressed!
You have GOT to teach me how you do that with your clothes.

1631

1632

Alright, I'll investigate Vincent some other time.
SNAP
POOF
Thank you.
How long can I keep this?
Chuckles needs it back next weekend for a bar mitzvah.
Yep!
A whole week? That's a generous clown!
Now, go home an' get your freak on with that blow-up sex toy!
Ugh, at this point I'm not even horny enough to care.

Know what'll put you back in the mood?
What.

Balloon penis hat!
I can't say no to this.

1633

GIRLS' NiiiiiGHT!

I haven't seen you in forever!
I know!

I hope you guys don't mind I brought Melody along.
Oh, of course not!

But--how is she gonna communica-
Penis

There's an app for that.
Penis Penis Penis
Butts Butts Butts
unfortunately.

1634

So, what's new with you, Maureen? I haven't seen you all year.
Oh, y'know. love my job, love my cat, still in love with my husband...

Well, that all sounds—
BOOOORING
HEY! I LIKE boring! Boring can be NICE.

Besides, what's new with YOU?
I--
feel OLD
still live with my MOM
bought a $75 blow-up sex toy
with arms
miss Zach
because I'm LONELY

nothing.
See? Boring can be NICE.

1635

Hey, where's Erin?
Oh, this isn't really her thing.
Especially the wedding planning part.
Oooh, I forgot we were doing that tonight!
You're the only veteran here, so I hope you brought some solid wedding advice!

Don't invite Candy.
Done.
snrk

Why isn't Mimi out here?
Oh, she's at a bout. She should be home any min—

I'm home!
Yaaaay!
Baby, what happened?!

Oh, some blocker stuck her skate in my eye, but you shoulda seen what happened to HER!
She TOTALLY ate the floor! Her lip was way worse than mine.
Got some of her blood on my tutu.

Anyway, who wants to see my big, frilly wedding dress?!
ME

1636

Here, I took a picture of it with my phone.
See?
Oooh!
Ahh!
Aww!

You're gonna look so cute in that!
Can I--

NOOO!!
THEA!!
AAA!

You're not supposed to see!
Well, no problem, you smudged my glasses all up!

1637

Are there any other traditions we're adhering to for this wedding?
Naw, just that one.
I want my dress to be a surprise!

OH, and I wanna do the "Something old, Something borrowed, something blue" thing.

Oh, and I wanna throw my bouquet!
So, all of them.
AND A GREAT, BIG CAKE!

1638

Are you guys gonna have bridesmaids?
Just Maya on my side.
And just my momma on mine.

OH, and Gabby! Gabby's gonna be our flower girl.
VERY important!

Aww, does Gabby know about it yet?
Oh my god, it's ALL she talks about. Maya's taking full advantage of it.

If you don't eat your peas, you can't be a flower girl.
I-I'll eat ALL of the peas, mommy!
PAT PAT
That's right, you will.

1639

1640

Anyway, we can talk more about wedding stuff later.
Yeah, what's goin' on with you Single Ladies?
oh...
umm...
NNGG
?

If you are asking about sex,
I am getting mad laid.
YAAAAY!
yaaaaay.

1641

Hey wait, didn't you have a date with—
·: Siiiigh :·
yeeaahh

He doesn't want to date me because I'm dating Erin.
I told him we're open, but — I have to respect his decision, y'know?
ooh
damn
I'm sorry, Jamie

You guys realize she's talking about "Mall Santa" from New Year's, right?
That's more like it.
OOH!
DAMN!
I'M SO Sorry, Jamie!

1642

Well, how 'bout you, Clarice? Any romance budding behind the bookshelves?
:groan·: If only it were that simple for an under-cover DOMME.

Even if I meet someone I like, he's most likely NOT gonna be the sub of my dreams.
or submissive at all
And the WORST way to find out is, y'know, first-hand.

I don't even know how you VANILLA people do it.
Missionary.
from behi-- missionary.

1643

Hey, sweetie!
Hey, Snuggle-Muffin! Did you have a good time with the girls?
mow

Yeah, a little sad, though. I think Clarice is really lonely.
Oooh, that sucks, I like Clarice.
PURRRRRR

Yeah, me too. At least it made me realize how lucky we are that we found each other.
Aww, yay!

And how lucky we are that we both like boring sex!
Awww
...
yay

We did some wedding planning for Thea & Mimi.
I've got a little wedding envy.
Heh, you wanna get married again?

Y'know what'd be better than a second wedding?
A second honeymoon?

Oh my god, a FIRST honeymoon!
Bingo.

How did we forget to go on our honeymoon for this long?
We were too busy havin' tons-a sex?

1644

Do you still wanna do Dinosaur Land?
YEEEE!!

I'll take that as a "yes."
Yes!
We've gotta make it real FANCY, though.

Hmm, I don't think Dino-saur Land DOES fancy..
No, I mean we've gotta STAY somewhere fancy.

Ooh, like a Honeymoon Suite!
Like a TREE-HOUSE!

1645

A treehouse?
Yeah! They have treehouse hotels now!

That can't POSSIBLY be sturdy enough for us to, uh.. y'know...
What kind of treehouse isn't sturdy enough for sex?

The one at my parents' house?
GASP! You had SEX in that thing?!
NO!! I just..

...jerked off too hard once.
Does this coincide with the story about the hornets' nest?
it was a REALLY bad day.

1646

Here, check out the treehouse hotel I found online.

You've already picked one out?
Yep!
Lookit how FANCY these places are!

oh my god
Right?? This one has a jacuzzi...
Paradise #

oh my god
Wait-- no, stop looking at the prices!
Baby, please let me just MAKE you a treehouse.

1647

1648

Excuse me, are you... "Chuckles"?
Shoobily doobily!

Ah... assuming that means "yes," I have your air pump.
Ooooh thank you! Did he behave?

yyyyes?
And what kinds of animals did you make with him?

um...
I wasn't using it to make balloon animals.

dirty girrrrl
BYE

1649

Hazel?
Hi, Mom.

Hazel--
Hi. How are you feeling?

Uh... nervous, now. What's up?
Well... sweetie, we need to talk...

Mom, I don't even make enough MONEY to be using drugs.
Oh GOOD, that's always my first concern with you!

THANKS. That's very flattering.

1650

So: what are you worried about?
Oh, it's just-- I found something in your room--

MOM! What have I told you about going in my room?
Well, but I was just dusting, so I thought--

WAIT— did you go in my closet?
I DID, and-- oh Hazel, I just don't think we should have any more pets.

pets?
Well, I don't know what kind of pet it was, but it was DEFINITELY a BOY pet.

1651

Mom—
look.

It's harmless.
I found it in the street.
It was hit by a car.
I'm gonna nurse it back to health
And then set it free.

Okay?
Okay.

Can we never speak of this again?
We will never speak of this again.

Jamie?
Hey, buttmunch!

You-- y'know that blow-up sex toy I bought?
Yeah! Did you get it blown up?

Yeah. I think my mom saw it.
GAASSP!!
oh my god!!
What did you say??

I told her it was a wild animal and I'm nursing it back to health.
I think she bought it.

...
Jamie?

mute.
HAHAHAHAHAHA HAHAHAHA AHAH

1652

Dude. Your mom is playing you. She's not that dumb; she's a librarian for goodness' sake!

Well, wait -- does this sex toy LOOK like an animal?
Um, I guess it could be mistaken for a turtle --
with a dick on it...

GASP!
Hazel, are you fucking a blow-up turtle?!
NO!!

It's okay, you can confide in me! Remember that teddy bear I had in high school?
I do NOT want to know what you did to Mr. Fluffles!

1653

Hazel, face it, your mom knows you're fucking a turtle.
it's not a turtle

Look, just act like it never happened.
I guarantee your mom doesn't wanna think about it, either.

Wait, how did she even FIND it? Don't you lock your toys in a box?
This one won't fit now that it's inflated.

Why don't you just deflate it between uses?
Oh right, and visit Creepshow the Clown every time I'm horny?
Yeah!
And then inadvertently develop a clown fetish.
I'll pass.

1654

This is worse than a naked-in-front-of-class dream.
Aww, it won't be that bad, I promise.

Seriously, just act like it never happened. That's what I did.
Whoa, what? When did this happen to you?
purrrrrrrrrr

When I was 17! I thought Mom wouldn't know what a vibrator was, so I left one out on my nightstand.
And she knew what it was?

Well, she said we "needn't discuss" what she found on my nightstand, then hid her face behind a newspaper.
OH. Yeah, she knew.

1655

1656

Hazel, about your "pet"...

I think we should keep him after all.

I didn't realize it was a kitten!
mroww

Kind of a-- goopy kitten.
mroww

1657

Th-- this is the pet you found in my closet?
It looked so strange, I thought it was a pink lizard!
prrrrrrr

You must've done a good job healing him; he looks very healthy for his-- uh, breed.
Haha, yeah! Good as-- new--

And this is the only thing you found in my close
We needn't discuss the other items I found in your closet.

1658

KNOCK KNOCK KNOCK

Jamie?
I didn't know where else to go...

What's wrong?!
It's my labia.
They're just--
they're just so--

AAA Jamie they hurt so much!
EEEE!!

Just kidding! It's a cat.
the FUCK!!

1659

So, this is the "wild animal" my mom found in my closet.
This is your sex toy?!

No! It's a cat!
Like, an actual cat.
Not a sex-cat.
Oh! So she really DID find an animal!
Well, that must be a relief.

Glooooop
pat

You're SURE that's not a sex toy?
If this looks like a sex toy to you then I never wanna know what's in your toy box.

So, you're gonna take this little guy to the vet, right?
'Cause I think his dad mated with a ball of Silly Putty.
Hey hey! Just because he's skel-etally-challenged doesn't mean you get to make fun of his mom.

He prolly just needs a shot.
So do I.

1660

HAZEL
WINTER CLOTHES

Mom, what's this box with my name on it?
That's your mailbox, dear.
HAZEL
WINTER CLOTHES

I get mail?
I've been putting your mail in there since you moved in, dear.
WINTER CLOTHES

You realize I'm not in your brain, right?
You're in my heart, it's almost the same thing.

1661

Junk mail, junk mail...
Whoa, these are all from Pussy Whipped.

Are these--
all--
checks?

HOLY SHIT

BOOZE!
BOOZE!
POOF
POOF

ahem
INVESTMENTS!

1662

Yo.
THEA. Holy BALLS.
My Pussy Whipped checks!

Oh-- are they okay?
They're HUGE!
And there's like, TWELVE of them!

Did you JUST now get all of your paychecks for the past year?
Yeah, my mom kinda forgot to tell me where she was putting my mail.

Did you just assume we weren't paying you for your articles this whole time??
Well, I've been getting drunk and bitching about life for free for years.
So, yeah.

1663

1664

Okay — DON'T deposit those checks, they're probably expired.

Can you tell me how much we owe you?
Uh, looks like...
$

$?!!
Geez, we really ARE paying you well.

I guess you always were Esther's favorite...
I'm her favorite?

She doesn't pay ME that well when I write articles.
Thea?
Yeah?

Can you tell me again, the story about how I'm Esther's favorite?
click

1665

RIIING
click
Yes?

Hey Esther, it's Thea.
Hey girl, how's the next issue going?

Oh just fine, but that's not why I'm calling.
Did you notice that Hazel hasn't cashed a single check we've sent her?

Of course not, I have a secretary.
Did your secretary notice?
Of course not, I hired her for her looks.
Hey!!

1666

I'm kidding. Louisa's as smart as she is beautiful.
That's better.
But no, we didn't catch that.

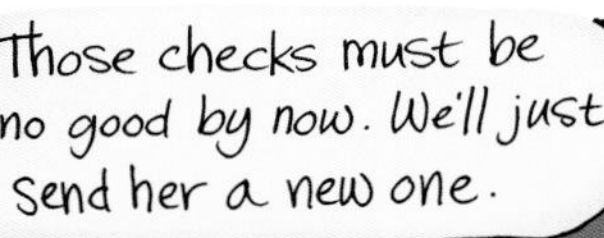
Those checks must be no good by now. We'll just send her a new one.

Well, you can make it out for $. That's how much you owe her for the year.

Wow, really?
Maybe I should give her a raise.
Are you kidding? You pay me a fraction of that for my articles!

Thea, y'know what's really funny?
What?
Everything Hazel writes.
click

1667

Hey, wifey!
Sigh.

Sigh? Why sigh?
Mimi --
Do you think I'm funny?

...
Is this a trick question?
Well THAT'S a big "no."

No no no! You're funny!
I laughed for a whole minute when you poured OJ on your cereal this morning!
I meant intentionally funny!

Baby, I DO think you're funny. I wouldn't marry someone with no sense of humor!
Well, thanks.
But... what about my writing?

Your writing?
Yeah. You've read some of my articles, right? What'd you think of the jokes?

... and BOY are my arms tired!
BA-DUM CHHH

Oh hey, is that my phone?
Mimi!

1668

You don't think my articles are funny.
AUGH, I didn't say that.

° sigh °
It's okay. I know comedy isn't my forte.
I just wish Esther liked my writing more.

Oh, but honey, she loves your editing skills!
As she should. You're a GREAT editor.

In fact, I'd argue that Hazel's articles wouldn't be half as funny if you didn't edit them.
Ooh baby you know just what to say to me.

1669

So, FIVE stars?

Yep!
Unlike you, I've never read his earlier work, so I had nothing to compare it to.
Ah, then you'll LOVE his first book.

Shall that be our next one?
Indeed it shall. I re-read it this morning; you can have my copy.

This is the greatest book club ever.
It goes a lot faster when you limit it to two people.

1670

Wait, is this a first edition?
Yep! And I really meant it when I said you can have it. Look.

Oooo.
It's signed.
Wait--

He signed it "for Clarice?"
Joshua, I--
I know. Strange coincidence, right?

Oh.
Right.
He died eighty years ago, but he must have known you would read it someday.

1671

1672

Joshua, this is too kind of you.
Not at all! That book was clearly meant to be yours.

Well, thank you.
I'll read it tonight and we'll have something to talk about on Monday.
Well, actually...

I was thinking, if you don't have plans tomorrow...
K-CHNK
BOOM BOOM BOOM BOOM BOOM

Recovering from an injury?
Indeed!

1673

OW OW OW OW
Oh dear, it really got your finger.

I-- I think I need to go home.
I think you need to go to the hospital.

N-no, it's not THAT bad, see?

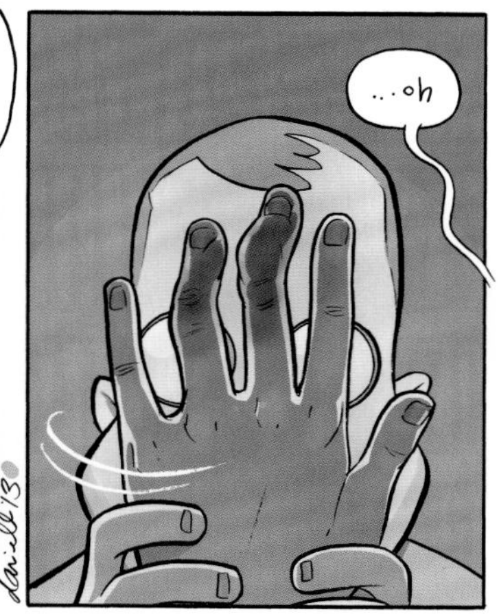
...oh

1674

The nurse said they don't have many patients right now, so it shouldn't be too long.
oh thank GOD

Thank you so much for taking care of me, Joshua.
It's no trouble. I had no plans for this afternoo-

-bus flipped over, twenty patients coming in.
Hustle!

-evening.

1675

This is a hell of a way to spend thousands of dollars on a friday night.
At least you won't be the one spending them.

Wait- what?
Why?
That shelf was loose. I'm certain worker's comp will cover the expense.

Oh, that's right. And I have health insurance now.
Gosh, I'm so used to my other job, where I have to-

M-my other job, where I have to dance.
Ah, I forgot you were a dancer.
It's easy to forget.

sigh
Has it really only been an hour?
I'm afraid so.

I did grab your book, in case you'd like to read it.
oh!

...oh.
If you'd like, I could--

nod
Introduction:
The summer I spent on the coast of Maine was, unbeknownst to me at the time, an apology from—

1676

clarice?
clarice?

Clarice, they're calling for you.

oh..

Oh, I'm sorry!
It's alright. You were tired.

Did I miss anything?
I read the first two chapters.

Ooh, and I slept through the whole thing.
That's okay, I rewound it.

1677

11:47
Hey

Whatcha readin'?
Oh, an old fantasy novel. How are your fingers?

Broken.
And how's the rest of you?

Medicated.
Let's get you home.

1678

Do you have any dietary restrictions?
N-no, why?
I figured you'd be hungry, so I picked up some wraps.
They should be easy to eat with one hand.

Oh, and I'm happy to drive you home, but I can call a cab if you'd prefer.

You're really good at this. Have you considered starting a service for people who hurt themselves a lot?
I have, but I wasn't sure where to advertise.
Ham or swiss?

1679

1680

Hey, you were saying something earlier about tomorrow...
Oh, yes!

I'm not sure you're familiar with her work, but Mara Doddridge has a signing–
GASP!

I LOVE Mara Doddridge!
Oh! So you must already know about the signing at Four Seasons.

Actually, I thought she was dead.
Well, assuming she's still alive tomorrow, would you like to go see her?

1681

This is me.

Looks like a nice place to live.
It is! It has a lot of character.

Would you like to, uh...
umm...

Well, see you tomorrow!
See you tomorrow.

1682

ow

ow

1683

BZZRT
llen
zky
trick
Did someone order a surrogate left hand for the day?
ha ha

You're not left-handed, are you?
NO, thank goodness.
So you haven't had too much trouble being one-handed–?
Well--

You'll notice I'm wearing the same clothes I wore yesterday.
I won't tell a soul.

wow.

Helluva turnout for an Appalachian poet.

She's quite well-known, you know.
I guess so, but-- her work is so OLD.
Didn't she start writing in the 1940's?

Sure, but she started young.
Still. Do you think that's her, the old gal in the wheelchair?
She must be at LEAST 80 by now.

Actually, I'm 87.

1684

OH—
GOD—
I'm sorry, Ms. Doddridge, I didn't mean—
Oh, it's alright, dear.

At least you didn't think I was dead!
ha!
HA—
NOOOO no no

Well. I hope you enjoy the reading.
It'll be a short one, as I'm so OLD.

I hope you'll stick around for the snacks and prune juice
And nap time!
ha!

1685

Well, at least she has a good sense of humor.
AUGH.

On the bright side, there are two empty seats left, and they're right up front.
Why don't we—

oh.

Ironically, the only other place to sit is in the children's section.
AUGH

1686

...and thank you all for coming to listen.

CLAP CLAP
Wow.
Her poetry is ten times more powerful when it's read by her.
Agreed!

Would you like to have her sign a book for you?
OH, haha, no, I think I've embarrassed myself in front of her enough for one day.

Oh that's a shame, I was gonna sign yours from "Ye Olde Coot!"

1687

1688

I hope you know I'm just teasin' ya.
Oh, heh, I know, I just— really look up to you as an artist.

Ooh, well thank you, dear.
All teasing aside, it was nice to see some young faces in the audience. If you'd like a book, it's on me. Just come over to the table.

Wow, I didn't think 32 was considered "young."
I think any age is "young" when you're an "old coot."

1689

"from Ye Olde Coot."

What a perfect Saturday. Thank you for every-thing, Joshua.
You made the event more special to me; thank **you**.

Now, is there any-thing you need help with before I leave you with just one hand?
Nah, just my clothes–
B-but I think I can figure that one out
haha
So, no.

OKAY SEE YOU MONDAY
See you Monday.

1690

DING-DONG ♫
Hey, Ms. Tellington! Is Hazel home?

Oh! Jamie! Are you dressed up? I can't tell.
Sorta! Didn't Hazel tell you? We're having a Back to School night!

Oh!
We're gonna paint our nails and listen to old mix tapes an' act like we're back in high school!

Does your mother know you wear skirts that short?
Of course she does, Miss T.!

1691

Hey, Haze!

WHOA, hey there, **Ass-tits McGee**. Didn't our high school have a dress code?
Psht, you sound like your mom.
You ready for some 90's revival?

I've got My So-Called Life on VHS. What've you got?
I've got NIN, REM, Radiohead, Spacehog, a year's worth of Seventeen Magazine..

Is it okay that I miss everything about high school except high school?
I think that's normal.
GASP! Pogs!

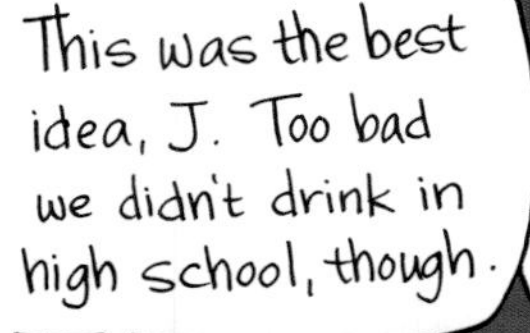
This was the best idea, J. Too bad we didn't drink in high school, though.
Oh, I brought something even better than booze. Check it out.

I'M A GOOD GUY FOR A GAL

Remember
BLAST SODA
?
BLAST SODA

Oh my GOD
Where did you FIND that?
It's been in my mom's basement for ten years!

I've got beers in the fridge.
Okay!

1692

It's probably for the best that we didn't drink in high school.
urp
We might've taken these articles seriously.
"IMPROVE YOUR MOOD! 1. Put on your FAVORITE OUTFIT, then pretend your STUFFED ANIMALS are saying nice things about it."

"2. Hug an ACTUAL TREE."
haha!
"3. Have ice cream, for dinner!"

That's brilliant.
Let's go.

1693

Heh, it's so weird hiking our old high school trails with a booze buzz.
Day drinking is a sacred and wonderful thing.

hee hee
It feels wrong to be in broad daylight an' not really know where we're going!

Actually --
where ARE we go -

JAMIE
Well how did we end up here?
Jimmie Cone

1694

You sneaky scamp.
I thought we were gonna pick up a pint at the Quick Mart.
Oh c'mon, it's PERFECT! We're reminiscing about high school, and here's this ice cream guy who crushed on you in math class...

UGH. Jamie, I'm not going up there.
It's okay, you don't have to! I just wanna size him up.

In fact, you stay here, I'll be right back.

Chocolate fudge sundae with M&Ms, please!
Duh!

1695

1696

Hello ♫
Hey there! I'd like to order two sundaes...

Say, is that one guy here, with the V-name--?
Oh, you mean Vincent?

Yeah!
Sure, I think he's taking out the trash.
Vincent?

Hazel?

1697

Oh-- uh-- hi?
Vincent.

Oh I know! I remember. Chemistry class.
Advanced calc.

RIGHT! I know, I remember.
And you wrote in my yearbook.
And we were friends.
RIGHT. I'm a little forgetful.
I know, I remember.

1698

So uh, how's the ice cream biz?
It's good. Same as always. I was wondering when I'd see you here.

Ha, yeah, I've been... watching my weight, or something, so not much ice cream for me these days.
ha ha
PAT PAT
Well, I meant, I was hoping you'd come to see ME.

Uh-huh, uh-huh.
You kinda left without saying goodbye that night at the bar.

Did I?
The bartender made me a drink called the "I'm very very sorry."
She said she named it after you.
Did she?

1699

Um... man. I'm really sorry. I could've sworn I'd said good-bye.
Well, I could've just as well called you to follow up and I didn't, so--

You-- have my phone number?
I believe so. Is this still it?

Yeah.
Cool, I wasn't sure if you'd changed it since high school.

You've had my number in this thing since HIGH SCHOOL?
Oh, of course not! I've had to re-enter it by hand on at least six phones now.

Okay, well, I should get going—
Hey!

Who's your new friend?
Oh, actually, old friend.
Hi Jamie. I'm Vincent.

Oh! You know my name!
Sure, I remember you from high school.
Alright, let's go.
Bye, Vincent.

So uh, I'll call you?
Yeah, call her!
Oh WOOPS, you got ice cream on your tits.

1700

Ooh, good thing I got a spoon.
Geez

Jamie, what the FUCK? I don't WANT that guy to call me. I'm not trying to hook up with him!

Well, I talked to the cashier, and she said he probably hasn't gotten laid in YEARS, and I figured YOU could stand to get laid—

And I mean, she DID give us double sprinkles...
Double sprinkles does not mean someone gets laid!

1701

Besides, what do you mean, I could "stand to get laid?"

oh come ON, Hazel.

It's been almost a year since you and Zach broke up. I'm surprised you've lasted this long without having sex.

And seeing as you'd already given Vincent your number--
I never gave him my number. He's kept it in his phone since high school.

OH.
Yeah.
Like what we did when we found Donnie Bellwood's number?
That was different. Donnie Bellwood is the hottest man alive and someday we may be good enough for him.

1702

Well, I'm sorry if I made you feel uncomfortable. I really was just gonna size him up and then get us some ice cream an' leave.

Nah, it's cool. I'm seriously not interested in that Vincent guy, but I mean... you're right, it IS weird that I haven't had sex in a year and I'm not doing anything about it.

Aww, it's just like high school again!
Neither of us is getting laid and we're not really trying to anyway!

Except now we can buy sex toys without a fake ID, so it's not as terrible.
WORD.

1703

1704

HONK HONK
That's my ride. Later, Vincent!
Have a good night, Katie.

Hey girl, how was work?
Slow as hell. But I did my good deed for the day.

Oh yeah?
Yeah. I'm trying to get my manager laid. I think I helped him get some girl's number!

God, can you believe people his age still bother?
I know, it's kinda pathetic.
sigh

1705

WOOO, DUDES' NIGHT OUT, PUSSY-LOVERS' EDITION!
WOOO
Darren says hi and he thinks we're all gross.

Ha ha, HEY, I love sausage! But only the kind in my pants!
Haha, yeah, I love sausage, but only the kind I put in my mouth!

Wait, those both make us sound gay.
No they don't. I just like to eat sausage.

Yeah, but you said you like to put sausage in your mouth.
To EAT. I like to EAT sausage. Like, put it in my mouth and chew.
NEW TOPIC PLEASE

1706

Hey, speaking of extra sausage
GROAN
You don't mind that we didn't invite Jim, do you?

Nah, I understand. I've kinda stopped hanging out with him myself. He can't stand to hear me talk about Melody.

Okay, cool, so this probably won't offend you...
What is it?
Angel made it.

It's called the "I'm very, very sorry."
She said it was based on someone I know.
Obviously!
Pfft, OBVIOUSLY Jim!

1707

So, how ARE things with you and Melody?
Oh, y'know,
The Best

Awww, you look just as in love as you did when you started dating her.
I am. And the sex keeps getting better and better, too.

Oh man -- if she's deaf -- does that mean she's, like, super-quiet in bed?
Ah, no, that's actually the only problem.

Wait --
is she super-LOUD?
(yes)
Ask him how many times the cops have been called.

1708

Whoa, have people seriously called the cops on you guys?
It only happened ONCE.

Did they think you were having a FIGHT, or—
Nah, it doesn't sound like she's SCREAMING, it sounds more like--

We're getting calls from your neighbors about a possible--
EXORCISM?

DEMON POSSESSION?
A very NICE demon possession!
That's a pretty accurate way of describing an orgasm, actually.

1709

Wow, so-- I mean, if she screams like a banshee during sex -- doesn't that kinda break your concentration?
Nah dude, it weirded me out at first, but--

We've been doing this for awhile, y'know? So, I associate the sounds Melody makes with her pleasure, and -- now it turns me on.

Huh, yeah. Okay.

So, if you heard an ACTUAL exorcism going on, you'd get—
There's a haunted house two blocks down-
NO
NO

1710

... good seeing you at Jimmie Cone, and if you're free this week, well, now you have my number, so...
:ahem:... um...
maybe you'll call me?
:click:
Voicemail

Oof.
Yeah.
Well, I DID tell him to call you.
Yes, and I fully blame you for this.

Y'know what's weird?
What?
Turns out I had his number this entire time,
except it's under "Victor."

Geez, do you NEVER purge your old contacts?
Who else do you have in here?
"Josh Who Has My Pants?"
Oh, I remember that guy. He had my pants.
Did you get them back?
Yeah, but I forgot to change his name to "HAD."

1711

So, what's the protocol here?
Do I actively ignore his message?
Um... uhh...
I don't knooooow
PURRRRRRRRRRR
Oh c'mon, you must get hit on by thousands of people you don't wanna date.

Yeah, but only in person. I'm very protective of my phone number!
Well, still, you're a veteran at rejecting people nicely.
Come on, What Would Jamie Do?
hmm...

Jamie would change the topic and buy you an apology beer.
Good answer.

1712

Hey Angel, what's this extra cocktail? Is this for us?
yup!

What is it?
One of my classics. I call it the Return of the Fuck Buddy.
Hah, is that-- wait, who is this for?

Remember that girl you went home with last weekend?
N-- no?

She sure does.
Hi, Zach.

1713

H-hey! ...Elise!
Oh, you remember my name!
You never texted me back.

Ah-- right, sorry, I'd meant to. You left your jacket and your toothbrush at my place--
Well yeah, I was hoping for a return visit.

Oh.
Like, tonight.

♪ With a cherry on top! ♫

1714

Hey guys, I'm gonna split early. I uh, bumped into a friend--
Oh, a FRIEND
Yeah, all MY friends run their hands seductively down my chest when we talk, too.

sigh Alright, she's more of a fuck-buddy. But let's keep it on the D.L., please. I don't need the whole town knowing about my sex life.

Especially Hazel.
Dude, it's been nearly a year. If Hazel can't handle hearing that you sleep with other women, then...

...then... maybe we should move to another room!
Yeah, who wants to play darts?

1715

Hey Angel, you got any drinks with straight-up Benadryl in 'em?
GUH

How did I forget about my stupid cat allergies?
Here, this has hot sauce in it. At least your sinuses will be clear.

Let's go in the other room so nobody can see me like this.
um..

OH
Let's go in the other OTHER room.

augh
Are you okay?
Yeah, I just-- didn't expect to see him here tonight.
There aren't even any specials on Tuesdays.

GOD, I hope he didn't see me. My face looks like a goddamned Halloween mask.

Was that Hazel?
Yeeeaah, we weren't sure you wanted to see each other, so--

That's weird, there aren't any specials here on Tuesdays.
Are you kidding? Tuesday's special is "there are no specials, so you get the whole place to yourselves."
That's pretty special!

1716

I'm gonna go talk to her. I don't want things to be weird.
Uh-- okay, man...

Hey, Hazel?
sniff

I just wanted to say hi. The guys thought I shouldn't say anything at all, but I don't want things to be weird between us.

Oh– yeah, it's cool. Thanks.
Cat allergies?
Yeah.

You guys touchin' tips over there?
No, we're doing very hetero, manly things.
Oh good, if I want a pedicure, I'll come over.

1717

Wow, that went remarkably well.
Yeah, I guess things will never really change between us.

So you're feeling okay?
Yeah. I'm fine.

See you at your place, Cabbie!

How are you feeling now?
WAS. I was fine.

1718

I-- didn't think she was gonna yell that.

right in front of Hazel.

Hoo boy.

Hazel, don't do anything rash.
Hi! What're you up to tonight?
Oh, y'know. Just out lookin' for a good time. You?

Who's that dickbag she's with?
I think his name is Revenge fuck.
No good can come of this, Zach. Run.

1719

1720

So, you single?
'Cause my ex-boyfriend is over there, and he's going home with a strange woman tonight --
Oh I SEE
ugh
Hey Zach. Sorry about Hazel.
:Sigh: It is what it is. I'll let myself out the back.

Well, that ended poorly.
It couldn't have ended more poorly than that.

Hmm, I wonder if they have specials on Tuesdays.
Mecklenburg INN

1721

Looks like your ex took off. You still down for a romp?
It's not revenge sex without the sex, is it?

'Atta girl.
H-- hi--
Let's see what those skinny legs of yours can handle.

I'll have a drink with alcohol in it, please.
I've already prepared your "I'm Very Very Sorry," as a chaser for this "WTF, Worst Timing Ever, Dude."

1722

Was -- was that Hazel's boyfriend?
HA! Yeah, for TONIGHT!
ahem
By which I mean, NO.

Oh. Okay. Um, I didn't know she was like that.
She wasn't like that in high school, she just... crushed on everyone but me.
I always wished she'd have crushed on me.
I'm wearing polka-dot boxers today!

Why am I telling you all of these things?
You don't drink very often, do you.

1723

Mmm give it to me, big boy

...
Are you okay?
Hm? Yeah

You seem really distracted.
Hm? What makes you say that?

You're softer than a sack of baby food.
Geez! Thanks!
RIIING
You are NOT picking that
Hello?

You're seriously leaving.
Sorry, Elise, some drunk guy needs a ride.

I need a ride!
Not that kind of ride. Besides...

You're right, I am kinda distracted. I'm not in the right mindset to give anyone a "ride" tonight.
I'm sorry.

Don't forget to take your toothbrush.
Shut

1724

All aboard the Drunk Bus!
Thanks for coming, Zach. Hope I didn't interrupt anything.

Nothing I didn't want interrupted.
So, where's this fare?
Here

Oh. I thought you were a rug.
So did I, but rugs can't puke.

Well this will be fun.
Here's a bucket and a 100% tip.

1725

So... Vincent, was it?
Mm-hm
Did you have one too many of Angel's cocktails?

I suppose two is "one too many" for me.
I don't drink very often.
Ah, I see.

Truth is...
I wasn't really there to drink. I was hoping to see someone.
Someone very special to me.

And did you?
Yes.
That's why I was on the floor.

And you're on the floor now—
I'm on the floor now because I'm very, very intoxicated.

1726

So... I take it things didn't end well with your "someone."
Things can't end well if they never even begin.

sigh
I met her years ago. I was homeschooled, but I took an AP class at the public high school.
She needed a tutor, so I helped her with her homework almost every day after school.
I guess I can't say we were CLOSE, but she told me everything— about her parents' divorce, all of her aspirations, the boys she liked...

I hate to interrupt, but you haven't told me where I'm taking you.
Oh, are we still parked? I thought this was just a really smooth ride.

1727

1728

Anyway, long story short, I fell in love with her, but I never told her. Years went by, now she's back in town, and she barely remembers me.

I know I should move on, but--it's hard to let go of someone who still makes your heart jump, you know?
Yeah. I hear ya, man. I'm still hung up on my ex.
She's stubborn and set in her ways, but -- she's passionate and smart, and when she allows herself to be vulnerable with you...
it's worth all her hard-headedness.

Wow — we could practically be talking about the same person.
Haha, no way man, I'm sure yours is **way** less of a hot mess than mine.

1729

It's been nearly a decade. She's probably not even the same person anymore.
I need to move on.

Well, you seem like a good dude. Shouldn't be too hard for you to meet other women.
Ha! **Girls,** maybe.

I took over my family's ice cream shop when my father got sick.
All I see all day are teenagers and young college girls.

That sounds both great and terrifying, and I already regret saying "great."
Welcome to my world.

1730

KNOCK KNOCK KNOCK
Trick or Treat!
Go away unless you have candy.
I have candy.
Oooo, Nerds!

Where's your costume?
I'm wearing it. Guess what I'm dressed as.

Some one who actually went home with that guy at the bar and had revenge sex?
Bingo.

1731

I can't believe you slept with that guy. He looked like he'd just stepped off a yacht.
y'know what? We both got what we wanted and we'll never see each other again.
I call that a win.

fair enough!
Okay, so, I'm taking you to a party tonight, but it's a SCARY party.
So I brought an extra costume.
Oooo, is it **scary**?

It's too Scary.
You look cute as a brunette!
Yeh look better'n usual!

Who on earth do you know that lives in the old Alexander Mansion?
You'll see.
KNOCK KNOCK

Good evening.
Please make yourselves at home.
Thanks, Candy!
thanks ...

I thought we didn't like Candy?
We "like" Candy for the next eight hours.

Oh.. you mean "like" as in "Social-media-like."
Yeah, but instead of hitting "dislike" at the end of the night, we just leave.

1732

So-- Candy, you live here now?
I wish.

My friends Matilda and Genevieve here are para-normal investigators. They're being paid to deal with the spirits in this house.
Hello.
Hello.

WHOA. You guys are like-- real-life Ghostbusters?
UGH.
That's SO not PC.

But-- you bust ghosts, right?
That's like asking a vegan if they enjoy deboning a chicken.
It's very ghost-negative.

1733

Hello, hello!
Are we late for the paranormal activities?
Not at all!

I see this is a GHOULS-only party.
This is NOT a party.
It's an investigation of the spirits that reside within this house.

There will be no SMOKING
SMACK

And no DRINKING.
SWIPE

Where'd you get that drink?
You gave me a costume with pockets in it.

1734

Soooo-- is this place, like SUPER haunted, or--
Yes.

Oh.
How do you know? Do you have some sort of equipment?
We ARE the equipment.

You ARE the equipment?
Shhhh.
C'mon, that's bullshi--

Shhhhhh.

1735

1736

AAAAAAAiliili!!
Do you see that?!

Who's there? Is that my kitteh?
Here, kitteh kitteh kitteh kitteh kitteh

awwwwww

WHAT HAVE YOU DONE WITH MY KITTEH

AAAAAAAA!!

1737

GRAB
DRAG

STOP. SCREAMING.
You're upsetting the spirit.
WE'RE upsetting HER?

She's doomed to roam the halls searching for her beloved kitteh.
It's very tragic.

Can we just GIVE her a cat?
Not it!

1738

You can't appease a GHOST cat lady with a LIVE cat.
Sadly, you'd need a dead cat with unfinished business.

What cat DOESN'T have unfinished business.
I have one.

I said a DEAD cat.
Yeah. I have one.
It's dead and it goes DOOOOOM

Is she for real?
Yeah, she also has a talking cactus, a cat made of Silly Putty, and a job that pays her to use her English degree!

1739

CREEEEAK

So... did you bring, like, a NET, or--
We don't CATCH ghosts, Hazel.
We work WITH them so they can cohabitate with homeowners peacefully.

So, you're more like... couples counselors?
Correct.

What's that?
Enya.
To put everyone in a state of calm.
Define "everyone."
Let the Orinoco flow, let

DOOOOOOOOM
Ahh, there you are, spirit.

DOOOOOOOOM
Here, Candy, hold this.
Oh! Is this sage? I know a thing or two about smudging–
NO. Smudging is disrespectful to evil spirits.

SNIFF
SNIFF

DUUUUUUUDE
It's catnip.

1740

I can't believe Ghost Kitty followed us all the way back to the mansion!
Do you think the old cat-lady-ghost will take him?
DUUUUDE
Only one way to find out.

FLING
Kitteh?

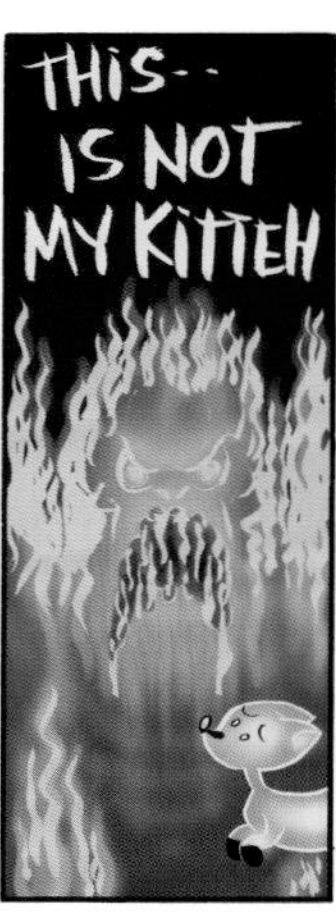
THIS.. IS NOT MY KITTEH

EEEEEE!!
Abort! Abooort!!

This one's much better than that stinky ol' fleabag.
PURRRR

1741

Hey, Joshua! Did ya do anything fun for Halloween?
Hmm, I suspect you would find it fun...

Every Halloween, I make a batch of mulled cider and re-read Frankenstein.
It's my favorite tradition.

Did YOU do anythin
CLAP CLAP
CLAP CLAP
CLAP CLAP

You only asked me so I would ask you.
Uh-huh.

1742

So, I went to a haunted mansion with some friends—
Ah! With Beatrice, correct?

Oh--
Yeah, how did you know?
She told me.

Beatrice... talked to you?
Beatrice talked to me, and she was warm and inviting.

Okay, I went to a haunted mansion with a different Beatrice.
I believe a different Beatrice has worked here at the library all these years, as well.

1743

1744

So anyway... I'd always KIND of believed in ghosts...
Are you telling Joshua about the apparition we saw?

uh... yeah... but apparently—
I already told him about it.

Right.
And then we talked about his favorite ghost story. Right, Josh?
This is correct.

Oh, you mean the legend of Wizzard Clip?
Yeah! How'd you guess?
Clarice taught it to me.

1745

Hey Josh, are you free this Saturday? There's a calligraphy workshop at
WELP

I gotta get back to work.
oh..

Clarice?
Are you alright?

Y-yeah, I just-- Beatrice is smiling and being nice.
Ooh... yes, that can be very disorienting.

1746

Hi, Clarice!
Tucker!

Hi, can we talk? How's your love life?
oh!
uh, great!
My parents are in town, so I'm taking fiona out to meet them this weekend! We're going to a fancy—

Wait, were you just asking that so I would ask you how your love life is?
uh-huh

1747

Heh, alright: Clarice, how's YOUR love lif
Let's go in here.

uh...
okay.

Tucker, I haven't told ANYBODY about this, but...
I think I'm in love with a library patron.

GASP!
Is it that Joshua fellow?
SHHHH
yes

AAHH, Clarice, that's wonderful!
NO IT'S TERRIBLE!

What could be terrible about being in LOVE?
Tucker! You know what I do for a living!

Can you IMAGINE if Joshua found out I'm a professional Domme? He'd be terrified! He'd think I was a -- a sexual weirdo.

And I mean... I don't even know that he'd WANT to date me anyway.
GAH, maybe Beatrice would be a better girlfriend for him after all.

Uh... Beatrice?
Yeah, she fell outta her cocoon and transformed from an awful worm into an awful moth.

1748

I thought you liked Beatrice?
Oh I do, but it's not lost on me how awful she can be to other people.

Isn't she especially awful to Josh?
It's JOSHUA-- UGH, that's another thing, where does she get off calling him JOSH?

She's being all sweet and flirty with him all of a sudden. It's like the moment I fell for him she just swooped on in—
RAP RAP RAP
Excuse me

If you're not doing homework you're not s'posed to hog the study rooms.

Excuse me, it can be homework OR research and this is definitely reasearch so bug off for two more minutes.

1749

Aww, I wouldn't worry too much, Clarice. You're a way better catch than Beatrice.
Well, but that's-- it's not--
sigh.
Thanks, Tucker.

I'm more concerned about Beatrice acting all fishy toward Joshua.
FINALLY.

She used to HATE him. I wanna know why she suddenly likes him so much.
Hey.

So, now I know why you like Joshua so much.

1750

TALK.
I found out about his alter ego.

What do you mean, his alter ego?
Y'know, franklin Quimby?

The book reviewer?
Yeah! I never knew that was him!

Because it ISN'T.
You don't have to pretend you don't know, Clarice. He told me.

Between this and your sudden range of facial expressions, I'm very confused.
They're not facial expressions, I've got a persistent itch near my eye.

1751

1752

How did you find out Joshua is a book reviewer?
Well, you know how he always checks out the same books I want to read?

They're the books I want to read because I listen to his podcast, and he always discloses which books he's going to read next.
I'm a HUGE fan of his!

I found out he's local, put two and two together, and flat-out asked him if he's Franklin Quimby yesterday.
And he said yes.

Wait... if you listen to his podcast, how did you go this long without recognizing his voice?
Because his podcast voice is sooooo dreeeamy!

1753

So... that's the whole reason you're being nice to Joshua now? Because he's famous?
What? Clarice, I'm not SHALLOW.

I just didn't know he had all that IN him until now. I figure maybe if I'm nice to him, he'll let his inner Franklin Quimby out.

You just wanna hear his podcast voice.
No, I wanna talk about books with him, too.

Just...
just don't hurt him, Beatrice.
Okay, I won't hurt him by talking about books, gotcha.

1754

You're a TERRIBLE accountant, Earl!
WHAP

You try and you try, but you just can't stop FUCKING UP, can you?
n-n-no, Mistress

You COWARDLY piece of SHIT
SMACK
AAAA!

You're a FAILURE and no one will ever love you.

Sorry, I-- got a little personal there at the end.
I noticed!

1755

LOCK

POOF
So... you gonna look up his podcast and get off listening to his voice?
STOP IT. You know I don't fantasize about people unless I KNOW they're interested in me.

POOF
Yes you do.
Who asked you??

Franklin Quimby
SEARCH
typa typa typa
click

click
Welcome, fellow readers. You're listening to Franklin Quimby, and this is review number eighty-seven. This episode
click

Holy moly, he does have a nice voice.

Franklin Quimby reviews 50 Shades of #888888

SHUT
Sigh

1756

Okay, so, we're shopping for our moms, my sister, your grandma—
And you.
MALL

Aww, Erin, I meant it when I said I don't need anything!
I know! But if you see anything you want, you can tell me.

SANTA CLAUS
this way!

Well, Ho Ho Ho!
I'd say "But where on earth would I keep him", but I can think of a few places.

1757

Should we go say hi?
Um... yeah! I mean... I think so?

Would it be too weird for you?
A little. But... I mean, Keith and I are just FRIENDS, so it wouldn't be THAT weird...

BLAARGH

Would it be as weird as two elves puking in a fountain?
No, it would be less weird than that.

1758

Ho-ho, it's alright, kids, Santa's got this under contro-ho-hol!

Hey, "Santa!" What's—
Jamie! Oh, thank God!
If you aren't busy, I could really use your help. Both my elves AND the photographer ate some bad cookies, and—

Wait... are you saying they're LITERALLY tossing their cookies?
Better than literally losing their shit!

1759

1760

Oh! By the way, this is—
Erin!
Yeah, good guess!

Ho-ho, Santa Claus knows the names of ALL his best elves!
(costumes are behind Rudolph!)

He knew who I was!
I guess he remembers you from the New Year's party!
huh, where's Rudolph?

I'm Rudolph.
Don't eat the cookies.

1761

Alright, 3, 2, and smile for Santa!
Dude, I wanna be an elf ALL the time!
I know!
Who wants another magic trick?
MEEE!

HEY, whoa, put that kid down!
Emergency Backup Elves are here, everyone calm down

Awww, we just got started!
GOOD.
But, she was gonna show us a magic trick!
There's magic in your heart, kid. You can find it by staying in school, and upgrading to an 8x10 portrait package.

1762

Do you still need me to photograph?
Nope. We're trained in all aspects of the Mall Santa business.
Step away from the camera, ma'am.

Huh... how do you turn this on?
It IS on.

Where's the picture?
I turned off the LED to save battery life. Use the viewfinder.

What's a viewfinder?
The-- the part where you look through the camera.

You can look THROUGH the camera?
Were you born in the nineties or something?

1763

Hohoho! Since Jamie is a PROFESSIONAL photographer, perhaps she could stay...?
Sure thing, Santa!
elf off

Sheesh. Coupl'a killjoys.
That's Corporate for you.

Pfft, what, like Corporate North Pole?
Those aren't fake ears, Jamie.
GASP!
Are you saying... ...you answer to a higher Santa??
I could tell you, but I'd have to run you over with a reindeer!

And that about does it!
Whew! That line was nonstop! It's tough being Santa!
SANTA will return tomorrow!

It's tough being Santa's helpers, too. I really owe one to you and Erin.
Aw, it was fun! And Erin still got all of her shopping done. She's heading back now.

So... now that we're alone, I'd like to tell Santa what I want for Christmas.
Oh! uhh, w-what do you gulp want?

I want to see you more often.
Ho-Ho! Just leave out a plate of cookies, and I'll be right over.

1764

BRIIIIINGG
Jamie
would like to Eyeball Time...
Decline

H'lo?
HAPPY NEW YEAR!!
Where ARE you?!
End

uh-- I'm--
GASp!
Hazel, did you SLEEP THROUGH NEW YEAR'S EVE??

wha-- na--
N-NO! NO, THA'S NOT POSSIBLE!
It's-- it's--
Hey, y'know what my new year's resolution is?

It's-- 6:30 am on December 31st.
More prank calls.
Now that you're up, wanna grab breakfast?
NO.
END

1765

Happy December 31st!
shut it.

Oh, c'mon. When was the last time you were up before 7 am?
I just wanted you to see the sunrise once this year.
Why? It's the same thing as a sunset, only brighter and more annoying.

But now you have the whole day ahead of you!
I already HAD a whole day ahead of me. It was shorter, and I was less pissed off.

1766

Are we still on for tonight?
Yep! I've got the Jenga and Nirvana ready!
"Jenga and Nirvana?"

Yeah! We're gonna party like it's 1994!
Heh. Okay, that I can get into. My mom kept all my CD's and band tee shirts from ten years a--

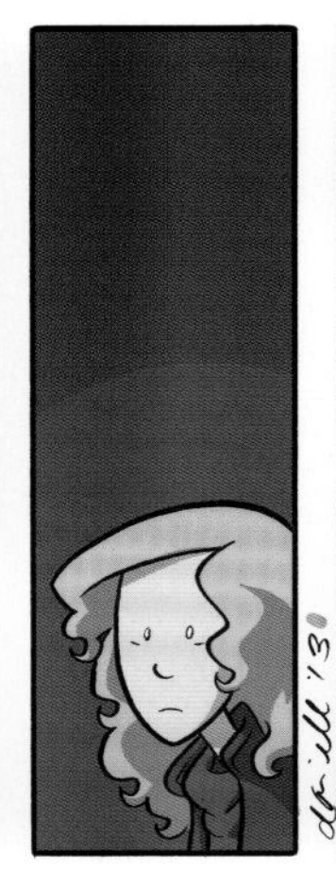

Twenty.
Twenty years ago.
It's okay, we can drink like it's 2014.

1767

1768

Happy New Year!
GASP!
Nuh uh. Jameson, were you a ska kid?
Of COURSE he was. Look at the guy, he was practically born in those checkered pants.

I thought we could SKANK in the new year with a little BOSSTONES and Reel Big fish!
Whoa, Streetlight Manifesto!
You know what we need is some Five Iron Frenzy...

WAIT. ohmygod.
Are we like those old people who talk about how great disco was?
You mean our parents?
Psh, ska is WAY more accessible than disco!

1769

Ace of Base?
I can skank to it!
I was in kindergarten when this came out.
LA LA LA CAN'T HEAR YOU
HEY, it's 11:59!

Here's to keeping the spirit of the nineties alive!
3...2...1...HAPPY NEW YEAR!!

ding ding
text
text
insta-gram
text
ding!
snap
ding ding
tweet
text
text
tumbl
video call

1770

Haze?

Ooh. Would you like a new year's kiss from your BFF?
Nah, it's not the kissing that's bugging me. It's the nineties.

The nineties? Are we playing too much ska?
No... I mean, yeah, kinda, but--

I'm remembering high school, and it just--feels so RECENT.
But it wasn't recent. Time is really speeding up, y'know?

We should switch to Jeff Buckley.
No Jamie, that's not--
actually, now I really wanna hear Jeff Buckley.

1771

I never thought I'd hear you admit that you miss high school.
Oh GOD, I don't.

But I do miss the endless possibilities. I thought by now I'd have lived in a dozen cities, become an established writer...

I mean, my life isn't half bad, y'know? I write for a cool magazine, I work at a booze shop.
All my friends live nearby.
But, I'm not getting anywhere. I don't know what the next step is.
I don't even know how to step.

Why don't you start by stepping back indoors?
That's not gonna help me.
No, but it's really flipping cold out here.

NEW YEAR'S SHOTS!

Say your resolution before you take your shot!
I'm saving up for our honeymoon!
Ooh, me too!
We hafta save up for our wedding first.

I'm giving up shots!
Uh, that's kind of counter-productive.

Not if I wanna break my resolution before I have a chance to start it.
That's brilliant and I'm stealing it.
Cheers.

1772

BZZZRT BZZZRT
nng

I-- I can't SEE!
Why are my hands taped?
BZZZRT BZZZRT

I thought it'd be funny.
It's HILARIOUS. Help me get it off, my phone's ringing.
BZZZRT BZZZRT

EWW, not with your FEET!
wait..
BZZZRT BZZZRT

Erin?
Why are my feet taped?

1773

Dammit
He-hello?
Hi, is this Hazel?

Yes-
Hi Hazel, I'm Roberta from Daring Literary.
We're looking for someone to write a snarky book for twenty- and thirty-somethings, and we REALLY like the work you're doing over at Pussy Whipped.

oh-
Thanks!
Would you be interested in writing for us?

Um... well wait, WHAT kind of book do you want me to write?
Oh, really anything. If you write it, we'll publish it.

...
Are you also a Nigerian Prince?
Hah!! There's that untrusting cynacism we've come to expect from you!

1774

What was that all about?
Some literary agency wants me to write... a book, I guess?

Dude, yay!
I dunno, it seems fishy. How'd they know who I was?
whap

Uh, the Internet?
I am BARELY on the Internet.

When was the last time you googled your name?
Never have. I asked Jeeves once, and he answered "Hazel's High School Poetry LiveJournal" so I stopped asking.

1775

1776

I guarantee there's more than just your old LJ up there now.
The Internet is like, REAL big.
Yeah, but I don't put anything ON it.

That doesn't mean other people don't.
Hazel Tel
Aside from Pussy Whipped, who would put stuff about me on the Internet?

Huh. 2,810 people?
what
Oh! Here's the photo Jameson took last night after you passed out and I taped your hands!
WHAT

Hah, fifty-six "likes!"
Like
fifty-seven!

1777

How am I on the Internet two THOUSAND times?

I hope it's all photos of you passed out.
You would.
What is "Bookface?"

Oh! It's a great website where people can review books!
Why am I on it? I've never written a book before.

You can review authors, too. Looks like they're all reviews of your writing.
UGH. I don't want to read reviews from a bunch of assholes on the Internet.

They're almost all positive.
WHAT DO THEY SAY

1778

WOW these are--
Really nice!

I find Ms. Tellington's wit and sarcasm endearing.
★★★★☆
Aww.

A fresh, honest, and clever voice for intelligent women in their twenties.
★★★★★
Huh!

Not the most unique writer out there, but I enjoy her work all the same.
★★★☆☆

ASSHOLE!!
What would HE know?!

1779

Incoming call: Hazel

H'lo?
Good morning! Did you know your #1 columnist has a 4.5 star average rating on Bookface?

Yes.
oh
Am I the only person who didn't know about Bookface until two minutes ago?
Yes.

Even your mom's on it.
YOUR mom's on it!

Ask your mom how to set up an account.
I'll ask YOUR mom how to
END

MOM
Happy New Year!!

You too, what is Bookface and how do you do it?
Ooh, I've been inviting you to be my Bookface friend for years!

Do I have to be friends with you to be on Bookface?
We can share book recommendations, author reviews, and I can even IM you and we can have real-time book club discussions!

We real-time live in the same house.
You can pretend to live in London, and I can live in Paris!
I'll type with an accent!

1780

BOOKFACE
Your BookFace account has been registered!
Please check your e-mail and click the link we've provided to confirm your BookFace account.
Whoa... e-mail?

I forgot all about e-mail.
click
BookFace Accounts Welcome to BookFace!
TEH Bank Deposit Notification
Devin Jessup Waiting on your respo
Shokolada Hellooooooooooooooo
Patricio Vasquez-Aguilar do you even check your e-mail anymo
Rainee Scott Rainee has invited you to join ChainedIn
aaronackbar We gave the pony to someone who respond to e-mail. Sor
Gabby Harrison New Year's plans?
aaronackbar No really, you won a pony (not spam - actual contest)
Topher McCulloch Merry Christmas!!!
Jeffrey Dill Happy Hannukkah!
aaronackbar You won a Pony!!!!
Huh... deposit?

to me
You have received a payment of $
Pussy Whipped Magazine. If this
Holy-- I forgot all about this deposit!
I'm like, RICH!

POOF
POOF
I'm not listening to EITHER of you.

1781

B--
BOOZE!!
Yeah, you're kinda predictable, Bad Hazel.
You got anything better, Less-Bad Hazel?
um
uh

M-maybe a a helicopter?
A HELICOPTER?
Investments.

WHOA. Who are you?
I'm Grown-Up Hazel. I've been waiting to come out your ENTIRE LIFE.
Invest that money and start saving for your retirement.

Y'know, with a HELICOPTER I could fly to work.
NO

1782

I'm kidding, I'm kidding.
I can save some of this money, I've done it before.

You were NINE. You put all of your allowance in a piggy bank and then lost it, because you never cleaned your room.

You only "saved" that money because you're neglectful.
Pft, I'm not NEGLECTFUL.
mrroow

GASP! Goopy kitty?
Oh HEY there's that mutated cat you found and then NEGLECTED.
HAZEL
WINTER CLOTHES
I didn't NEGLECT it! I was SAVING it.
FWUP
PURRR
mmf!

1783

1784

Wooo
Yeah, Mimi Massacre!!
Kick 'er ASS!!

Don't let 'er get past you!
Don't--
That's okay, you'll get 'er next time around!
ahem
Riveting WARM-UP they're having, isn't it?

You bet!
I'm here to support my WIFE down there.
You don't say

Yeah, I actually don't know a THING about roller derby!
You don't say
Woo
get 'er!!

1785

Were you cheering me on during warm-ups again?
It all kinda looks the same to me.

Pft. dork.
Hey, do we have a date?
Yup! April 12th.

Ya hear that, girls? Wedding's on April 12th!
Woo!
PARTY!
BOOZE FEST!!

Did—
you just invite the entire team?
Well no, two blockers and a ref are out sick, but we'll send them invitations later.

1786

Mimi, I thought we said this was going to be a SMALL wedding?
Oh!
Yeah, the actual exchanging-of-rings part, but...
I thought we said the reception would be bigger?

Yeah, but the fire hall can't hold that many people--
The fire hall? I thought we agreed--

We should have the reception behind my mom's house!
Ha! In a trailer park?
Yeah, let's do that!

I thought you were joking!
I thought you were serious!

1787

You-- wanna have our wedding in a trailer park?
Thea, I was raised in that trailer park.

Yeah, but then you got a re-spectable job and moved OUT.
My MOM never did. What're you saying about HER?

I-- didn't--
You kinda did.

Am I sleeping on the couch tonight?
No, I am.
That couch is SO comfortable.

Mimi?

I'm sorry.
I know.

I didn't mean to say that about your mom.
You know how much I respect her and all she's done for you.
I know.

But I hope you can respect EVERYONE from my old trailer park that way. They're ALL like family to me.

Here, get on the couch, I know that's half the reason you came down here.
GOD this couch is so comfortable.

1788

sniff sniff

mmmmmmmmcoooooffffeeeeeeeeeeeee
oh.
you made a list.
Don't look at the list until you've had your cup of coffee.
Then, the list.
Then, infinite coffee.

1789

So... this is your invite list?
I keep forgetting you're far-sighted.

This is my list of reasons for wanting to have a wedding.
I realize it's all magic and pixie dust for me, and sort of a pointless waste of time and money for you.

So I broke it down into logical explan-ations for
GASP

Is that an infographic?
I knew you'd like that.
Jesus I love you.

1790

So, which of these is most important to you?
Oh, I boldfaced 'em.
These are the big ones:

·To introduce you to my family, and prove to them that I made a great decision when I picked you.
awwww
·To assure the people who love me that I'll be in good hands for the rest of my life, and that they won't have to worry about me.

·To make all my lesbian friends jealous.
Well now you're just sucking up.
Go on.

1791

1792

These are all really good reasons to have a wedding. I can't believe I'd never considered any of them before.
Aside from the "endless booze" one, of course.

Then again, I don't really HAVE a family to show you off to. Maya's the only one who matters.
I know, sweetheart.

I don't want to spend too much energy lamenting the family I DON'T have, though.
I'd rather focus on the family I'm about to have.

Speaking of which, don't hug any of my aunts indoors. They're all gassy as hell.
Noted.

1793

So, if you can warm up to the idea...
This is what I had in mind for the reception.

Oh! Well THAT'S lovely
That's the trailer park

EENH
What exactly is it that you dislike about trailer parks?

I-- I just think they're --
I mean, having our wedding there would--

Humiliate your parents if they found out?
Hmm, you're making this more appealing to me.

1794

Hey, Jamie! Look, I made you a SCARF!

That is NOT a scarf. You don't even know how to knit!
Okay, you got me.
TOSS

But... look at this KITE I made you!
That's not a KITE. It wouldn't last a second in the air!

fine, fine, let's just open this bottle of wine I got you.
POP

Goopy Kitty!
mrrow!

1795

Where has Goopy Kitty been all this time?
In the mud room, I guess. Explains why we haven't had a mouse problem.
PURRR

Hey, remember how you made that comment about Silly Putty?
I'm sorry, that was very Silly Putty-negative of me
No no, look:

HeLLO i Am
ON a Quest
$EARCHING 4 MY
Goopy Family
PLS HALP
ME
WHOA!
Right?

"40% off all lingerie until Valentine's Day"?!
Jamie.

Do you think he's related to Special K's goopy kitty-daddy?
Chyeah, duh.

Do you still have Rupert's phone number?
You mean Davan? Yeah, I think so.

I guess we should just call him and
WHAP
OW!!

Oooh, look, fluffy turned Goopy Kitty into a slingshot!
Oh looook, fluffy got a badge in being an asshole!

1796

Nooo, fluffy, what did I say about matches?
moow?
MATCHES

Geez, has he ALWAYS been this evil?
Aw, he's not evil! He's just curious. ALL cats are curious.

Not about weapons and fire.
Oh c'mon, Hazel, cats don't understand what they're curious about.
They don't understand why they do HALF the stuff they do.

Let us pee just outside the litter box, as an offering to Lord Satan.
Praise be to Satan!

1797

Hey, by the way, are you doing anything for Palentine's Day?
Is Palentine's Day like Valentine's Day for your pathetic single friends?

Yeah! Since Erin and I don't do sexy stuff, we wanted to have friends over after dinner.
How charitable of you. I'm in, but I have to be back home by midnight.

What're you doing at midnight?
Nothing. Sleeping. None of your business.

SLIDE
LOVES

1798

BOOZE!
BOOZE!
POOF
POOF

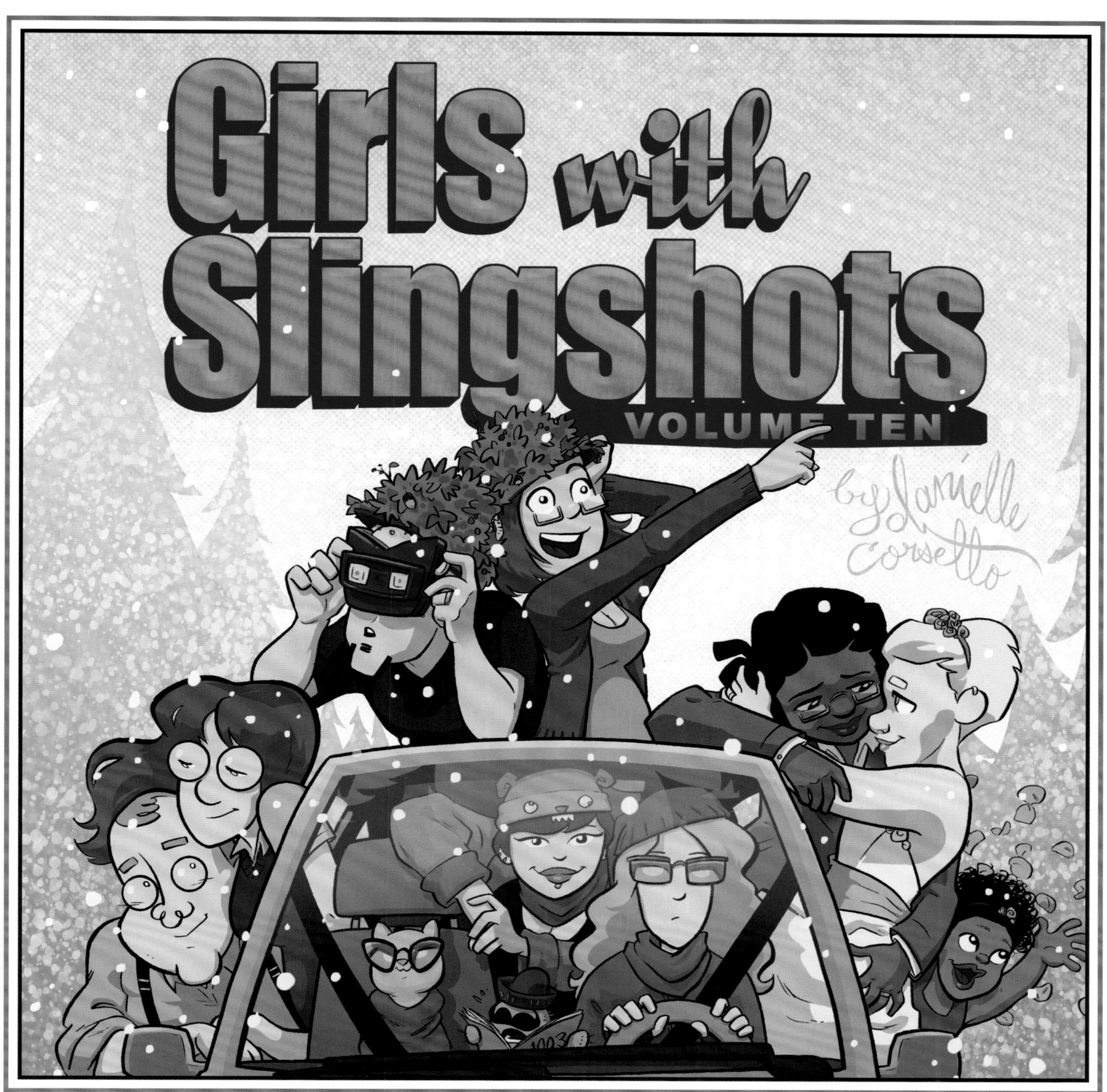
Girls with Slingshots
VOLUME TEN
by Danielle Corsetto

VOLUME TEN

strips 1799-2008

1799

Hi, Clarice!
Hi.
SELF-HEL

Have you had a chance to read --
Nope, been too busy.
MOVING ON from Heartbreak

Ah, that's alright. I've been pretty busy, myself—
Hanging out with Beatrice?
Dealing with JEALOUS

No, I haven't seen Beatrice in weeks.
oh!
R-really?
Recovering from making a FOOL of yourself

1800

I'd actually meant to ask you, ah... for a bit of advice, regarding Beatrice, if I may--
Oh?

I don't really have much experience-- romantically-- and, uh--
oh

We were spending a lot of time together, she and I, and--
oh
I'm afraid I may have led her on.
oh

I don't know how to tell her I'd just like to be friends.
OH!

1801

I haven't seen Beatrice outside of the library for the past two weeks, but last night she sent me an e-mail...
mm-hm?

She said she knew I liked her, because of a... love note I wrote in a book?
bump
thump

But... she MUST know it wasn't from me. I would NEVER deface a library book.
OH! It wasn't defaced; it was written on a Post-It note.
Probably. I'm sure.
thud
thump

Either way, it wasn't from me. But... how do I tell her that?
Just tell her it was all a stupid prank, played by some stupid idiot who didn't think it through.
Probably. I'm sure.
thud thud thud
thump

1802

I hope I don't seem ungrateful, turning down a smart, pretty girl like Beatrice.
nooo.

The trouble is, I believe she likes me for someone I'm not—
franklin Quimby?

oh!
y-yes, how did you—
I've often wondered why you told Beatrice, but not me.

I hadn't assumed you'd ever heard of my show.
Well!
I hadn't, until Beatrice told me.
thud

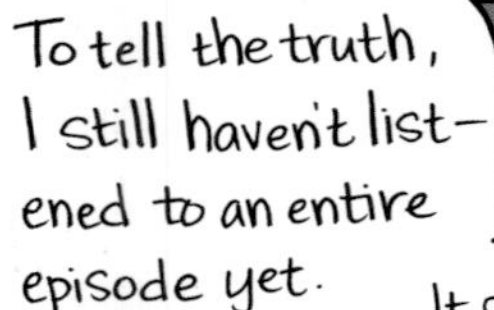
To tell the truth, I still haven't listened to an entire episode yet.

It seemed... kind of weird to hear it without telling you.

See? This is why I like you. You've been kind and thoughtful toward me since the day we met.
Heh. You like me, do ya?
nudge

Of course I like you, Clarice.

Actually, I wanted to invite you to sit in on my next recording, but since you haven't read the book yet–
I'll read it tonight!
CRASH

1803

KNOCK
KNOCK
KNOCK
OPEN

Hey, Clarice! I was just closing up—
Do you have time to go to the Meck?
CLOSED

Sure! What's up?
A man I really like invited me to his house and I'm nervous and I could use a drink to take the edge off.

Whoa! You're going to his house TONIGHT?
No, in two days. I have 48 hours of edge to drink off.

1804

So who IS this mystery man?
Oh, he's -- a library patron... a book nerd... the sweetest man I've ever met...
BEEP
BOOP
SECURE–

WOW! Clarice, I've never seen you like this!
I knooow! You're the only person I feel comfortable gushing to about him!

Ooh, man, I am so sorry, but... Hazel knows about it, too.
What? That's not even POSSIBLE– you're the only person I've told.

If it makes you feel any better, I was pooping the whole time I was listening.
Speakerphone.
NOOO

1805

Hey, Angel! Let's get a Simmer Down Now for Clarice here!

Oooo, what does Clarice need to "Simmer Down" about?
None of your business.

Hey, can we keep this crush of mine on the down-low, please?
Oops, sorry!
HEY, ANGEL!

Let's get a BIG FAT CRUSH on a LIBRARY PATRON for that lady right there!
My pleasure!
Simmer down, now.

1806

1807

Could you two PLEASE keep your voices down? I'm really nervous about this.
Aww, what's there to be nervous about? You're a bangin'-hot dominatrix!
Yeah, I'm not an ounce of gay and even I know you could have any man you want!
Has it occurred to either of you that some men don't want a woman who's into kinky sex?
This guy only knows me as the mild-mannered librarian Clarice, not the whip-wielding domme Clarice.

Couldn't you just -- try to have sex with him WITHOUT hurting him?
That's not—
Could you tape pillows around him?
Or give him a shield to protect himself from you?
GUYS THAT'S NOT HOW BDSM WORKS

1808

... and he held my busted hand up the whole time to reduce the swelling.
awww

See? It's way better to just focus on all the good stuff now. You can worry about compatibility later.
Yeah, you're right. Thanks for listening to me get all mushy, guys.
Don't mention it.

Do you really not mind, Hazel? I mean--
I no longer drink myself into a coma when I'm reminded that I don't have Zach in my life, if that's what you're getting at.
So, no.

She's replaced booze with word games.
LIKE HELL "CLIT" ISN'T AN ACCEPTABLE WORD, ASSHOLES

1809

KNOCK
KNOCK
KNOCK

Clarice!
I found your house!

Indeed you did!
May I get you anything? Water, hot tea?
Ooh, what service! Tea, please.

Certainly. Make yourself comfortable in the study. I'll bring the tea right in for you.

Is... this not the study?
That's the library. The study is the other room with all the books in it.

1810

I hope you like English breakfast.
Oh, I do--
So, uh, the podcast is doing REALLY well for you, then?

Oh! It's doing well, but it didn't buy this house. I inherited everything from my parents.
Oh! I'm so sorry- it's lovely, though.

Thank you. The study was mostly my father's.
So many books on gardening and flowers.

That, and his collections of Garbage Pail Kids stickers.
OH
My father liked to keep us guessing.

But, we can talk more about the house and my parents after we record.
click

I hope you like men in earmuffs.
ha!

Oh
Am I joining you?

Oh, I'm sorry! I suppose I never actually asked you. Would you like to --
I hope you like women in earmuffs.

1811

... this is review number one hundred and nineteen, and tonight we have a very special guest.

As you know, this podcast is devoted to reviewing only media borrowed from my local library--
WOW, I didn't know that!

Ah--
...
...heh, I'm not used to having two people--
OH, I'm sorry!
That's okay! You're hearing the voice of local librarian and fellow book-worm, Clarice.

Clarice and I are going to share our separate reviews of this week's book
Which will probably start off radically different, cause a hot debate, and then merge into one strikingly similar opinion
as per usual.
As per usual.

1812

... so what this book is mostly about - as so many books are - is the power of fear.
Hm. Yes, it could be taken that way.
But-

Our protagonist leads this double life he's afraid to share. And when he finally meets the one person he wants to let in--

-with everything to lose, he makes himself fully transparent to her.
And she doesn't leave.

So, I think what this book is ultimately about
is the power of courage

1813

I'm sorry- I'm SO sorry, but- I can't keep pre-tending to not have these feelings for you.

I'm-- you don't have to apologize, I'm --
I'm --

1814

1815

I never thought this would happen...
That you would feel this way about me, too...

It was unbelievable enough that Beatrice took an interest in me... but YOU--
GASP
I didn't even consider--
are we LIVE?

OH, nonono! I'll edit all of this out!
oh thank god

Well, I may keep it as evidence
In case I wake up and think it was all a dream.
heh. Send it to me, too.

1816

We should, ah, perhaps take these off, and finish the pod-cast tomorrow...
Tomorrow?
Are you suggesting I stay the night?

UH
OH GOD, THAT WAS TOO FORWARD

N-no, no I have a guest room...
A guest room? Is that what you call your bedroom?

OH GOD I'M SORRY I CAN'T STOP BEING FORWARD
L-let's just start with the couch...

1817

uh

Is this too fast?
um
n-no, I think...

I think you should know...
Clarice, I haven't really...
I've never really been in a rela-tionship before, so...

Joshua, I haven't--
It's been a VERY long time for me, too.

Do you want me to slow down?
um...
n-no...

Good morning, beautiful Clarice.

I'd have served you breakfast in bed, but frankly something tells me you're too sensible for that.
I thought you might like some tea, though.

Breakfast in bed is overrated.
And messy.

Clarice, I-- can't tell you how much it means to me, your patience with me last night...
I hope I didn't disappoint you.

1818

Oh Joshua, I'm not disappointed! I'm just glad you were upfront about
BEEP
BEEP
BEEP

oh

Ronald at 12:00
bring paddle,
new ball gag.
I forgot, I...

...have an appointment.
at the library?

mm
Well, if you can spare an hour, I'll make you eggs and fruit before you go.

HEEEY BIRTHDAY GIRL!!
My birthday was yesterday.

Yeah, but you ignored all my texts and phone calls, so it doesn't count!
It was yesterday. I am NOT a birthday Girl.

You sure LOOK like a Birthday Girl!
I am NOT wearing that.

I brought Birthday Sushi for a Birthday Girl...

1819

Step into my Birthday Office.
TWEEE

So, what's it like to be 29?
More embarrassing than being 28?

What's so embarrassing about it?
Dude, I'm almost THIRTY. Who's in their thirties and still lives with their parents?

A lot of people who were born in the eighties and live in an overpriced suburb of New York?

Yeah, well, that's not gonna be me. This year I am growing up and moving out.

1820

Oh! There's a great app for apartment hunting. You just set up an account and list your preferences
Bluhhh too much wooo ork

1821

Hazel, I think you're too comfortable.
I'm sorry, what? Those two last words don't go together.
krak

I'm serious. The only reason you feel stuck is that feeling stuck is comfortable.
You're settling.
I'm not THAT comfortable.

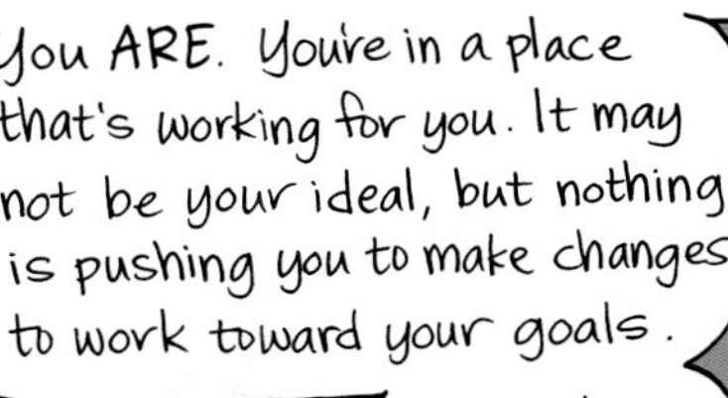
You ARE. You're in a place that's working for you. It may not be your ideal, but nothing is pushing you to make changes to work toward your goals.

And you're too unmotivated to make those changes yourself.

Look, you haven't even changed the wall calendar to March.
I don't have to! There's a little version of March right there at the bottom of January!

1822

Besides, who are you to judge? You still work at the florist's and live in your college apartment.
And do you ever hear me complain?

Haze, I like my life. I've never had any really big dreams beyond this. But you ALWAYS have.
I thought you wanted kids?

Wull yeah, but that's a long way in the
You're just as old as I am.

I am eight months younger than you.
That only matters when you're five.

1823

Anyway, back to growing up and moving out... what steps are you taking to move?
Um... steps?

Like, budgeting? Do you know what kind of apartment you can afford?
Oh! My old one.

Okay, so you want something in the $850 range.

No, I want my old apartment back.

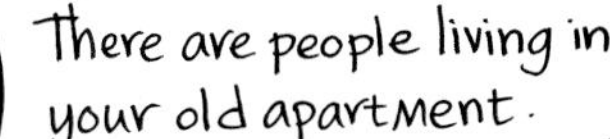
There are people living in your old apartment.

Yeah, but I think you're right–I should stop settling and start going after my dreams.

Picking out an apartment that people aren't living in isn't settling.

Ha! Spoken like someone who doesn't have big dreams like I do!

1824

huf puf
I'm sorry I'm late!

I got two last-minute articles that I practically had to re-write...
And there was an actual LINE at the dry cleaner's...
and...
Sangria?

Um.
Sure.
Where are the decorations?
In the back of my car.

We're getting married tomorrow, right?
Yeah! We have a whole day to relax!

Is this... the pond?
Yep!

Can't you see it? We'll have an arch of flowers here...
Exchange vows over there...
And our guests will sit here!

I-- thought you said everything was ready?
It is! The pond filled up after the snow melted, the tulips are about to bloom...

Mimi! Our wedding is in 24 hours and nothing's prepared and there's a pile of trash where we're supposed to exchange our vows!
That's not trash, it's my neighbor Charlie!
Hey, Charlie!
Heyo!

1825

How are we gonna-- WHEN are we gonna--
Thea, calm down. It's only 4:30. People are coming to help us once they're off work.

I thought this wedding wasn't a big deal to you, anyway?
It-- it wasn't--

But, now that it's here, it's--
It's a big show we're putting on for everyone else, and I don't want people to think we're a joke.
Well THERE'S your problem!

You need to think of it as a big show everyone ELSE is putting on for US!
You're the guests of honor!
Thank you, Charlie!

1826

That's not really how people think of weddings, though, Mimi.

So? Not everyone thinks of them as being gay or in a trailer park, either.

Look, everyone who's coming to this is coming to support us. We didn't invite anyone who's coming to judge us.

Just for this weekend, don't focus on everyone else's satisfaction. Focus on what would satisfy you.

A shower, and another sangria.
That's the spirit!

1827

Ahhh, much better!
I can't believe your mom has a jacuzzi....

Mimi?
over here!

Whoa.

WELCOME
Don't worry, we'll all get cleaned up before dinner.

1828

1829

Good morning, my beautiful bride.
mm good mo–

oh!
heh, you gonna bust out the handcuffs, too?
No...

You're not supposed to see the bride until just before we get married.
Technically, we're already married.
shh, just go with it.

1830

It's a good thing we stayed here last night, or this would've made for an interesting drive back to the trailer park.
hee hee

Oooh, y'did the blindfold thing! That was my idea!

You girls have a seat an' I'll fix you some breakfast.

We should feed each other.
I bet it'd be easy!

1831

I gave your weddin' clothes to Miss Ellis next door. You gonna run out an' find your sister?
Yes, ma'am

You know you can call me Mama, baby.
Aww!
okay.

AUNT THEEEAA!!

WHUMP
Whoa! Is this your flower girl dress?
nope!

That's her pre-flower girl dress. She already stained her pre-pre-flower girl dress.
we had blueberry pancakes.
I see.

1832

You sure know how to make a pantsuit look good, sis.

You sure know how to make a double mastectomy look good! Damn!
Can I just tell you how much I don't miss carting around a dozen pounds of tit?
I mean, I can't recommend the "having cancer" part, but...
I can basically fit into anything now!
I can basically only fit in this when I inhale.
How long can you hold your breath?

Mommyyy, Aunt Mimi says it's time to go!
BAP BAP BAP
okay! thank you, baby!

Are you gonna cry?
Pft. We're already married. I got all my tears out at the courthouse.

I put tissues in Gabby's basket.
Sis, I'm not gonna—

WELCOME

oh god she's so beautiful

1833

Okay, Gabby, there's the music. You ready?
I've been ready foreverrr!!

Aww!
ooh!

Why did she stop?
She peed herself out of sheer joy.

1834

We gather here today...
it's okaaay
sniff

Oooh they look like the cover of a politically-correct bridal magazine!
Are there ANY men at this wedding?
Shore there are!

But Ah'm the only one that's YOUNG an' SINGLE.
AH, what a shame that I'm the biggest lesbian here, or we'd have had such fun!

1835

As you may know, Mimi and Thea were married in a private ceremony last year, so we're skipping the vows—
Ah, actually...

Skipping the vows was MY idea, because... ah... I wasn't sure I wanted to let a bunch of strangers in on something so... personal...

for the past ten years, my sister and my niece have been the only people I consider family, and...
really?
shh

...and, I look out at you all now, and... I'm just so happy to call you all family now. Thank you for supporting us.
aww!
aww!

Does this mean we're reciting our vows?
No, I didn't memorize them.
Good, me neither.

1836

1837

I still do.
I still do, too.

3, 2, 1–
FLASH

Whoo! I need to unbutton this.
Whoo! I need three people to get me out of this!

1838

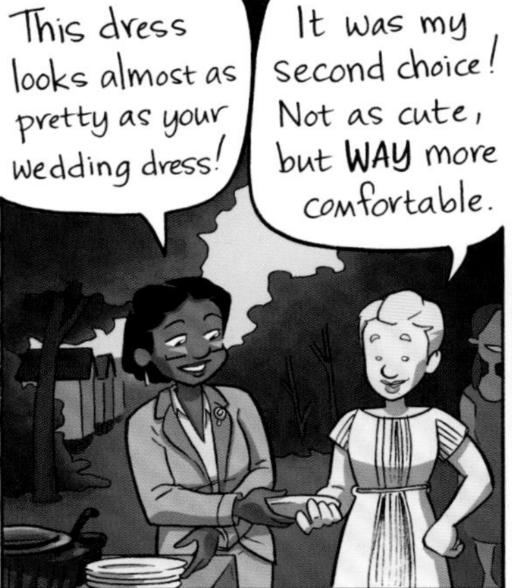

This dress looks almost as pretty as your wedding dress!
It was my second choice! Not as cute, but WAY more comfortable.

OH, and it doesn't need to be dry-cleaned!
Ha! You're so practical.

Well, I needed something easy to wash for our next event.
Next event? What, our first dance?

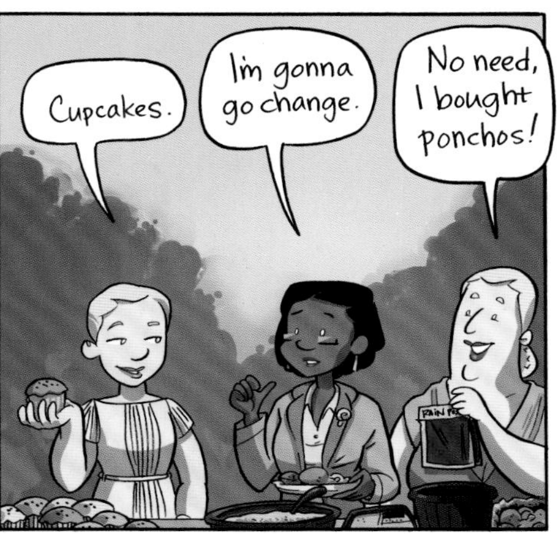

Cupcakes.
I'm gonna go change.
No need, I bought ponchos!

1839

Y'ready?
woo!
Be nice. You know this isn't really my thing.
get 'er!

I know, baby.
give 'er a facial, Mimi!
ha ha!

ooh!
aww
you guys are too nice!!

See? We barely even needed the ponchos.
clap
clap
clap
woo!
aww!
CUPCAAAKES!
clap clap clap clap clap clap clap clap

Woops
Ya jinxed it.
Cup-cakes!
WUMP

1840

You ready to toss that bouquet of yours?
What, into the fire?

Not unless that fire wants t' fight!
AW YEAH, that bouquet belongs to a derby girl!

Alright, ladies!
No elbows, no tripping!
HNGF

NNG!
MINE!
No!
BITCH!
HNF
Got it!

I always wanted t'be a derby girl!
Honorary.

Hey wifey, you were right.
I love it when you say that.
g'night!
If your trailer's a-rockin'...
snrk!

There wasn't a single person at this wedding who was here to judge us. Everyone here was here to support us.
WELCOME

This would've been completely different if my parents had been invited.
um...

So, Maya and I weren't sure when to give this to you, but...

1841

...this seems like the right time. It's from your father.
What?

Dear Theadora,
Congratulations. She seems like a good girl.
I am sorry things have been distant. Let me take you and your wife out for lunch one day.
Your mother does not need to come.
Love,
Papa

Are you okay?
M-hm
Are you mad at me?
No. I love you.

But I'm a little mad at myself.
Don't be. He isn't.

Hey, Jamie!
Hey, Clarice! What brings you here?
Flora's Flora
OPEN

Oh, just wanted to say hi--
Bullshit. Spill it.

I have a boyfriend!
And?

And what? I have a boyfriend.
That's all?

That's all? That's HUGE!
Oh I know, I just wanted to see what else you'd tell me. Yay, you have a boyfriend!
clap clap

1842

So, BOY-FRIEND! I take it your visit went well?
It went SO well! I told you he has a podcast, right? Well, we—

Oh, I know. I listened to it yesterday. You two have great chemistry!
You-- listened to it?

Wull YEAH. Romance Detective, remember? You two sounded different at the intro and near the end, though.

Oh-- that's probably because we recorded those parts the next day--

AHA! I knew it! You slept over!
That's not what I said!
And yet I'm still right!

1843

1844

So, did you guys... put dog collars on each other, or whatever you do?
Jesus, no, nothing like that. We're taking things very slowly.
Wow, really? That must be hard for you.
It's... actually kind of relieving. It's been a long time since I've slept with anyone...
Besides your clients.
I don't sleep with my clients, Jamie. There's very little I do with my clients that a vanilla person would consider "sex," in fact.
So... did you guys... put on leather masks and stick each other with lawn darts
WE CUDDLED.

1845

Did you guys JUST cuddle?
We cuddled, and we kissed, and it was wonderful.
Oh. I'm sorry, I guess I don't really "get" BDSM culture.
That's okay, I don't really "get" what you and Erin are doing. Come to think of it, most of the people you and I hang out with have some sort of weird sexual thing.

I've started leaving my pants undone, see, in case I need to use the bathroom in a hurry.

Except Hazel, She's just weird.
How long have you been here?

1846

So, now that this guy knows you're a dominatrix--
uh-
cough
well...

He doesn't know?
It-- hasn't come up. I'm still afraid to tell him.
Oh! You've gotta try what I did with Erin when I was too afraid to tell her I wanted to get it on with dudes.

What'd you do?
I turned her into a sloth!

When I said I don't "get" you and Erin, it was an understatement.
I'm doing it to you right now! Helloooo little guy!

1847

CLARICE.
Exactly how did someone who's NEVER LISTENED to Franklin Quimby manage to become a "special guest" on his podcast?

uh

He just-- asked me.
Really. Why you?
We'd read the same book, so—
I read ALL of the same books he reads. Why'd he ask you?
what the heck does a sloth look like?
Don't change the subject.

Well?
Be-- because--

Beatrice he's in love with me and I'm in love with him and we're dating.

Ha! That wasn't so bad.

WHAT?
YAH!!
1848

I-- I didn't know how to tell you--
You're DATING Joshua?

Beatrice, I know you like him, but--
·:snort·: What? No I don't, not like that!

Oh. ... Really? But--
Actually, I was worried he wanted to date ME, so this is kind of a relief.

Well -- then why are you so upset I was on his show?
Uh, because I want to be on his show?
Duh. This isn't exactly the Dewey Decimal System here, Clarice.
1849

I have to admit, I'm really surprised. I'd always assumed Joshua was your type.
Ha! Really? No.

What IS your type?
Oh, tall, stout, dark, long hair... dressed like a Renn faire man...

Not dumpy, pale, balding, dressed like an engineer...

uh, no offense.
You're just reassuring me that we'll never compete for men. Go on.
1850

ding ding
Hello, Heather!
Hazel.
Your regular box of Zinfandel, Mister Perphect?

No, not tonight, Holly
Hazel.
Tonight, we need something special, to celebrate...
A successful bowel movement?

Our little Donovan pooped in the potty!
Wow, I did NOT expect, nor did I hope, to be that accurate.

I tell you what, children will just never cease to surprise you.
That's why I'm on birth control.
1851

1852

I'm so glad you carry boxed champagne!
Well, we know how much you Perphects love your boxes.

Speaking of boxes, that's our second reason to celebrate; we finally unpacked our last box! We're officially moved in, after all these years!
Hey, congrats!

Just in time to move out, amiright? I mean, you don't want to live there forever...
Well, actually...

That's our third reason to celebrate— we just closed on the apartment!
I know!
WHAT

1853

Of course, we're trying not to let the apartment overshadow Donovan's potty victory.
How did you--when was it even--

Oh, it was on the market for MONTHS! But no one was biting, so we offered the owner $20k less than she wanted...and she accepted!
NOOO

Yeah! We can hardly believe it, either!

Say, what do I owe you?
What you owe me cannot be quantified by a number.
tap tap
$19.07

1854

I could've BOUGHT it.
Geez, maybe you could've. It's listed at $180...

They offered $20 less
WOW, $160k for a place like that? That's a steal!

Oh, it's a steal alright. And I'm gonna steal it right back from—

Can we skip the part where you concoct a wacky plan to make them move out, and start at the part where you cope with reality like a healthy adult?
FiiiiiNE.

1855

Hey, while I've got the app open, why don't we look at other places in town?
hm?

Dude... check it out. This place looks just like your old apartment!

It... it IS my old apartment—
apartments in your area
No, look: out the window. There's the park...

GASP
It's like my old apartment with a view of the park!
It's like your old apartment with a view of the park, and double the rent.

Well, that was over faster than college sex.
Nooo, just get a roommate, ya dolt!

Bluuuhh I don't want a roommate.
Oh come ON, you've never even had a bad roommate before.
Hey, Pussy Patrol!

Darren! Do you need a roommate?
Psht, I need a roommate like I need another hole in my butt.

Didn't think so.
Wait-- was that a--
yes.

'Cause I'm getting too much action for one butthole.
oh!
I am NOT living with him.

1856

Aww, that's okay, Pookie, I wouldn't live with you, anyway.
Hey!! Why?

There are some friends you just shouldn't live with. Namely, the ones you wanna keep.
Aww, alright.

So, why are you looking for a roommate? Did your old lady evict you?
Nah, I'm evicting myself.

I'm almost 30 and I live with my mom. You know what that says about me?

It says your mom loves you, you don't pay rent, and you never have to clean the toilet?
It says I have to masturbate only at night, in silence, after she goes to bed.

1857

These places are all hecka expensive, Haze. You're gonna need a roommate no matter where you live in this town.
Noooo

You could always live OUTSIDE of town. The rent goes down by HALF in Knotty End--

BLEAH, GOD, I am NOT living in Knotty End.
Oh c'mon, just because it's an unfortunate name for a town--

It's not that, it's all the-- round things.
Roundabouts?

Yeah! You have to pay attention and think when you drive through that town!
Unlike all the other times you're behind the wheel. I see.

1858

WAIT wait wait. I've got a TON of money saved up. I don't need a roommate!

Hazel, that money's not gonna last you forever.
How much was that one place across from the park?

More than you can afford long-term!
Maybe I'll go over tomorrow and check it out myself.

Are you doing that thing where you pretend you can't hear me because you know I'm right?
I hope you don't mind paying my tab!
You're buying me lunch tomorrow!
Thanks Jamie, you're a peach!

1859

1860

Did you buy me lunch?
Of course I did.

Aww, you DID hear me!
Of course I did.

You didn't really check out that expensive apartment, did you?
Of course I did.

Hazel!! I thought you said you HEARD me!
But I didn't say I CARED.
Now, let's eat the sushi that Not Caring bought.
SNAP

1861

Hazel, you can't afford that place on your own.
I can, for about a year.

:sigh: I guess you could just get a roommate after you waste all your money living alone.
Yeah! See? It's not an entirely irresponsible move.

Did you meet the owners?
Yup. Got the paperwork going and everything.

Did-- they ask for references?
Yeah, they why are you doing that with your face?

1862

Hazel-- no offense, but once they call your past landlords--
Ah, c'mon like anyone really checks refere
RIIING

hello?

HAHAHA HAHAHA HAHAHA NO.
END

That was the owner.
What'd they say?
He just laughed and said "no."

Hazel you were EVICTED from your last apartment and you BURNED DOWN THE KITCHEN of the place before that
Yeah, but I was quiet and never threw parties!

1863

Man, that was so long ago. I'm almost surprised your old landlord remembered you, except--
I guess I'm kind of BURNED into his memory.
Yeah. How did it happen, again?

Hm, no incense holder. Guess I'll use this old shoe.

This thing's always too sensitive.
SNXXXX

And what's worse, the whole place smelled like a burnt SHOE!!
I love it when you ask questions you've memorized the answers to.

Hey, for real-- I'm sorry.
Why? You didn't want me to live in that apartment anyway.
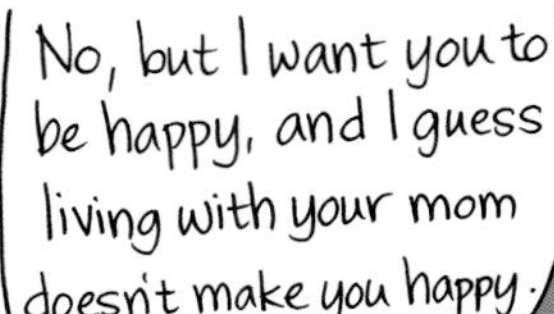
No, but I want you to be happy, and I guess living with your mom doesn't make you happy.

:sigh:
It doesn't make me UN-happy.
I'm just embarrassed about it.

Hazel, who do you think is judging you for living with your mom?

I dunno. Everybody?

You.
:sigh:
I know.
I assure you, we all have WAY more legit stuff to judge you for.

1864

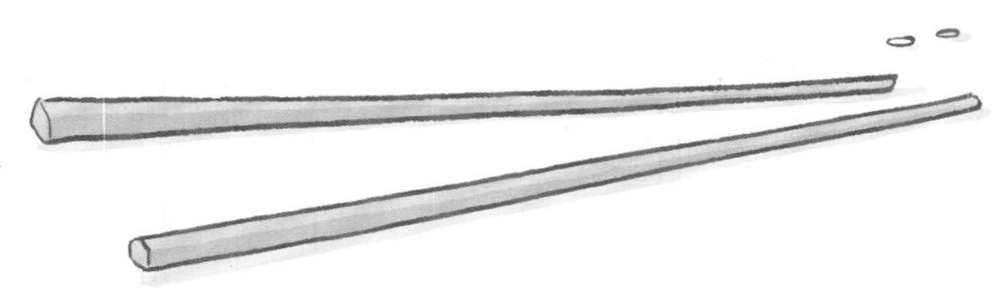

It's hard to believe we've already reached that all-important "can we shop for groceries together" stage of our relationship.

I'm ready.
EATERS' CHOICE

Alright. What's your grocery shopping strategy?
Oh, I don't know that it's much of a strategy...
PRODUCE

I just list everything by aisle number.
1 onion
1 celery
2 soup
2 ketchup
2 olive oil
3 pepper
4 ★
Whoa. That's a strategy alright!
What does the star mean?

Oh, I always allow myself one new treat.
I usually know what I'm going to get, but the star makes it feel more impulsive.

Did you ever think you'd have a girlfriend who finds you more attractive because of the way you write your grocery lists?
I was never really sure I'd ever have a girlfriend, Clarice.

1865

Do you want any help?
Nope! I just want someone to feed, and you're pro-viding that.

You don't like cilantro, correct?
BLEH, cilantro tastes like SOAP!
ha ha

You know... I think I know more about you than I've ever known about any other person in my life.

Well... there's still a lot you DON'T know about me.
And I look forward to learning every single thing as you see fit to share them.
I just hope one of them isn't "I hate crawfish étouffée," because that's what I'm making.

1866

1867

Mm... Joshua, this meal is INCREDIBLE!

Do you cook like this all the time?
Sadly, no. My everyday diet mostly involves bread and lunchmeat.

Then how on earth are you so good at cooking?
Oh, have we reached the stage in our relationship where we come clean about our secret double lives?

wh--
what do you mean--
Clarice, you should know the truth... I moonlight as a gourmet chef.

...
was that ...a joke?
Oh-- yeah, sorry. I, uh, don't moonlight as a comedian, either. Clearly.

1868

I forgot to ask; how did your meeting go this afternoon?
Meeting?

OH.
It went... It went well.

um
Joshua... I need to tell you something...

But I'm having trouble turning you into a sloth, so it needs to be in the dark.
O--
okay.

1869

Is this dark enough?
I think so.

Are you okay?
Yeah...? I just--

·sigh·
There's something I've been dishonest about, Joshua.
These meetings I've been going to--
They're not for the library. I have a second job.

What is your facial expression right now?
I'm not sure. Does "wondering if it involves a sniper rifle" count as an expression?

1870

A second job is nothing! Unless...
unless you ARE an assassin...
NO, no no...

I'm a professional--
um... what I do, it's greatly misunderstood, so... uh...

It's okay. You can tell me.
No, I can't. I'm so afraid of what you'll think of me.

Well, you're not an assassin...
No.
Do you kick puppies for a living?

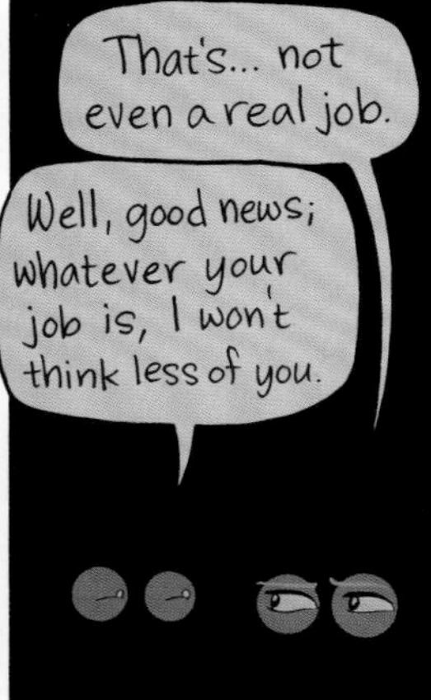
That's... not even a real job.
Well, good news; whatever your job is, I won't think less of you.

Clarice, um... I actually have something to confess to you myself, and I intended on telling you tonight...
Do you think it would help if I told you mine first?
Um... I think so?
...Yes.
Okay.
The reason I've been hesitant to... ah, have sex with you... is...
I've had a sort of... unusual sexual past...
I was in high school. My best friend Reggie instigated it... um... just oral sex, but...
We only did it a couple of times...
Well, I never had a girl-friend, and-- I don't know why, I knew I was straight, but... I wanted to be sure...
So, I hired a sex worker. And, ah... technically, that's how I lost my virginity...
But...
Clarice, I want to really lose it to you.
Joshua... have your eyes adjusted?

1871

Clarice, I didn't expect this to happen tonight..
Do you regret it?
I regret none of it.
Well, except.. I feel as though I distracted us from your confession.
As of tonight, you know ALL of my secrets. Can you tell me yours?
♡sigh♡
I feel like I can tell you ANYTHING right now.
Joshua, I'm a professional dominatrix.
HAH!
OH-- that wasn't a joke.
I think we should turn the lights on for this.

1872

WOW... really??
A real dominatrix?
Really.

I wish I would have known this earlier.
Wh.. why?

Well... we JUST had sex, and I had no idea that you were into... I mean...

...I didn't disappoint you, did I?

I really like it when you answer me with kisses.
Then keep asking me ador-able questions.

1873

1874

I have to confess, I don't know much about... your lifestyle, beyond that fifty Shades book.
EHH, that's not the greatest reference.

So I've been told.
Do you -- I mean, would you prefer that I be --
Do you need me to --
click

All I need is for you to love me.

I love you.
I love you, too.

1875

Hey, Mom?
Yes, dear?

What were you like when you were 29?
Oh! Well, let's see... you would've been six, so we were reading a lot of books together... you could ride a bike with training wheels...

Okay, yeah, but... what about YOU? Were you happy?
Oh sure! You made me very happy, sweetie.

Mom... did you ever stop to think about YOUR life, outside of mine?
Why would I have wanted to do that?

I guess that answers my question.
You know, Volume Six was my favorite of all your baby books.
HAZEL

1876

There's you and your Kid Sister doll.
Before you sewed her legs back on for me.

Huh. Not a single photo of Dad. Guess he was on a lot of business trips that year.
No. He was renting an apartment in Wolcott.

...
You mean, he wasn't living with us?
He didn't live with us for three years.

WHAT?! How did I not notice a thing like that?
Well, you didn't seem to notice when Buddy died, either...

Buddy is DEAD?!! I thought he was out on business, too!
sigh It's time you knew the truth.
Buddy wasn't an investigative reporter, Hazel. He was just an ordinary cocker spaniel.

1877

Why are you telling me all of this now, after all these years?

Well, I thought you'd have figured it out by now. Buddy wasn't THAT smart...
Not the dog. I mean about Dad.
You seemed to be okay thinking he was just out on business.
I decided that you didn't need to know he'd moved out.

Why did he move back in with us after three years?
um... money.
...Hazel, I don't really want to talk about this. It was so long ago.

Mm... okay. Are you at least happier now than you were when you were 29?
Sweetie, I've been happier every day since we moved down here and became a family of two.
A-HEM

Hey, Angel
Do you have a drink for weird, somewhat traumatic realizations about your childhood?
Are you kidding? It's the base for half of my recipes.

I call it "tequila."
thanks.
OUCH, straight tequila? How traumatic was this realization?

I don't wanna talk about it.
Really? Because what Angel calls "tequila" I call "tell everyone all your problems naked."

1878

I have no idea where my father was during half my childhood.
I don't even really know where he is now.

Wow, looks like you were right about the tequila.
At least you're not naked.
Do you have any contact with your dad anymore?

Not really. He sends me a birthday card every year.
the jerk.
Hey now. At least he remembers your birthday, right?

Yeah... but it's just... not enough, y'know?

Like, he could at least put some money in it.
OH, there's no money in it? Nevermind, your dad's kind of a jerk.

1879

ding ding
Baked good delivery for Joe Shmoe!
Ex-cellent!

I made twice as much as last time --
--twice as much--
SEND
tap tap

--so if you can't sell everything, you and Maureen can just keep--
bloop bloop
bloop bloop
the--
bloop! bloop bloop bloop bloop bloop bloop bloop bloop!

Wow. Busy day?
I mass-texted everyone who asked about your next shipment.
bloop!
We're sold out. Can you bring more tomorrow?

1880

Hey, Jamie!
GASP! Surprise Erin visit?!
PURRRRRR

Can I use your oven?
Hurr hurr, of COURSE you can use my--

Aw man, I'm sorry, I always make sex jokes at you...
That's okay! I just replace genitals with hearts whenever you do that.

Aww, Erin, that makes my vagina swell up two sizes.
Eww, you don't hafta make it a challenge!!

1881

1882

So, did your oven break, or–?
Naw, it's just filled up and I need more space.
beep

WHOA! Baking frenzy!
Yeah, Jameson's selling what I'm making faster than I can make it.

Hm. And you're sure you don't wanna make this your full-time job?
Jamie, I paid a fortune for that Masters of Biological Sciences degree...

Do I need to replace your measuring cups with beakers to convince you that baking IS science?
You find me a recipe that measures ingredients in millilitres, and I'll--

actually, why **don't** I use beakers?

1883

Don't get me wrong; I would become a baker in a **HEARTBEAT** if I thought it could sustain me for years to come.
But Erin...

You've made more money selling baked goods to **one** store in the last few days than you've made by using your degree for the last few years.

Besides, when I run a search for "**masters of biology jobs**," the first thing that comes up is "**No. 5 Worst Master's Degree for Jobs.**"
Aww man, worse than **HISTORY??**

1884

What is it about science that you like so much?
Well... I like being precise and careful in the lab...

I like seeing everything as an experiment, rather than as a **success** or a **failure**...
BUTTER

I like that mistakes can sometimes provide an unexpected solution...
And I love that nearly everything you discover can be used in some way to make people's lives better.

You just described baking.
false.
Does it **LOOK** like I enjoy being precise and careful in the kitchen?

1885

Two Japanese iced coffees to go!
Thanks, man!

Jameson, you are such a joy to have here.
Oh! Hey Pauline, I didn't know you were coming in today.

Oh, I just thought I'd come in and do inventory early.
I, uh, already did inventory yesterday.

Oh. Well then, I guess I'll start placing orders—
I did that, too.

Well dag nab, what'd I come in here for?
To sit down with a fresh cup of your favorite brew
and also maybe to sign my paycheck so I can cash it?

Jameson, it's finally catching up to me.
What is?

Old age.
I could've sworn the weekend had just begun!
I forgot to put out the trash, forgot to put out the mail, never watered my garden...

Heh. Or maybe I'm just having a bad case of the Mondays.
It's Tuesday.

Oh FOO.
Also you're pouring salt in your coffee.

1886

°sigh°
Y'know, you're the closest thing I ever had to a son.
Aww...

No, I really mean that. Now listen, son: I'm too old t'be runnin' a hip little café downtown.
It should be run by someone hip and young.
It should be run by you.

W-wow! Pauline, I-- I seriously question your judgment--
Oh, no! Please say you'll run it; I KNOW you'd do such a good job--

OH! I think so, too; I meant on the "hip and young" part.
But yeah, of COURSE I'll run the café!

1887

Hey, Sugarpie?
I have some really big news!

Pauline wants me to--
what's wrong?

Nuh uh

Are you sure?
I peed on ALL of these!

1888

Maureen! I can't believe it!
Neither can I!

Oh, honey! You look so upset!
I'm just-- I'm not ready! I'm totally not ready!

I know we want kids, but...
I wanted to think about it, and research it. I'm not ready!

Sweetie, we have nine months to research it.
EIGHT and a HALF!

1889

1890

So, I guess we're the 0.3% the Ring doesn't work for?
Well, not exactly. I went to take it out, and it wasn't in there.
Do you think it fell out?
No, I would've felt that. Maybe I forgot to put it back in after sex? ...but I always put it on the bathroom counter...
mrrow
Man, he LOVES that new toy you got him.
I didn't get him a toy.
AAAAAAAAAA

1891

The cat stole your NuvaRing?
The cat stole my NuvaRing.
I didn't realize you could get pregnant so soon after it's taken out.
Well, you have a three-hour window. But I think mine was out for two weeks.
Two weeks... you mean, date night?
Remember? We fell asleep right after sex, all snuggled up together?
I must've forgotten to put my Ring back in.
Man, that was a GREAT night.
I came REALLY hard.
Y'think?!

1892

Are you feeling a little better about this?
Yeah. I feel a lot better now that you're here.
Aww, sweetie. You know I'll be with you every step of the way.
I know. You're gonna be the greatest dad.
Can I take you out tonight? To celebrate?
Hm, I think I'd rather stay in... but maybe...
we could play that game you don't like to play with me?
Sure, baby, I'll play Scrabble with you.
YESSSS being pregnant is AWESOME

1893

Hey, didn't you say you had some big news?
OH! Geez, yeah, I almost forgot!
Pauline wants to retire. She wants me to run Joe's!
WHAT?!
Yeah! It's gonna be so much... uh, work, but...
We're gonna have a business, AND a baby.
Wow. Yeah, now I understand what you felt after you peed on all those pregnancy tests.
Immense bladder relief?

Hello! I'm looking for
a pinot grigio that pairs well with Billy Joel.

I'd like a nice
[descriptive words about beer that you read in an article about beer that you did not understand]

Can I get
a 6-pack of Pabst because moustache V-neck hipster.

"A Judgy Yet Accurate Analysis of People Who Buy Booze."
Are you writing this for
a cocktail only sophisticated people drink, but with rail liquor.

1894

Grey Goose is not a rail liquor.
Yeah, but it's funnier this way.
SAVE

Hey, whatever happened to that book you were supposed to write?
Uhh, yeah, it's... coming along.

What do you have so far?
Um... it's just stream-of-consciousness stuff right now. Brainstorming.

Oh. Does it look kind of like...
typa typa type

...this?
That's a blank document with the words "My Book" at the top.
So yes.

1895

Y'know, Daring Literary is getting to be a pretty big deal. You should pounce on their offer to publish you while it still stands.
I knoooow, I know.

I'm just STUCK. I don't know what to write about. They didn't give me any boundaries. I can write about ANYTHING.

That's how you work for us, and everything you write is great.
Yeah, but— (thanks) those are articles. I can't write a whole book about, like, "Ten Things I Don't Get About Women's Clothing."

Hazel, you could certainly fill a book with what you don't get about women's clothing.
Ooh, I could devote a whole chapter to tiny pockets.

1896

Well if you want any help, you know you can always ask me.
Thanks, "Boss."

Don't you put quotation marks around that.
I didn't, "Boss."

I'm an editor. I can HEAR punctuation.
Hey, Thea, guess; what I just did.

That is NOT how you use a semicolon.
AUGH STOP
Should of seen the look on your face; your face LITERALLY exploded.

1897

1898

♩♫

Oh–
Oh! Hi!

I'm just stepping out for a few hours.
Okay.
Are you wearing lipstick?

Leftovers are in the fridge!
Okay.

Are you wearing perfume?

1899

Well that was weird.
ACH! Yehr poor mother!

Huh? Why?
Don't yeh know what she's doin'? She's goin' door t' door, beggin' th' neighbors not t' press charges on her pervert daughter for pleasurin' herself on th' public swingset while drunk an' in th' nude!

Wh-WHAT? But, that never happened! It was only a dream!
Aye, an' Ah suppose yeh think all that butt-secks yeh had wit' Zach was only a dream as well!

DAMMIT McPEDRO, STOP READING MY DREAM JOURNAL
Ah liked th' part where he grew breasts an' turned into a penguin, that was creative.

1900

Seriously, what was my mom all dressed up for?
Heck if Ah know. She doesn't talk t'me, e'er since Ah started t' compliment her derrière.

UGH.
I don't blame her.
Ah did hear her say somethin' to th' ferns... Somethin' about a gentleman caller...

What, like the UPS guy?
Ehh, yehr not familiar wit' the term "caller," are yeh?

Oh! Duh. Telemarketer.
Whate'er helps yeh sleep at night, lass.

Luscious

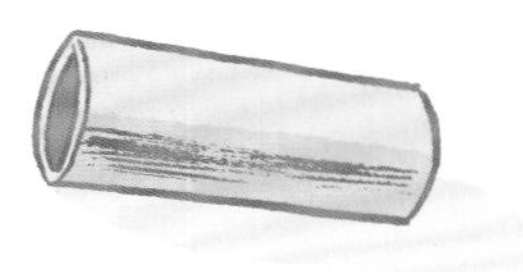

Here.
thanks.

Oh.
It's you.
blub
Don't act so excited.

How did you get so big?
Me? I'm very important.
bloop

That doesn't really answer my question.
What are you writing?

1901

Oh...
...I don't know yet.
Explain.

Well, it's... not that I don't have anything to say... I do, I just... don't know if I'm ready to say it... so...
CRINKLE

OH MY GOD
Hazel-- you forgot--

AAAAAAAAAAAAAAAAA
I need to feed the fish!

God DAMMIT why did I eat half a box of HoHos before bed?
The question is, why didn't you eat th' WHOLE box? These are delicious!

bloop

Whew. You're fine.
You ARE getting pretty big, though.

Y'want a Ho Ho?
McPEDRO. Don't feed him human food.

She said to the cactus eating a HoHo.
Bye, I'm gonna hang out with my own species now.

1902

What a BEAUTIFUL day!
m-hm
tap tap tap tap

Your dad picked the perfect afternoon for an outdoor lunch!
m-hm
clink clink clink clink

It's okay to be a little nervous, sweetie.
I'm not nervous! I'm just... wondering where he is...

Well, we're here 20 minutes early, so... probably 20 minutes away.
m-hm!
crunch crunch crunch crunch

1903

1904

There he is!
crunch munch

Hey there, Mister-
OH, 'hem, you can just call me Henry.
Henry!

Papa-
Theadora, 'hem-

Let's sit down!
PAT PAT

1905

So, ah, I hear from Maya you're editing a magazine?
Yes! It's going really well!

Well, that's good. What is the magazine called?
Oh, it's -- uh, it's... one you wouldn't know.

Oh, I see ALL of 'em out on the rack when I pick up my coffee. Try me!
It's... actually not in print. It's only online.

Huh. So, can I go to the website and
NO!!
ha ha, no, it's... under construction...
for as long as you have an intrest in it.

1906

Well, I'm 'hem very proud of you, for what it's worth.
Oh, Papa... that means a lot to me. Thank you.

And, ah, what is it that you do, Miss Mimi?
hurk!
Oh, I'm a pharmaceutical rep for an erectile dysfunction medication called "Heads Up!"

Ha! Ha ha oh Mimi
What? That's my job.

Well, ah, I hear that kind of drug can fetch you a lot of money.
One might even say it can fetch you a lot of CLAMS.
ha ha oh Mimi nooooooo

1907

Ha! Well... Mimi, I knew I'd like you just fine since that first time we met up.
Aww.
Ah, look, about that: I'm very sorry for the way my wife treated y'all. That was no way t' treat our daughter and her partner-

Ah, is that the right word? Partner?
Oh! We say "wife," but either one is fine.

Theadora? Are you alright?
You are so cool. I didn't know you were so cool. How long have you been this cool.

1908

D'you still love pickles?
OF COURSE I do!

Heh, so does your little niece, y'know.
Mpf--
That's right! Guess it runs in the family.

I bet she made for a real cute flower girl.
Did--you wanna see photos?

OH, did you bring your wedding album?
Yup!
Two of 'em!
tap tap

1909

So there's little Gabby
ooh
Before she peed herself...
Photos 372/998
swipe

...aaand there she is AFTER.
ha!
haha!
okay, enough boring you with photos-
swipe

And here we are at the altar-
oh-
Okay, that's good--
swipe

first kiss!
How is your salad?
Great! How's your burger?

1910

Well, ah... things certainly have changed for, ah... for--
marriage equality?

Yeah. Ah, so, are you both--do ya have all the same--
Yes. Everything you and Mom are granted through marriage, so are we.

Ah. Hm, that's good, that's fine... I think what you have is a little different than what me an' your mother have, though...
NO. It's the same thing. It's a marriage.

Well, ah... what your mother an' I are about to have is a divorce.
WHAT?
WOO!!

1911

ahem
Sorry. Sorry I "WOO"ed.
That's quite alright, Mimi.

It's been a long time coming, someone just needed to pull the trigger. And I was getting tired of waiting for her to pull it.
We're separated right now. I live just a town over. And I want you to know that you're both welcome into my home.

...particularly if you have any decorating advice.
We'll bring the frames.
You bring the pizza!

1912

'hem...
Theadora, thank you for agreeing to meet up with me. I wasn't certain you'd accept.
oo wait!

Oh, Papa. Thank you for reaching out to me through Mimi and Maya.

It means the world to me.

Heh, I'll have to get used to being hugged.
a LOT

1913

50
40
ah--
thumpk
50
40
--OH!
So close!
How many tickets have we got?

49, plus...
13...
...plus 884 from the last 8 months, means--
--we only need 18,516 more for the sumo wrestler blow-up suits.
I'm telling you, the giant kitten-shaped bean-bag chair is only 15,000...

1914

I can't believe we've been playing Skee-Ball for eight months!
Yeah, you'd think we'd have more tickets after all that time!
ARCADE

Hmm.
Keith, thank you.
for what? You've won WAY more of these than I have--

No, I mean, for hanging out with me so much.
Oh! Don't thank me - you're the one who asked Santa for more us-time.

Yeah, well, Santa could've given me a candy cane and told me to fuck off.
But then Santa would've become the sad man who plays Skee-Ball by himself.
Besides, Santa doesn't say the f-word.

1915

So, how's everything at the kid-zoo?
Oh, awesome. They LOVE Jasmine.

Wull yeah, what's not to love about a professional sword-swallower. How long is she in town?
Uh, longer than she'd originally planned, actually...

oh REEALLY!
Heh, I, uh... asked her to stay with me friday, and she asked if she could stay for the weekend...

oh.
Really?
Well... yeah, what's not to love about a professional sword-swallower?

creeeak
Hey, Sweetie!

How was Skee-Ball?
FLOP

I just made double-chocolate chip cookies. Y'want one?
Keith has a girlfriend.

Ooooh.
Y'want two?
yes, please

1916

Is it that Jasmine girl?
yup.

Well, you called it.
Sigh
you knew it would happen at some point, sweetie.
I know.

And I'm happy for him, and I know it wouldn't have worked with him and I, I just --
It still HURTS.

This is why they call it a CRUSH. You can't help but feel crushed.
UGH. Couldn't they have called it a... a million dollars or something?

1917

uh...
hello?
Jamie, c'mere!

What IS this place?
The library just bought it for, like, book reasons, but-

They're not gonna use it 'til next Spring, so Mom wants to throw the Halloween party here! What do you think?

Are those chalk outlines on the floor?
Yeah, they gave the library a HUGE discount for that.
Heh, idiots - chalk isn't even that hard to clean up!

1918

I thought we were meeting at a dive bar?
Oh-ho, but we ARE! Remember how there wasn't any booze at last year's party?

Yeah..
Well, same thing this year, BUT--
PUSH

SHOOM!
WHU..
SHWIP!

Instant bar!
It's like Adult Narnia.

1919

1920

$5 for both.
Wow, so cheap!

So, what's wrong?
Huh? I didn't say anything.

Yeah, but you're at, like, 20% Jamie Joy capacity.

You-- noticed that?
I may not be the most observant person, but noticing Unhappy Jamie is like noticing pepperoni and brick on a pepperoni and mushroom pizza.

1921

Keith has a girlfriend.
Ooohh.
Well... I mean, so do you...

I know, I know. And Erin's wonderful. I just... wish I could find a second lover.
EHH...
I wanna be supportive of you, Jamie, but... god, I do NOT get what you're doing.
"I want a second lover"? It just sounds...
selfish.

Think of it this way: is it more selfish to have multiple lovers who fulfill you in different ways...
or have one lover and expect them to fulfill you in EVERY way?
c. keep drinking and hope the latter exists somewhere.

1922

I know it seems weird to you— before Erin, it would've seemed weird to me, too— but it feels right to US.

And I know it wouldn't have felt right to Keith, either. He's super into monogamy.
Who's his girlfriend, anyway?

A professional sword swallower.

This situation is rife with jokes which I, as your friend, will now refrain from making.
Which is essentially the same as making them, so thanks.

°sigh° I finally find the kind of guy who'd be a perfect dad--
whoa
WHOA
Did you wanna have KIDS with this guy??

Well, maybe!
It's not unheard of for someone to look for good co-parenting traits in a potential lover, Hazel.

It's just weird to you, because that's not what you're looking for.
I am looking for the kind of guy who won't acknowledge that children exist, unless he needs them to get out of the way.

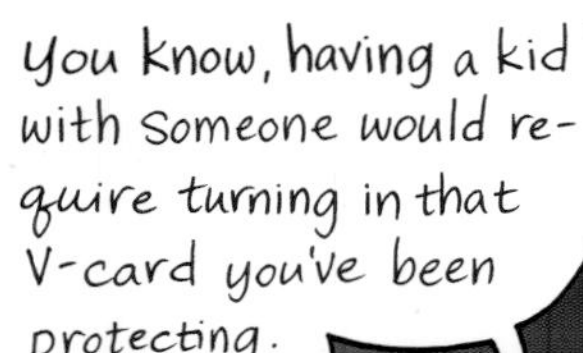

You know, having a kid with someone would require turning in that V-card you've been protecting.

Yes, I understand how it works.

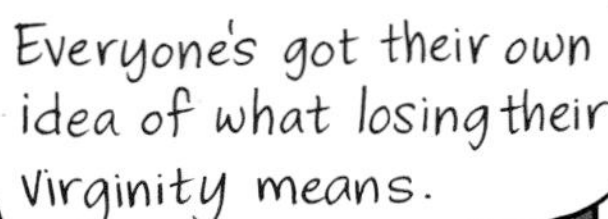

Everyone's got their own idea of what losing their virginity means.

Mine's anything that could get me pregnant.
That's why I've held off for so long.

I don't wanna have sex with some irresponsible dude and then wind up preggo with his kid.
You never consider that when you pick out sex partners, do you?
I'm comfortable going on record as saying that when I'm looking for sex partners, I literally never think about kids.

Children's BOO!k Halloween Bash
$5 or book donation

Hello! $5 or a book donation, please.
BOOKS!

Well that's a fitting costume.
Books!

"A Beginner's Guide to Beer"
"An Introduction to female Masturbation"
I don't need 'em any more.

I'm showing these to your mom.
Go ahead! They're both signed out "to Clarice."

1923

Isn't Alice supposed to be blond?
The book was in black and white.
Aren't you supposed to be a children's book character?

I am. I'm representing the adult form of the Very Hungry Caterpillar.

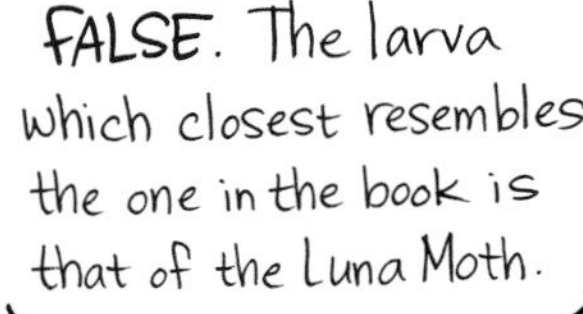

OH! ...huh. I thought it was a butterfly.

FALSE. The larva which closest resembles the one in the book is that of the Luna Moth.

The person who made that book was clearly a moron.
Gosh you're fun. Why don't you go help Carol with the punch.

1924

A red-headed Alice, oh la la!
At your service. And you're...

uhh, Aryan race Jungle Book?
OH, hang on

Pop

OH! Calvin and Hobbes.
Bingo.
AUGH they're stuck

1925

1926

Your mom's murder palace cleans up pretty nice!
Is something wrong with your eye? You look like me.
I went full Calvin and one of them got stuck.
Hey, y'wanna check out the Spooky upstairs?
There's "DO NOT CROSS" tape all over it.
My mom just put that up to keep out the kids.

Hazel, we ARE the kids.
No, I mean the ones that make bad decisions.
Oooo, let's use this rickety old dumb-waiter!

1927

SKREEEET
Ha! It worked!
GUH

Wow, it really IS spooky up here
I think this place was abondoned in the 60s.

Ooo, spooky furnace room
Furnace Room

HAHAHAHA
HAHA
HA HA HAHAHA

HAUNTED FURNACE ROOM
M-maybe old furnaces just sound like creepy laughter?

1928

flip the lightswitch!
I'm not sticking my hands in there!

flick

flick!!

1929

BARTENDER
HUFF PUFF
YOUR STRONGEST DRINK

That was a hundred times scarier than a ghost.
Are you alrigh
HUFF PUFF
BARTENDER! your strongest drink --

What, now you DRINK too?
Your strongest KOOL-AID drink!

What is going ON? I thought you were a... a GOOD mom!
HAZEL! I AM a good mom!
I just...

Honey, I've been single for fifteen years. And I met Simon here, and we just...

:sigh: I should've introduced you much earlier.
Hazel, this is my boyfriend, Simon.
Hi--

Dude I am NOT touching your hands after what I saw.
RIGHT. Right, I'll just go wash these.

1930

I'm sorry you had to meet Simon like this.
Not as sorry as I am.
Ladies.

This is your strongest drink?
We only do beer an' coffee here, toots.

Wait... if you got a coffee, why'd you say that thing about "Kool-Aid?"

Oh, I don't know. It's something your father used to say when he'd drink around you.

Is there anything you guys HAVEN'T hidden from me?
We were upfront about how your parakeet died!
Granted, you were there when your dad stepped on him.

1931

Well, this has been a fun talk.
I -- should get back to the punch stand...

Don't do anything too curious, George.
cringe

So?
She has a boyfriend and my parakeet is still dead. Next topic.

Admit it...
My mom got felt up at a party. OF COURSE I'm jealous.

1932

Hellooooo, Hangover Nurse!
Shh, Jameson-

Mama had a rough night.
Aww, my bad. Hangover Latte is on the house.

I don't remember anything.
That's okay, pookie, the face-Books remembers everything! See?

I said I don't remember any-thing. I didn't say I WANT to remember anything.
Oo, you may wanna de-tag yourself in a couple hundred of these.

1933

1934

You do remember "the incident," right?
Against my will, yes. It's everything AFTER the mixed-species groping that I forget.
Speaking of furries, who's the White Rabbit?
Oh! That's Clarice's new boyf, Joshua.

Wow. What an oaf.
ahem.

What a personality.
What a personality he must have.

1935

Good morning to you, too.
Sorry
Doughnut time!

My favorite time!
Hey, boo! Y'wanna doughnut?
Are we here in time for the doughnuts?

WHOA — is this a spontaneous doughnut party?
Naw, a spontaneous doughnut party is the reason we're here late.
Ours was cream-filled!

1936

Wow, EVERYONE'S here! This NEVER happens!
I maaay have texted you all about fresh doughnuts...
Hey, let's get a group photo!

Squeeze in!
Ready?
Get in there, Erin!
3
2
WE'RE PREGNANT!
snap!

maureenbloggirl TFW you tell all your friends you've got a bun in the

Mazel tov!
I KNEW IT!
AAAAAAA BAAABIES!!
Did you entice us all with doughnuts just so you could get us together for this photo?
yup!
ha ha Hazel, your face
Wow, so, you're BOTH pregnant?
Yeah! Well... you know what I mean.
No, I don't. Did you miss your period?
Hazel-- I'm just being supportive-
Oh! So you're gonna make yourself throw up every time Maureen does?
N-no, I--
You're gonna alter your hormone levels so you can gain a bunch of weight and cry all the time?
Look, I--
You're gonna go through a procedure that's as painful and life-threatening as child-birth, because you're both SO PREGNANT?
WE'RE pregnant because I told him to say that.
?
Oh! Nevermind. Congrats!

1937

Hey, Erin?
How did you know?
Oh -- what, that you're pregnant?
yeah!
Well, you've tried every single thing I've made so far, EXCEPT for anything with rum in it.
oh!
... oh.
And, of course, there's that unmistakeable GLOW
EEEEE AM I GLOWING??

1938

So how far along are you?
Three months!
wow!

And when does Jameson announce HIS little bundle of joy?
Huh?

When are you gonna tell the gang about your new baby?
Man, really? Just because I had four doughnuts--

I-- I meant the café.
OH
next week.
But I really am doughnut-pregnant.

1939

1940

Wow, next week! Does that mean the paperwork's done?
Nah, it's gonna take awhile. But Pauline's letting me act like I own the place already.

Is that why you gutted the kitchen?
Yep. We're gonna need a bigger fridge, new countertops, shelves, floors, cupboards, a bigger sink...

This baby's gonna cost more than your other baby, isn't it.
Yeah, but if things don't work out, at least I can sell this one without getting in trouble.

1941

Well, I get why you wanna replace everything else, but keep this oven or I'll steal it from you!
Oh yeah?

Yeah! Check out these meringue cookies I started this morning. Perfecto!
Good! It's yours.

Wh-- the oven? I-- was just kidding. I don't have space--
No no, I mean, it's yours, but it stays here.

This is a very confus-ing gift.
I want this oven to stay here, and also for you to stay here.
More confusing.

1942

Are you inviting me to WORK here?
YES

Wait -- for real? I can do ALL my baking here, in this kitchen?
YES
THAT

How much would you want for the space?
A 5% raise in my commission.
That's all?

And I get to lick all the whisks.
Well DUH, I'd assumed that.
DEAL

1943

ACH! The holidays are upon us! Are yeh ready for 'em?

Of course y'aren't! Let yehr old pal McPedro get yeh started with some BOOZY COCOA

two scoops of your favorite hot cocoa mix
1/2 oz. Bailey's Irish Cream
fill mug with hot water
mini marshmallows!
and finish it off with a peppermint stick

...or equivalent
MY "WHERE'S WALDO" VIBRATOR?!
bzzzzzzz

Y'know what'll really get yeh in the holiday spirit?
A pretty wreath!

Yeh can make yehr own usin' fir branches, a wire form, an' some embellishments, like ribbon an' berries.

But yeh don't hafta stick to traditional materials or shapes! Let yehr creative side take over for a wreath that screams

McPEDRO

1944

Nothin's more Christmassy than trimmin' the tree!
DOOOOM
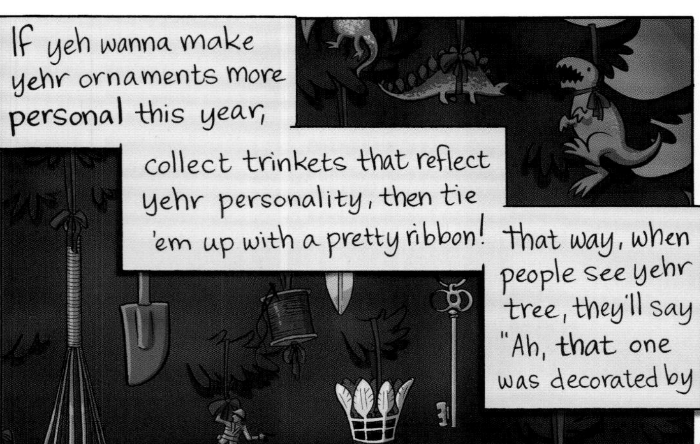
If yeh wanna make yehr ornaments more personal this year,
collect trinkets that reflect yehr personality, then tie 'em up with a pretty ribbon!
That way, when people see yehr tree, they'll say "Ah, that one was decorated by

McPEDRO!!
?
Bzzzzzzz

1945

Wanna make a special fruit cake for yehr special somebody? Let ol' McPedro show yeh how t'
Hey

I made a special fruitcake for my special somebody already. Merry Christmas, little buddy.
GASP!
Ooh!

Are-- are these--
DICK-SHAPED JELLY CANDIES! Suck it, Christmas pervert!!

Ah used th' exact same ones! Except Ah baked yours in th' shape of a
OH GOD DAMMIT

1946

Hey Erin!
Can you make more of those chocolate cherry muffins? We're out!

It's not even 9 a.m. yet!
I know!

Holy shmoleys.
The place is PACKED!
That's at least 80% your fault. People LOVE Muffin Mondays!

I wish I could put this on my resume.
Send a few of these along with your resume, you'll get any job you want.
I'll hire you!

How's that job search going, anyway?
Oh, I'm taking a break from it.
I'd rather put my focus here for now.

Y'know, it's funny -- I spent so much of my childhood staring through a microscope...
...and so little of it admiring my mom's baking...

Who knew someday I'd get my kicks breeding different strains of yeast to make the perfect sourdough?
umf!
This science tastes even better than your LAST science!

1947

Hey Joshua, it's snowing outs-
GASP!

You built a fire!
And I have the kettle on for hot cocoa.

And I brought down your favorite blanket...
and your book
purrrrrrrr

Sometimes it's hard to remember you're a big, bad dominatrix.
Are you kidding? You're serving the heck outta me right now!

1948

So, how was your day?
Day?
Oh, um...

If you're GOOD, Mistress will pop this ripe zit in your face.
UNF!

Twilight Sparkle doesn't believe you're a REAL pony
WHIPPAH
WHINNY LIKE A PONY
nnneeigh!

...nice?

1949

Did you do anything... ah, unusual, or-- fun?
sluuuurrp

It's okay, darling, you can talk to me...
sigh
...no, I can't.

I met you as a librarian, not a dominatrix.
For years, I've felt like I needed to hide this side of myself from you, and now--

--and now, it's hard to SHELVE those feelings?
OOH-HO-HO, you think you WROTE THE BOOK on NOVEL puns, don't you.

It's okay if you don't want to share the details of your domme life with me right away, Clarice. I can wait until you're ready.

But I'm not going to stop asking questions, because I want you to know that I'm interested in ALL of you,
not just who you are in public.

Is that okay?
That is MORE than okay.

Good. Because this fell out of your jacket last night and I'm dying to ask what it is.
Before we have this discussion, I SWEAR it's clean.

1950

tikka tikka tik

Dear—
AA

Are you thinking about moving out?
WHAT? N-no, what gave you THAT idea?
SHUT

Well, there are red circles all over the rental section of the classifieds—

MOM

I'm a human being in her twenties. I don't search "the classifieds."
Well then who did?

scrrriiitch

1951

Okay, I'm glad you're not moving out.
Well--
pat pat

°Sigh°
I might as well come clean.
I've been looking at apartments online.

But-- why would you want to move out of our house?
Mom, I'm almost 30. I can't keep living under your roof.

But, it's YOUR roof, too.
If it were MY roof, you and your monkey handler wouldn't have been allowed to do what you were doing under it last night.
for three hours.

1952

W-we weren't--
gulp
three hours?
I timed it.

I--I thought you were out of the house--
Nope! Other side of the wall.
...that thin, flimsy curtain of a wall.

Oh Hazel, I'm so sorry. If I'd known you were home, we wouldn't have been so loud.
Well, at least you didn't ask me to join you this time.

Oh, but you used to LOVE playing along on recorder!
Mom, I was EIGHT. I'm not gonna play recorder while you and your boyfriend sing Christmas carols for three hours.
Three hours!

1953

1954

Well, if that's the reason you're leaving, Simon and I can sing at HIS house from now on...
That's not the reason I'm leaving. I just-- I'm too old to be living here.

Oh, but you always seem so young to me.
Yeah, well, I seem young to me, too. But... I need to have my own space.

sniff I knew this time would come *sniff* that my Hazel would grow up...
What? Mom, this isn't NEW. I lived on my own for years.

Oh I know, but *sniff* back then, I always knew you'd move back in with me.
That's a nice way of sayin' she always knew yeh were a feck-up.

1955

So! Where we movin' to?
◦sigh◦ I dunno. I couldn't find any apartments I liked.

Ah think the PUDDIN' CAT found some places for yeh.
Goopy Kitty! You're the one who circled all those?
mmvrf

Hmm, what's this?
A word search?

Heh, dumb kitty. None of these are words.
Except for
LOL

1956

sniff
Wow, you sure smell like an adult female. Y'got New Year's plans?
Simon's coming over to ring in the new year with me.

Right. Welp, I'll be at the Meck with Jamie. Be back around 1:00.
Oh... you're not STAYING out?

...WHY.
I-I just, we may HUG at midnight, and... we could still be HUGGING...

FOR AN HOUR?
SIMON'S A VERY GOOD HUGGER

1957

I'm pretty sure by "HUGGING" she meant—
LA LA LA can I stay at your place or what?

Of course you can.
Thank you. I don't wanna hear them-- HUG.

Aw, Hazel. Your mom's an adult now. You have to accept the fact that she's gonna HUG sometimes...
Who's giving hugs?

Hazel's mom!
NO
?
Ooh I want a hug from Hazel's mom!
STOP

1958

Have you had a chance to check out all the eligible kissers in the bar?
Yeah, I've decided to make out with this bottle instead.

Oh c'mon, I've seen at least eight unattached cuties walk in.
Either you have better vision than me, or lower standards.

I'm getting too old for the "kiss a stranger at midnight" game anyway. I don't even know —
— why I'm spending New Year's Eve at a bar.
Judging by your generous tips, it's to keep me employed, so thank you!

1959

10 — 9 — 8 — 7 — 6 — 5 — 4
Go oonnnn, go find someone to kiss real quick!
You're right, I should get another beer. This one's a terrible kisser.

— 3 — 2 — 1 —

HAPPY NEW YEAR!

SMOOCH
CHUG

1960

Excuse me!
Ha ha Sorry! Impulse!
2015

Angel! Another Woodchuck.
uh-- Happy new year, Hazel.

cough
Sorry, I can't turn my head to the left. Happy new year, whoever you are!

That's not what I ordered.
No, it's a shot I call "Don't Be An Asshat To My Favorite Patron"
with a great big chaser of "Please."

1961

ahem
Sorry, Victor, I was just kidding.
Happy New Year.
sigh
It's Vincent.
It's okay.
Damn! **Vincent**. I almost had it.
It really is okay. You're not the first person to forget my name, you know.

Besides, we haven't been friends in over a decade. We may as well be strangers; I barely know anything about you now.

Well, except that I don't remember anything about high school.
Which is funny, since I'm trying to FORGET everything about high school.

1962

Why DO you remember me so well? I mean... we only had that one class together...
I tutored you.

I needed a tutor?
HA! You-- I'm Sorry, you just... you weren't exactly a natural at calculus.

You were great at algebra, but -- well, it didn't matter. The sessions always shifted from math to your life, your parents' divorce, the move from Connecticut...

Hold on— is that why I got a D in AP Calc?
No offense, but even if we'd talked about math, you would've gotten a D.

1963

If you're so great at math, how come you're serving ice cream for a living?
Jimmie Cone is my family's business; I only work there in the summer. I'm a high school math teacher the rest of the time.

Oh! Well geez, no wonder you can't forget high school; you're surrounded by teenagers all year long.
Yeah. I know.

Do you teach at Catoctin?
Yeah! How'd you guess?

You're wearing their colors.
GAAAAH
go cougars.

1964

It doesn't help that I live with my parents in a suite that used to be my grandma's.
oh, ouch.

I feel ya. The only reason I'm still out here is because I live with my mom and she and her boyfriend are--
ugh. I don't wanna guess what they're doing.

Well, at least I don't have to worry about that. My parents are happily married, but my dad is too sick to get out of bed.

I feel like we're trying to out-miserable each other.
I've been forbidden from replacing Grandma's padded toilet seats.
You win.

1965

BZZZRT BZZZRT
nnf

BZZZRT BZZZRT
Swipe swipe

BZZZRT BZZZRT
AUGH, why won't you--
Swipe Swipe Swipe

BZZZRT
BZZZRT
wait.
Is this cardboard?
Gotcha!

BZZZRT BZZZRT BZZZ
But, how did you get it to--
Remote control vibrator.

I take it your new year's resolution is still "pranks."

BETTER pranks.

BZZZRT BZZZRT
Is that also a prank?
Oo no, that's your for-real phone.

BZZZRT BZZZRT

What about the Rube Goldberg machine AROUND the phone.
THAT part's a prank!

1966

SNAP
RREEEOWW
Hewwo?
gasp!

Good morning, Hazel! It's Roberta from Daring Literary. How are you?
Gweat.
pluck

Just wanted to kick off the new year by checking in on one of our favorite authors.
How's that book coming along?

Compawed to evewythig ewse at this vewwy moment...
pwetty good.
I forgot to give you a Benadryl!

1967

—looking forward to that first draft! Happy New Year!
You, too.
END

Upon reflection, I've decided to change my resolution
to treating your best friend like royalty for a year.
Yes, Your Majesty.

Who the heck makes a business call on New Year's Day, anyway?
Two years in a row, no less!

You know, you don't have to answer your phone every time it—
Do not question your Queen.
Yes, Your Majesty.

1968

Happy New Year, Hazel!

Oh. Hi. When did you move in?
Haha, oh, I didn't, your mother just invited me over for brunch!
Hi, sweetie!
Pancakes?

I made a batch of your favorite muffins! Would you like to join
I'm good thanks

AUGH
What? Headache?
No. They were GLOWING.

1969

1970

Substitute barista checking in!

Are you sure you're ready for this?
Coffee drinks are like the tee-ball of all mixed drinks. This'll be easy.

I don't know what that means, but thank you for, uh, "stepping up to bat" for me, Angel.
No sweat! You ready for your honeymoon?

About as ready as a small business owner who's not supposed to think about work for five days.
I strongly recommend remedying that with the major league of all mixed drinks. Start with tequila.

1971

...and don't worry, we won't count that as your carry-on.
snrk!

Watch out, she's smugglin' drugs!
Haha
Sir, come with me, please.

Oooh can I feel your belly?
WHAT
Boy or
When are you due?
I bet it's a boy!

If I have to deal with one more person —
That's why I'm taking you to hang out with dinosaurs.

1972

I can't believe we're finally going to Dinosaur Land.
Actually, Dinosaur Land is closed for the season. We're going to Dinosaur Universe!

uh.. what is that
It's the same thing (I think) except nobody seems to know about it, even though it was rated five stars!

Jameson. How many reviewers rated it.
uh.. I didn't.. does it matter?

Well, I'm the only reviewer to rate your Google skills, and I give you one star, so I'll let you decide.
That's -- actually pretty accurate, so-- no?

1973

One review for Dinosaur Universe, and they know an awful lot about the place. I bet my firstborn this was written by the owner.
BAG

sigh Well! There'll be dinosaurs.
And there'll be a treehouse!
Yeah!

Wait... you DID book the right treehouse, right?
um--
The one I sent you?
no--

GASP!
I booked the one you wanted, but were too shy to ask for.

I could stay in this treehouse all day.
Yeah.

Buuuut if we leave, I have a feeling we might see dinosaurs.
Hmm, let's consult the Magic 8 Ball.

"Reply hazy"
Shake it again.

1974

Are you sure you typed in the right address?
I think so. Why?
TURN LEFT.

I just... sorta expected signs, or... something.
YOU HAVE ARRIVED AT YOUR DESTINATION.

DINOSAUR UNIVERSE

See? There's a brachiosaurus!
That's a giraffe, painted green.

1975

creeeak
Welcome, welcome!

Welcome to Dinosaur Universe!

I'm Jerry. I created all this.
DINOSAUR UNIVERSE

$5 and a photo ID, please.
A photo ID? Why?
DINOSAUR UNIVERSE

Species profiling. At this time we only admit humans, and some service dogs.
Clearly.
DINOSAUR UNIVERSE

1976

Please wear these protective hats at all times—
wat

—an' your tour guide will lead you through th' park momentarily.
DINOSAUR UNIVERSE

I'm your tour guide!
To your left, there's a triceratops!

That's a rhinoceros.
You'll notice the triceratops has not growed its horns yet.

1977

1978

And over here we have a
It's like he broke into an old zoo and stole all their decorative animal statues.

Should we dip out while he's not looking?
Nah, I'm overcome with an illogical sense of compassion that I can only hope will subside after childbirth.
I don't wanna leave the old guy alone.

And then, when the ALIENS arrived—

We're leaving
We are STAYING

1979

Um, excuse me, the ALIENS?
Yup! This next part is what they don't teach ya in school!

The dinosaurs never went EXTINCT, you see. They were all transported by ALIENS to ANOTHER PLANET!
DINOS TODAY

So-- ALL of the dinosaurs are alive and well, on another planet.
Correct.

Which planet.
Bloopiter.
Which is just like Jupiter, only REAL.

1980

How did you-- acquire this information?
Oh, the aliens told me themselves.

Of course they did.
PLEASE tell us about the aliens.
Oh, I can do better than tell you—
ALIE PHOT

I can show you!

Nice swim trunks.
Woops! Wrong disc.

1981

See, that first one's when I saw their spacecraft in the sky...
k-chk
and then...

whoa!
That's where it landed, and the next one...
k-chk

is ALIENS!

THAT'S an alien?
It looks-- weirdly familiar--
Y'like pickles? 'Cause I think they look like gherkins with a eyeball!

And now for the big finale! If you'll follow me into my rocketship,
DAD!

Well hi, Lucy!
Hi! Who're your new friends?

Oh, I was just about to take them for a ride in the–
DAD, you know it's not safe. Remember what happened last time?

W-well that was just the once—
C'mon, let's get your meds.
You two wanna remove your hats and follow us to our safe, stationary house that's not a rocketship?

1982

I'm so sorry y'all were misled to to think that my dad's large-scale diorama would be anything like Dinosaur Land. And on your honeymoon, no less!
It's okay!
We had a blast!
snxxxxx

Uh, but I'm sorry if we triggered your father's, um.. dementia?
Oh! He doesn't have dementia.

Oh! Well.. that's good to hear!
Thanks for the cookies!
I'll be sure to take down that website so this doesn't happen again. Bye!

He doesn't have dementia?

1983

WHOA. Aliens?!
Yeah, it was CRAZY!

So, did that make it the WORST honey-moon, or--
The BEST. Plus, Jameson surprised me with an even cooler treehouse than the one I'd picked out.
WOW. Angel made us a lot of money last week. I guess making coffee drinks IS easier than bartending.

Actually, she had a REALLY hard time. There were a lot of complaints about the lattes.
Really? Then how did she make so much--

"Charm."
Titties.
·:Sigh:· Will I never grow out of this training bra?

1984

Hey, honey-mooners.
Hey, baby!

Ooo, speaking of babies, did someone get an ultrasound today?
Yep! Ten fingers, ten toes.

One shlong? One hoo-hah?
One third eye?
Five nipples?
We decided to let the sex be a SURPRISE

...for everyone else.

1985

1986

Hey, Hazel.

Uh, I've got all the paperwork we need to—

OH! Yes, great, thank you!
I'll, uh, let you know how it goes!

See ya!

WAY overdue calculus homework.
Oh yeah? Let's talk about it during study group.

1987

YOU'RE MOVING IN WITH HIM??

We both live with our parents, he wants to move out, I want to move out... it's just-- weirdly convenient.
You barely know him!

So? I barely knew um... whatsis
Scott.
Scott.

Scott didn't have a lingering high school CRUSH on you.
This just seems like a heartbreak waiting to happen, Hazel.

Aww, Jamie, I appreciate your concern, but--
I meant for him.

1988

Well, I have enough money saved up; if things get weird, I can always move out.
That's another thing– I thought you were hell-bent on blowing your savings by living alone?

Yeah, well— I don't have the greatest tenant history, or the most attractive employment record—
And he does?

Yeah! Did I tell you he's a tenured math teacher? And his credit score is like, higher than my SAT score--
Hazel, I hate to say this...
You sound like your father.

1989

What do you mean, I sound like my father? You never met him.
No, but I remember high school, and I remember how he used your mom for her money and her job security. Among other things.

Jamie, I'm not MARRYING the guy. I'm just sharing an apartment with him. You want I should find someone irresponsible to live with?
Mmn, okay. I just don't want you to—

End up like my dad.
Well--?

WELL? I don't have a spouse to use or a child to neglect, so you can stop worrying about it.

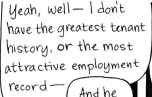

HAAAH

hey
HEY

HHAAAAAAAZzzoooiiuuu

1990

GASP!!
Hup!

WHOO
It was only a dream.

Besides, you're basically Mom's fish now.
If you died, it wouldn't really be my--

FWOOMP

Here ya go, little guy.
Sluuurp

I thought you were on a quest to find your family?
mowr
Didn't you find them?

tap tap
HELP WANTED

Ooh, I see.
You wanna get a job first, so when they see you, they'll know you're not a deadbeat.
Murrr

1991

1992

Maybe Choo-Choo Boo-Boo's human will know about your family. What was his name?
Randy?

No, wait--
Davan
pink cat, flask
dialing...
clik
Hello, stranger.

Hi, uh, Davan? This is--
Hazel. I know; I kept your number in case of an emergency. How're you and Sprinkles?

Oh... the same.
I'm actually calling because I have this... gelatinous purple cat here. Did your jelly cat have any OTHER babies?
murr

murr?
Not that I know of.

But there's a Pudding Cat Rescue near Boston. That's not too far from you, right?
About four or five hours.
sniff
HISS

Uh-- I'm sorry, is it ACTUALLY called "Pudding Cat Rescue?"
Yep! If you google it, it should be the only page that--

No wait. It's the SECOND page that comes up.
Do NOT click on the first page.

...
You clicked on the first page.
help
Good luck sandpapering that Rule 34 diamond from your brain.

1993

Pudding Cat
When your BFF
Livejournal
PuddingCatRes
Worcester, MA
Hours: M-F: 8-6 Sat & Sun: Closed
"We're just like normal cats, but squishier!" - Puddles
Hmm. Worcester...
That's only four hours away...

I don't have to be at work for three days...
I don't exactly feel like seeing Jamie...
Mom's boyfriend is coming over tonight...

And the cats in the cradle and the silver spoon

1994

Huh
I didn't really think to check the weather forecast.

murr?
You know, I used to live up here.

It's weird to be driving toward the old homestead. I haven't been here since...
hm

Since I started giggling at that sign.
ex 23
69
Wolcott
Prospect
2 miles

Yes! We made it!
Pudding Rescue
walk-ins wel

They close in 20 minutes.
I hope that's enough time...

Hello♫
Hi! I don't have an appointment,
but I have this goopy cat, and he's--

SHOOOM

1995

Oh, don't worry, most puddings react that way when they see other cats like them for the first time. He'll love his new home.

So-- he can stay?
Of course! We'll get some basic information from you, but you may as well say goodbye now, if you'd like to.

Um..

Hey...
Goopy Kitty?

Almost forgot your bandana, buddy.
RRRRRR

1996

sniff
Connecticu
Welcomes Yo
Connecticut
We're full of surpri

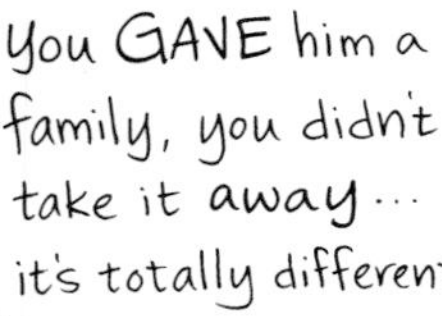
You're fine, you're fine...
sniff

He wasn't yours to begin with. You're not his parent.

You GAVE him a family, you didn't take it away... it's totally different.

What, d'jya kill off another vibrator?
SWERVE
HONK
JESUS CHRIST how did you EVEN get in here??
Ah was nappin' in yehr backpack.
yawn
Where are we?

1997

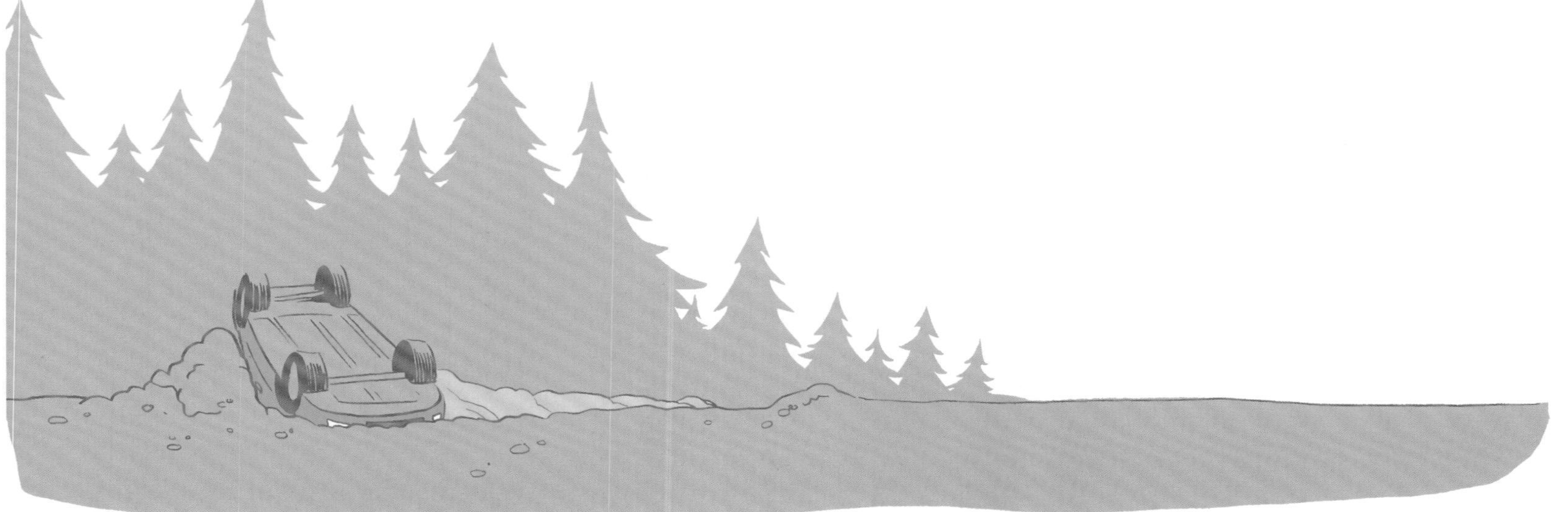

1998

AH think yeh did the right thing fehr Goopy Kitteh.
Well, thanks, but I wasn't crying. I'm just... allergic.
uh-huh

Eht's really comin' down out there, lass.

We'll be fine.

blik-blik
blik-blik

uh.. yeh sure?

We could get a hotel. Ah know for a fact yeh've got a clean pair o' undies in yehr bag.
creep.

Also, yehr car sounds like Bob Dylan.
I'll take that as a compliment.
WHRRRRRRRRRRRRRRRRR

If you wanna play armchair mechanic, the manual's in the glove compartment.

Hmm... trouble-shootin'... whirrin' noise when accel-erating. Could be any of the followin':
CAMRY
1993
CAM

D'yeh want meh t'read 'em? It's five pages.
forget it.

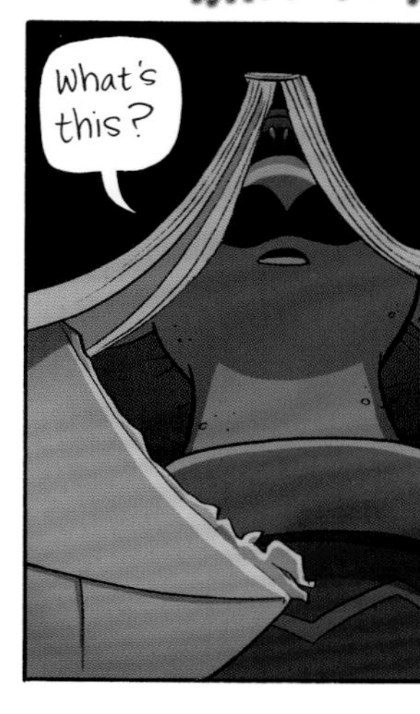
What's this?

Tellington..?
Gregory Tellington
36 Bilby Dr.
Wolcott, CT 06716
Hazel
POB
Wolcott...

Ah just saw a sign for Wolcott! D'yeh have family up here?

Let's find out.
ex2
69
Wolcott
Prospect
next exit

So, who lives here? Yehr uncle?
...my dad.
You have arrived at your destination.

Uh... the one yeh haven't seen in years?
That's the one.

...is he a murderer?

Come to think of it, I don't know WHAT he does.

Is he expectin' yeh?
um··
no··
What d'yeh think he'll say?
I--

1999

sigh
I dunno, McPedro.
His car isn't even here. Maybe I should just--

THUD
CRACK

GOD DAMMIT!!
What're you doing in my--

Hi, Dad.

Okay, so, there's a... a futon downstairs...
Thanks!
flik

Sorry it's not clean. The house cleaner's been sick.
cough
Housecleaner?

So. *ahem* Are you still living down near your ma?
Yeah! Um... still getting your card every year!

Oh, right right...
Ah, that's how you got my address.

2000

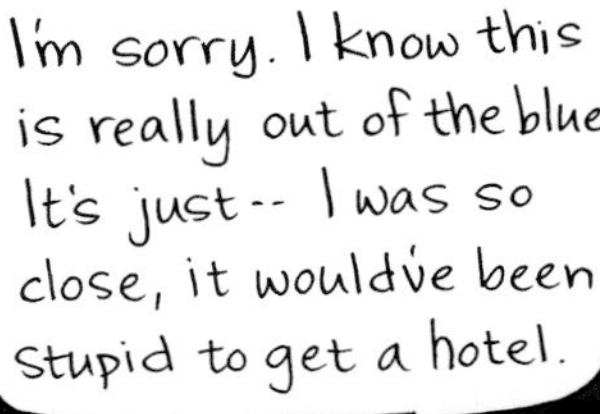
I'm sorry. I know this is really out of the blue. It's just-- I was so close, it would've been stupid to get a hotel.

Sure, yeah.

...you renting?
Hm? Uh, yeah, I'm about to move in with an old high school friend.

Throwin' your money away there, Sport. You need to invest.

I bought this place for fifty grand...
murder palace

But once I'm done with it, it'll be worth FOUR TIMES that!
no it won't, because of all the murders
SHH!

2001

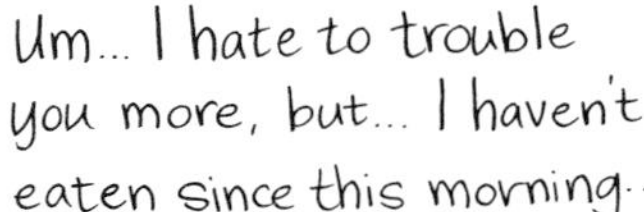
Um... I hate to trouble you more, but... I haven't eaten since this morning...

Hm? Ah--

Sure, sure... ah, how 'bout a pizza?
I could seriously eat a whole pizza right now.

Alrighty then...
Hello!
I'd like two large pizzas...

...for my daughter and me.

with sausage, salami, onions, pineapple,
and uhh...
pineapple?
how 'bout green peppers.
peppers make me gassy
but okay

There! Thirty-five minutes.
Wow-- thanks, Dad!

Sure. Consider it an early birthday present. You're gonna be, what, twenty-
Thirty.

Thirty.
wow.
Sheesh, a regular adult.

Good thing I got you a LARGE, growing girl like you!
I think I stopped growing ten years ago, but I'm okay with growing horizontally if it's for pizza.
pat pat

2002

So, uh... what are you filling your days with?
Do you have a job?

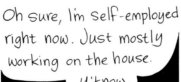

Oh sure, I'm self-employed right now. Just mostly working on the house. y'know.
Cool.

Hey, actually, we're BOTH self-employed! I'm writing for a magazine, and I just got a book deal with a really good publisher!
I knew about the magazine.

You did?
Sure. If you Yahoo our last name, your stuff is all over the place.

Actually, is there any way you can get it to stop doin' that? My freelance website is on the third page of "Tellington."
oh...
n-no, I don't think I can change that.

Hm, maybe I can write a letter to Yahoo...
KNOCK KNOCK KNOCK
Hey, could you get that? I've gotta use the john.

That'll be $52.22 and could I please borrow a snow shovel?
CHRIS
PIZZA

orites
Jamie
Mom
Thea

clik
Sweetie!
I've been trying to call you all day!
Hey, Jamie.

I'm so sorry for what I said about your dad.
It's okay.
You were mostly right, anyway.

Can I come over? I'd like to hug-pologize.
Um... I'm kind of not home right now.
Where are you?

... my dad's creepy basement?

That sounded a lot worse than it is.
Are you seriously at your dad's?

Yeah... it's a long story, but yeah.
Are you okay?

Yeah. I mean, mostly.
sigh
He's kinda... exactly the way he's always been...
...but somehow worse than I remember.

2003

Oh, hon.
It's okay. I think I needed to see him for who he really is.
And was.

He's family, but... he's not really MY family, y'know.
Not like you and Mom are my family
Aww, Haze.

You know I love everything about you, but my favorite is when you're vulnerable and sappy like this.
Shut up.

I wish I was there with you.
I wish you were, too.

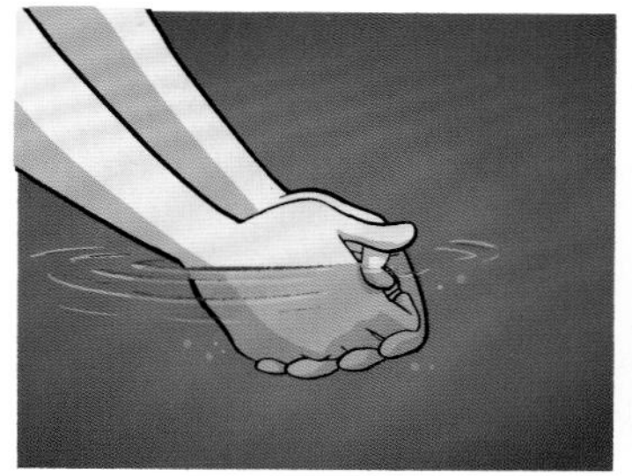

2004

Dad?

Hazel—
pizza in the fridge
if you want it.

Dad—

Dad—
thanks for leaving
one slice of the pizza
that I paid for

thanks for leaving
one slice of the pizza
that I paid for
and for the crack
in my bumper

Dad—
thanks for ~~leaving~~
~~one slice of the pizza~~
~~that I paid for~~
~~and for the crack~~
~~in my bumper~~
NOTHING

Dad-
thanks for
shoveling out
my car.

WHRRRRRRRRRRRRRRRRRRR R R R
ex2
69
Wolcott
Prospect
next exit

yawn
That was one helluva cactus nap.
W-where are we?
Ten minutes from home. I just needed to pick up some groceries.
Y'mean... we weren't murdered?
Pft. My dad is a lot of things, but a murderer isn't one of 'em.
That'd require him to actually follow through with something.
Whew! Ah dreamt he was vibratin' me t'death!
Uhh, which pocket were you sleeping on?
Th'one with yehr phone.
BZZZRT
BZZZRT
OH! Ha ha, right, of course.
Why is Jamie texting me so...
whoa-
MAUREEN HAD HER BABY EARLY!!1!11
it's a girl! everyone is doing great!
LOOK AT THE TEENIE BABBY I CANT EVEN
Wow. They did it.
They made a tiny baby human all by themselves.
What a great day to be born.
WHRRRRRRRRRRRRRRRR
OH GOD DAMMIT
GROCERY
PET'S

2005

What's wrong?
It won't GO.
pump pump
WHRRRRRRRRRRR

Good thing I've got Triple A—
DEAD

Good thing I've got a recharge-
Nope, ya don't.

AAUGH
Good thing I like walking.

tap tap tap

2006

Good thing my engine-savvy ex-boyfriend happens to be right there.
Good thing yeh haven't pissed 'im off recently!

2007

How much is a new transmission?
More than your car is worth. And it's not just the transmission.

I hate t'break it to ya, Haze, but—
Is she done?
She's done.
cLUNK

Wow. End of an era.
Thank you for looking at her.
I couldn't just walk by and leave you here.
Where were you headed?

Home.
...from Connecticut.
Connecticut?

WHOA-- is everything okay?
Yeah. Just... an overdue paternal visit...

Oh, ALIVE. Not in a casket.
You can breathe now.
WHOO thank you

My greatest fear for you has always been that your dad would pass away, and you'd regret never making amends with him.

Well, I can't say amends were made, but... it's a work in progress now.

Plus, now I've confirmed that he looks just like me... plus 25 years, a mustache, and a permanent scowl.
So: hilarious.

I'm not sure if you heard, but Maureen and Jameson had their baby.
Oh, I heard. Jamie texted me.
By which I mean her ovaries texted me.
It was mostly incomprehensible keyboard-mashing.
So you know about the video call at eight?
Video call?
Everyone's getting together at the café so Jameson and Maureen can announce the baby's name from the hospital.
Uh--
—I wasn't gonna go, in case you were there, but--
Oh man--
Zach--

Look, I don't wanna be those exes any more.
I miss you. I don't care if it's only as friends, I just... would really like to have you in my life again.

Besides, I don't want to keep you from Jameson. He's like, your only friend.
Psh, I have friends.
I've missed you, too.

In celebration of not being "those exes," do you wanna walk down to the café with me and help Erin decorate? I know how much you love baby colors.
Sure, let's spend the afternoon making that place look like Easter threw up in it.

2008

Uh-- can I leave my car here?
Yeah, it's free parking. We can get it towed later.

Just a few more miles and she would've made it all the way home.
It's okay. It's a fitting ending for my book.

You're writing a book?
Yeah... after the trip I just had, I finally have something to write about.

Will I be in your book?
No spoilers, Zach.

THE END

Danielle Corsetto lives in Shepherdstown, West Virginia with at least two cats and a rotating cast of housemates. Her most exciting daily routines include drinking a pot of tea in the morning, and visiting the post office in the afternoon. She enjoys long walks more than most people who say they enjoy long walks. She likes yoga more than she thought she would. She spends most of her time daydreaming and overanalyzing her experiences but always writes it off as "working."

If any of this sounds appealing to you, you may enjoy her autobiographical comic Stuck at 32 which is appropriately parked at stuckat32.com. She is not 32, but she once was.